ENDORSEMENTS

Denise Taylor has a gift for writing and a bigger gift of seeing the spiritual connection between the everyday and the hereafter. Through her struggle to save her daughter J onnae, she acquired an incredible base of wisdom. She sees the uncommon in the common and has the ability to teach it simply enough for everyone to grasp. Read "Heavenly Birth. A Mother's Journey. A Daughter's Legacy." You'll be totally inspired!

-Julie Ziglar Norman, Inspirational Speaker, Author, Founder of The Ziglar Women Faith and Family Conference

As a young child, I lost my older sister to leukemia. I know the devastation that can bring and the comfort that comes when someone shares their life experience. Denise has given us all the gift of meeting her daughter and learning the joy available in this life and beyond.

-Jim Stovall, author "The Ultimate Gift"

"Denise and Jonnae's story left me inspired to do more in regards to helping people learn to eat better in the face of so much disease and destruction. Denise has courage and grace, things that seem impossible to have in abundance when dealing with personal tragedy. I believe her gift is to help others find their way with truth. I hope I can do the same."

-Tosca Reno BSc., BEd. www.toscareno.com

Denise Taylor paints a portrait of inspiration, hope and unfailing love. This book has an amazing message of faith, and it will inspire you to face each of life's challenges with vigor and determination. *Heavenly Birth* is a blueprint on how to manage your daily life while faced with extreme adversity. If you only read one book this year, I highly encourage you to read *Heavenly Birth*. You will not be disappointed.

-Blake Bradley, General Manager,
Athletes for Christ / Shields of Strength

"Some of my NFL friends and I witnessed Jonnae's faith and courage first hand. Her life and Denise's message have made a big impact on us, as well as the teens we work with. This book will continue to bless all ages and walks of life."

-Byron Williams, NFL Alumni
President of BW Sports/Football Minicamps

Denise's testimony and Jonnae's spirit will forever live on. They've proven we always have the choice of victim or victor. I witnessed the impact of this story, first hand, when Denise spoke to the youth at my KY Derby football camp. The guys sensed her strength and embraced the lesson of, "We GET TO!". Because Denise and Jonnae chose victory in the face of adversity, we're moved to as well."

-Kerry Rhodes, NY Jets Safety

"Denise Taylor is an exceptional woman, with an even more exceptional story. I've heard her tell firsthand the amazing story of her perspective, and those shared firsthand by her incredible daughter. I'm certain the experience of reading this book will open your eyes to a profound new perspective of life, and death, in a way that is hard for most of us to comprehend."

-Rich Razgaitis, President, Univera Lifesciences

HEAVENLY BIRTH

A MOTHER'S JOURNEY, A DAUGHTER'S LEGACY

By

Denise Taylor

Do you want Denise Taylor to speak to your group or event? Email info@weGETto.org

HEAVENLY BIRTH

ACKNOWLEDGEMENTS

With more love and appreciation than words can adequately express, I'm grateful for those who have supported me through the gestation period, labor, and birth of this written work.

Thanks be to God for being all I need to experience a beautiful life. He's blessed me with so much, least of which is this incredible opportunity to share Jonnae's life and a message of hope. I'm excited to do so.

My parents, Ed and Jan Metzger, Johnny, and our four living children, Nolan, Austin, Layne, and Lydia made their own sacrifices as they put up with this "expectant mother's" emotion, exhaustion, and mood swings. With their understanding, patience, and unconditional love, I'm abundantly blessed.

My three amigos, Teresa Curry-Boyd, Rena Reese, and Terry Coyle, gave me invaluable guidance, wisdom, and encouragement. A true friend, one that is there whenever, however, with whatever, is a treasure. How very blessed I am to have these three.

In addition to author, speaker, and entrepreneur, John Terhune may not know he's a "birthing coach". He speaks of an "I will not quit" muscle. Strengthening mine proved to be most beneficial in "pushing" me through the intense labor required to give life to this book.

A mother's body lets go of the child when it's birthed into the world. I joyfully let go of Jonnae's spirit as she was born into Heaven. As I translated that to our family and friends with the release of a dove at her funeral, Chuck Branham, of *The Evening News*, captured it on film. I'm so grateful for this image and how it perfectly symbolizes Jonnae's Heavenly Birth.

After hearing that I refer to Jonnae's passing as her Heavenly Birth, Jillian Manus, of Manus and Assoc. Literary Agency, suggested the name for this book. As absurd as it seems now, the divine fit of *Heavenly Birth* was not immediately apparent to me. Time revealed it was indeed the God-given name for this creation, a blessing indeed!

Rena Reese, author, and founder of The Soul Salon International, Crystal Miller, and Daniel Sheffield were awesome caretakers when I required rest. Their expertise, when I needed advice or a break from editing myself, was invaluable to me and I'm forever grateful.

Terry Whalin and Intermedia Publishing, the group I sought to help me deliver this "baby," guided me in producing what you now hold in your hands.

People all over the world have encouraged and supported me this first year without Jonnae's physical presence. Their prayers and emails have blessed me beyond measure. I'm more than thrilled to offer something back as I share this journey with each of you. It is my prayer that you will be filled with a sense of wonder and grace as your eyes fall upon yet another one of God's precious miracles, *Heavenly Birth*.

DEDICATION

Above all else, love is the gift of oneself. Jonnae was selfless with her love for others and life. In celebration of her, this book is dedicated to those who seek healing, peace, and joy.

PREPARING FOR NEW LIFE

At age 12, my daughter Jonnae was diagnosed with Acute Lymphoblastic Leukemia. The onset of the illness was sudden, as no symptoms were foreseen. She awoke one morning with leg tremors and pain. By 1:00 p.m. the same day, she was diagnosed with blood cancer.

Immediately, in a very surreal reaction, I accepted whatever God's will was. I decided to combat her unpredictable future with positive attitude. I would stay focused on the good - no matter how much it seemed to be outweighed by the bad. Jonnae submitted to the same commitment, so we forged ahead together, seeking to keep an *attitude of gratitude*.

Jonnae tried to build a strong healthy body; I tried to hold onto mine. As she attacked her cancer with chemo, I attacked the obstacles of retaining fitness. As an emotional eater in the midst of a nightmare, I used my personal challenges as a way to exemplify to Jonnae, and all witnesses, what faith and perseverance can produce. However, over the course of a two-and-a-half year battle with Leuk, it wasn't my or Jonnae's physical bodies that were strengthened the most, but rather, our spiritual ones.

Only one month after completing her two-and-a-half year chemo schedule and being declared a "survivor," Jonnae relapsed. I began blogging every day to report on Jonnae's health and to express what I was feeling. I shared our journey of faith and fitness with a community of readers, consisting of family, friends, and strangers. I exposed our struggles as well as our victories, withholding nothing.

I shared Jonnae's suffering, her tenacity, and unbelievable courage and faith. I shared my struggles with binge eating and my frustrations as a mother who felt helpless. I talked about the constant presence of Our Father; we felt Him comfort and strengthen us in the darkest hours.

1

My focus on fitness may seem misplaced, given the circumstances, but it was the diversion I needed to escape the grip of my daughter's illness. At times, I appear to be a Bible-toting, scripture-quoting evangelist. I assure you I am not. To this day, I can't quote chapter and verse of scripture. When I share it in this memoir, it's simply because I sought answers and strength in every possible venue, and more times than not, it came through the Living Word of the Bible.

I used to see life through the world's cheap view finder, now I view it on God's high definition big screen. There's no comparison, and I have leukemia and Jonnae to thank for it. If she was supposed to live through leukemia, she would have. Her purpose was to teach through it. My purpose is to share what I've learned. Initially, that may be a thought that's hard to comprehend, but after you've walked this part of my daughter's leukemia journey with us, you'll understand.

> I USED TO SEE LIFE THROUGH THE WORLD'S CHEAP VIEW FINDER, NOW I VIEW IT ON GOD'S HIGH DEFINITION BIG SCREEN.

In seeking to use the power of words in a positive manner, I no longer refer to Jonnae's passing as death, but refer to it as her Heavenly Birth. I use analogies of pregnancy and birth all the time. The comparisons come naturally. I guess I'm able to see my role as a mother in many different ways.

Only weeks after Jonnae was born into Heaven, I was ready to move forward and begin sharing all that I'd learned–we'd learned–together. Some people were supportive; some expressed their concern. They didn't feel I was allowing myself adequate time to feel the loss.

Sometimes parents lose a baby and immediately try to get pregnant again. It's hard to determine the best way to heal and move forward. But God is the determining factor. If it's His will, when the time is right, He'll create a new life. He's done that in me. I'm not talking about a baby in the literal sense as a human being, but in the figurative sense, with this book.

The talk of my creating a book began in June, but it wasn't until October that God "announced" to me it was time. Much like the first trimester in a pregnancy, there was an excitement that came with the announcement, as well as the question, "Am I really ready for this?" The initial months didn't reflect much was growing, but I remained in faith and moved naturally with God, the Father and Creator of this *baby*.

I got excited as He scheduled my first *ultrasound*, an event in CA with agents, publishers, and professionals in the book industry. The picture didn't produce the results I had hoped for. It was like those first shots I saw of my real babies (ultra sounds have come a long way since then). Back when I was in the "baby making business" the pictures from ultra sounds only made out enough to see there was indeed a baby there. That's about all that was confirmed in CA, a book was there.

A month later, I felt an undeniable kick in my gut, evidence this book was undeniably developing. A due date was established. As the birth of this *baby* drew near, I found myself very much like a pregnant mother in the last months of pregnancy: exhausted, emotional, and just ready to push it out.

A mother sacrifices a lot in order to do what's best for the baby. The miracles I'll continue to witness as a result of the sacrifices, will be so worth them.

As we prepared for her Heavenly Birth, Jonnae and I experienced something miraculous. Those who walked the journey with us did as well. As I've labored with love, in preparing to give birth to this book, I've experienced miracles in abundance. I've been renewed. I have a new energy for this trek that began with Jonnae, but will continue with you. I hope you will accept the invitation, and embrace its content with me, as you learn to live a fuller life and prepare for your own *Heavenly Birth*.

"AN UNEXPECTED ANNOUNCEMENT"

SEPT 4, 2007

I implore you to pray fervently for my daughter, Jonnae. Her scheduled routine follow-up did not go well today. It seems as though the leukemia cells are forming again.

Tomorrow, she will have a bone marrow aspiration to confirm what the doctor believes to be a relapse. If indeed the leukemia has returned, we will need to activate an aggressive game plan. The doctor asked about my other children, which leads me to believe there is a possibility of her needing a bone marrow donor. Of course, that will be discussed tomorrow. She is scared, my family is in shock, and I want those who will, to lift us up in prayer.

The only thing I know for sure is God's bigger than any mountain. This is in His hands. I will accept His will, but pray that it is to heal my daughter.

SEPT 5, 2007

The way the doctors look and speak doesn't do much for one's spirit. I don't think Jonnae has picked up on it, but my husband, Johnny, and I have. Last night I told Jonnae we were going into extra innings. That wasn't accurate–this is a whole new ballgame.

If the bone marrow aspiration confirms what they suspect, an induction phase will start right away. It will be much more intense than the induction she had before. This time she will remain in-patient for the first four weeks. If she responds well and goes into remission, she'll have a bone marrow transplant. Our four other children will be tested to see if they are a match for her.

The doctors seem to be in mourning already. I'm not focused on their odds. Instead, I choose to focus on how big my God is. His will may be different than ours. Whatever is revealed, I will accept it the best way I can.

Earlier, I shared this thought with Jonnae. Peter was the only disciple who walked on water. The other eleven could have if they had believed. Once Peter started to doubt, his "power" was gone. It doesn't matter what I believe, what the doctors believe, or what anyone else does, or doesn't, believe. What matters is what she believes. She's created in the image of God and has the help of His divine power. If she believes and taps into it, she can be healed. To be a victor, she needs to keep her *eyes on the "Coach."*

Abby is my friend's daughter. She hit her first home run last week. After telling her uncle about her milestone moment, he asked her, "How far did you hit the ball, Abby?"

She hesitated and said, "I don't know. I just kept my eyes on the Coach. He sent me home."

What a perfect analogy. We will keep our eyes on Our Coach. He will lead us to victory!

Jonnae is strong. We've shed our tears of disappointment, but we are not giving up. We will fight till the end. When we were talking about fear today, Jonnae's only words were "The devil's not going to win."

SEPT 6, 2007

The tests have confirmed it. Jonnae has indeed relapsed. Aggressive chemo will begin tomorrow, or Monday. We're awaiting the arrival of a new antibody that begins on Day 1 with the rest of her chemo.

It's been an emotional afternoon. After the spinal tap, when her sedation began wearing off, Jonnae told me she felt God with her. I replied, "He's with you baby. I know it! Isn't it awesome?"

She said, "No mom! I don't just *know* He's with me, I *feel* His presence. I think He wants me to come to Heaven."

I wasn't expecting that. How can I tell her to keep her eyes on *the Coach* and then say, "No baby! Don't listen to Him"?

As calmly as I could, I said, "Honey, if you're ready to go, that's beautiful."

A tear rolled down her face. As she was still groggy and falling back to sleep, she said, "I just hate leaving everybody."

I went from feeling positive, strong, and like we're going to fight this thing, to feeling selfish and desperate, begging, "No God! I said I would accept your will, but I need her. Please don't take her."

Later, after the drugs wore off completely, we talked more about her vision. She's been thinking about today and the recurrent dream she's had in her youth; to grow up, get married, and have a family of her own. I told her I believe our dreams are placed in our hearts by God. They are not only ours, but His too. I don't think she's ready to surrender to Heaven just yet.

If God is ready for her, I want her to go peacefully. I don't want her feeling like she has to fight because I want her here with me. I don't want her going through more chemo and pain if He is ready to call her home. I wish I knew what the outcome is going to be. I'm willing to accept it whatever it is. I have to.

I smiled and said, "I know God wants you in Heaven, baby! Maybe you didn't hear Him say in 70 years."

THE FIRST "TRIMESTER"

SEPT 7, 2007

We're taking this one day at a time. After much reflection, I am feeling good this morning. Wherever this journey is taking us, I'm ready.

We still don't know if chemo starts today or Monday. I almost hope it's Monday. It is of upmost importance to begin the attack on leukemia, but I so dread the side effects of chemo. The doctor said it won't affect her odds, if we end up starting on Monday.

It is critical to get her into remission. Once we do, and we've found a matched donor for her, the bone marrow transplant will give her a fifty percent chance at survival. Of course, we are not focused on the percentages; that would be like watching the scoreboard. What's on paper doesn't matter; all that does is the will of God. We are watching the Coach. He is bigger than any statistic.

Chemo has begun. It's been administered over the last several hours. She's sleeping now. I don't know how long she has until she feels its side effects. This protocol is faster and stronger than anything she's experienced before.

This is déjà vu from her initial leukemia diagnosis in 2005-acceptance, strength, and a feeling that this isn't really happening.

SEPT 8, 2007

It didn't take long for the chemo to wreak havoc on Jonnae's small body. They just came in with concerns about her low resting heart rate. I don't understand the numbers, but one of them is half what it was during the day.

They have stopped her medicine temporarily to do an EKG. The new drug and chemo caused her to vomit, run a fever, have leg pains, numbness, and rigors, all in only a matter of minutes. The meds should have been done by now, but they slowed the pace of the drip considerably before stopping it all together. She asked me to pray with her and said she was scared. We read from the Bible and she fell asleep while we prayed.

I know I need sleep, but don't want to be sleeping if/when she slips away. I can't keep the thought from occupying my mind. My heart is heavy and I sense the end is coming. Maybe it's from what we witnessed yesterday. I hate these drugs! They may be necessary to save her, but they have no mercy on her body. It's so hard to watch. I feel so helpless.

When her body started trembling, she said quietly and peacefully, "Mom, when life gets tough, toughen your Faith! Remember? You bought me a keychain that says that."

Jonnae is doing much better. The infusion that was so hard on her is finished. Next weekend the chemo won't be administered so quickly and should not affect her as badly.

She got shots in her legs today. She's gotten them several times before. We call the drug "peg" (short for Pegasparginase). The required dose is stronger this time around and required her getting three of them at the same time. She was forced to get over her fear of needles years ago. She holds my hand and just as it is time for them to stick her, we start praying softly together. Today she didn't even flinch. I'm so incredibly proud of her strength and faith.

This experience is horrible. This cross is a heavy one to carry. But we both realize that we would never know our faith and Father, the way that we do, without this disease having instigated it. He is our source of strength.

Sept 9, 2007

Johnny gets frustrated with how intently I focus on Jonnae's needs. In addition to his concern for me, he believes I need to be home with him and the other children more. He encourages me to allow others to relieve me when our hospital stays are long. You can imagine the strain it produces.

Yesterday, Jonnae had such a good day, I was comfortable with her having friends stay at the hospital with her for a *slumber party*, while Johnny and I went out. The nurses would contact me immediately if any changes occurred. Johnny and I would return to be with her after church in the morning.

The church service was expectedly emotional. Jonnae had endured her two-and-a-half year protocol of treatment and we believed she was cancer-free when we scheduled a full day of events to be held on the church grounds. Today was the day we were to celebrate her victory and cancer survival with a large celebration attended by family, friends, and the community. Over the entire course of her chemo, Jonnae had saved things with the intention of sending them up in smoke, at this, her "survivor" celebration.

I heard something during Mass that made me anxious to get back to Jonnae. (I can go from steady to shaky in a matter of minutes.) One of the readings was a letter from Paul. He spoke of a father being reluctant to let go of his son, in death. The words he had written tore at my heart. I couldn't help but wonder if this was another instance of God's Word coming alive. I asked, "Is this for me, God?"

Later in the mass, as if to discern that indeed He was speaking to me, a song repeated the words to let go. It spoke of comfort after "mourning and grieving the loss of your loved one." As my dad's bold steady singing voice began to crack, and he tried not to cry, I knew he was interpreting the song the same way that I was. My dam broke and the tears flowed.

During announcements, Father informed the parish that Jonnae's cancer had returned and that we weren't having the celebration as stated in the bulletin. I broke down once again.

This morning my heart was saddened by God's Word. Tonight it's comforted by it.

We've made and hung these scripture posters:

For nothing is impossible with God. Luke 1:37 (NIV)

If you BELIEVE, you will receive, whatever you ask for in prayer. Matthew 21:22 (NIV)

9

Do not fear, only BELIEVE, and she will be saved.
Luke 8:50 (NRSV)

We walk by faith, not by sight. 2 Corinthians 5:7 (NKJV)

I can do all things through Christ who strengthens me.
Philippians 4:13 (WEB), also Jonnae's favorite.

I waver from believing she'll be a miracle to believing I'm being prepared to let her go. Normally, I'm not affected by the odds or others' lack of belief. However, she's spoken of God wanting her in heaven. As in church this morning, sometimes scripture even seems to reinforce it. A constant tug of war ensues within me. Strangely, I feel both sides are prompted by a gentle and loving Spirit.

In about a week, Jonnae will be feeling more of the chemo's side effects. Anticipating what I know is to come, I've taken a lot of deep breaths today. I desperately want to believe she will kick this thing. I never doubted she would before. Why is it different now? Is it because I'm exhausted, or is it something else? I refuse to let go of hope. I will not stop believing in miracles, or her ability to conquer.

Just last week, before this horrible nightmare began, she brought home an essay she had written about me being her pillar and how I've always believed in her. I still do. We've learned to focus on blessings and gratitude, even on the most difficult days. The strategy will not change.

SEPT 11, 2007

With each passing day, Jonnae is feeling more nauseous and tired. We are familiar with these effects of chemo and are dealing with them as they come.

She is such an amazing child. She loves to make me laugh and is so good at it. She gets her quick wit from Johnny. A friend just called to inquire about visiting hours. Jonnae heard me say they weren't strictly enforced. With sass, attitude, and a smile, she said, "I'm not in prison."

With this relapse, she has yet to host a pity party--not even a short one. When the time has come, she's decided to have as much fun as she can with her baldness. The first time she lost her hair, we made a temporary tattoo to put on her head for a special event. She's thinking of more things like that we can do, ready to make the most of it. She is quite good at making lemonade with her lemons.

I try to do the same. Here at the hospital, they know me as the mom with an exercise ball in the room, who does early morning workouts in the stairwell. My exercise is as imperative to me as brushing my teeth or taking a shower. Some people don't understand it, but it's how I get set for the day.

With eyes and hearts wide open to the gift of life, we are embracing it. I can't say, "If we can do it, you can do it!", if we don't do it first. So, we are, one moment at a time.

SEPT 12, 2007

When I played ball in my youth, it was extremely difficult for me to not swing at every pitch. Even when my coach would tell me to "take a pitch," I found myself swinging. Today was no different--I swung at the same pathetic pitch all day long.

I woke up today, ready to *step up to the plate and make contact with the ball*. It's all about fundamentals at this point. I don't have to *hit one out of the park;* I just need to *get a hit*. That's not my usual mindset, but when I'm struggling, it's best to go back to the basics.

This morning I made the mistake of reviewing Jonnae's chemo protocol and the study attached to it. The first sentence states: "Children who suffer early marrow relapse have dismal outcomes of less than twenty percent success rate."

That was a pitch I wasn't expecting. That statistic was hard to see in print. You might be asking why I hadn't seen it before; I chose not to.

Sometimes information is not a good thing. When I was preparing for the birth of my first child, I read a book on pregnancy and it scared me to death. I began wondering how anyone ever had a healthy baby. On my own, there wasn't anything to create doubt and worry. My focus strayed from my excitement and enthusiasm, to the *what if's*. So I decided I didn't want, or need, to be educated with details. Until I had directed my attention to the information, I hadn't had a problem with mindset and positive attitude.

My mom and husband combed through the pages of this study the minute they were handed to us. I don't need to know what everyone else has done. I only need to know what I can

> THE ENEMY HAS A WAY OF USING OUR OWN VOICE TO KNOCK US DOWN.

do and do it. That is what I try to instill in Jonnae. What her inner voice says is the only voice she needs to hear. I've also warned her to be careful. The enemy has a way of using our own voice to knock us down.

That's exactly what happened when I read that study this morning. As I heard the relentless chatter in my head, I *looked to the Coach for a sign* and got one: "Don't swing at that pitch!"

I finally asked myself, "Are you gonna swing at that stupid statistic and foul tip all day long? Or are you going to keep your eye on the Coach with Luke 8:50: 'Do not fear, only BELIEVE and SHE WILL BE SAVED?'"

That's the swing that finally produced a hit. I worked hard for that one!

For five months I've been training for a Leukemia/Lymphoma triathlon that's taking place in Florida. I was doing it as a way to commemorate Jonnae's cancer survival by crossing the finish line. I was going to give back to a society that had contributed to her cure and cross one too. While on a bike ride yesterday, I was engulfed in a tug of war. Do I continue or not? I've gone from being excited to celebrate her victory, to being completely devastated. On one hand I need the distraction the triathlon will provide. On the other, I don't want to leave her. I prayed to be able to set myself free from participation in the triathlon; to forget it and be at peace with the decision.

On my way back to the hospital, I realized what a difference

Jonnae's relapse has made for my team. Leukemia has hit close to home and, as a result, has made the purpose of their participation much more personal. They have a whole new drive. My going, my sharing this story, could empower everyone participating in the same way.

If I sacrifice my time with her to fight the fight, what I can't do by myself, we can do in numbers. I've never wanted so badly to not do something. This is where I test my "I WILL NOT QUIT" muscle, more than I ever have in my life. This is where I show her and everyone else, when you REALLY want to quit, you fight and go on.

The tug of war continued: *I don't want to leave her. Not knowing what the future holds, I want every second with her.* A tug from the other side responded: *There are others that didn't want to leave. You don't want to go any more than our soldiers who have gone overseas. They leave pregnant wives and miss out on births of their children. They don't want to leave and miss the first steps, first words, graduations and once in a lifetime events. They don't want to go, but they do. They go for the cause, they go for the fight.*

It's not that I need to, or that I want to; I've been *called* to. I must go.

I shared this with Jonnae, my family, and the doctors. They are supportive. I've never wanted so much to not do something. A couple of days will seem like a couple of weeks, maybe months, but it's a powerful mission. I need to use the pain, the disappointment, and the rawness of our story, to propel these willing "troops" to fight and fight hard, until this war against blood cancers is won forever.

On a much lighter note, my exercise ball has finally made it to Jonnae's hospital room. My family acted like they wouldn't be caught dead carrying the thing up here. The nurses have asked about it. They know from previous stays that I don't leave home without it. I told them I've missed it more than they've enjoyed joking about it.

It's been quite the conversation today. I'm determined to do what I can to maintain my fitness. Days are long and the clean eats aren't easy to acquire, but exercise doesn't have to be nonexistent. We have choices! I'm making mine! That is the only thing I have control over that cannot be taken away.

The exercise provides health for me and comic relief for the staff. It's always good for a laugh when they open the door to bring Jonnae food, clean her room, or check her fluids, to find my butt up in the air doing pikes on the ball or discover the sound they heard, from the other side of the door, was me jumping rope.

SEPT 14, 2007

The new drug that wreaked havoc on Jonnae last Friday didn't have the same effect today. PRAISE GOD! She's had a small headache and has been tired, but no vomiting, rigors, extreme rise in blood pressure, or leg pain.

The side effects of chemo that we are more familiar with have shown up quicker this time. Joint pain, double vision, loss of hair, and extreme changes in appetite, didn't occur for months, or even a year, before. After only a week, she's begun experiencing those things regularly.

She's getting a platelet transfusion now, and may need another tomorrow, pending labs.

Based on past experience, I suspect this week to be difficult. The mood swings, nausea, and fatigue, will be constant in challenging Jonnae's positive attitude. Oh, but I'm not worried! Fight and fight some more, that's what she'll do. It won't be easy, but our girl is good at "tuff." That's why we call her "Tuffstuff."

SEPT 15, 2007

I found myself reflecting on this crazy story while on a run today:

During our last transfer for Johnny's work, I had reverted back to unhealthy eating habits; primarily binging on food and not working out. I put on 20 pounds and was miserable. Crazy as it was, I entered a Toughman competition (a boxing tournament for amateurs), figuring if I couldn't get back into shape on my own accord, I certainly would before stepping into a ring to fight an unknown opponent, in front of who knows how many (I am in no way wired to be a fighter. Before my first fight, my husband even said, "Denise, if you draw blood, don't stop and ask them if they are okay").

I trained myself, best I could. I won my first three fights and then ran up against a 6' 2", black belt for my fourth. We had a lot of those Rocky/Apollo moments where we clocked one another hard at the same time. During the final seconds of the last round, she clocked me in the nose and nearly knocked me out. The judges called the fight a draw and asked us to come back the next night for a rematch.

I am not a quitter. However, if I didn't go back, I would be. It didn't matter that I had a broken nose and felt like I had been hit by a truck, I was going back. The black belt didn't come back, and I won the match by default.

This whole thing is the craziest thing I've ever done. They found someone else to fight me for the championship fight. This time, my opponent was a 230-pound female with some serious anger issues. In a defensive move, near the end of the second round, she decided she would rather wrestle than box. In response to her trying to take me down to the mat, I used my legs to brace against her. Her weight, plus my own, was too much for my right knee to bear. I tore my ACL right there in the ring.

With literally, only one leg to stand on, I stumbled until my body was supported with the ropes. With no way to defend myself, my opponent had her way with my face. My nose opened back up and the referee halted the fight. I convinced him I could go on (I'm a competitor. Maybe a stubborn, ignorant one at times, but I wasn't quitting). The bell rang to finish the second round. The final round began and I immediately fell to the ropes again. This time the ref called the fight. It was my turn to lose by default.

What is the point of reflecting on this? I've been defeated, or hanging by a thread in many trials and persevered.

Jonnae and I have returned home from the hospital. With my husband out of town and my parents on their way home, I succumbed to chaos and exhaustion and *lost a round in the fight* today. The tension and stress of keeping Jonnae and her surroundings germ free: dropping off prescriptions at the pharmacy, picking up groceries, leaving her in the car while I did so (because she can't be around anyone), running the other kids to and from practices, frazzled me. I usually take things in stride, but today I came unglued. Just as I would have years ago, I binged on everything I could get my hands on. The grip of addiction is horrible. Today, it won hands down.

It didn't take very long for the carb coma to slam me. I slept for a couple of hours before I managed to drag myself to the bedroom and throw on some running clothes. I wanted to at least get a single wheel back on track with a run in the subdivision. This memory of the boxing event came to me, while on the run, to fuel me for the rest of the day.

As I came back into the house, it occurred to me that I hadn't gone back to the pharmacy to pick up Jonnae's meds. Problem being, it was Sunday and they had closed two hours earlier. I went back to the hospital for a new prescription to take to a 24 hour pharmacy.

I waited in the pharmacy parking lot for 40 minutes before the medication was ready. The chaos of the day continued as I returned home to find Jonnae's dog, Sassy, had eaten chocolate from a gift basket left on the floor of her room. The kids were in bed, it was 11:30, and I had nine puddles of vomit to clean up. Now I'm ready to fall into bed and it's nearly 1:30am.

The day was exhausting in every way, but I've found myself down as the bell rings before. Many have counted me out when it looked as if I couldn't go another round, but I found a way to go on. I will not, WILL NOT, let the lost rounds keep me from fighting back. The near knockout will not take me out of the fight. As the saying goes, "What doesn't kill us makes us stronger."

SEPT 17, 2007

Fantastic news! My two oldest boys, Nolan (17) and Austin (13) are both matches for Jonnae's bone marrow. They will be tested further to see which one is best suited for her.

As for Jonnae, her ANC count is currently still zero, which means she is confined to our home and needs to wear a mask when we travel to the hospital. Wednesday, we go in for counts to see if her platelets are okay. They need to be a certain number for the bone marrow aspirations, spinal tap, and chemo scheduled for Friday.

I'm still quite unnerved about leaving for the triathlon Friday, before her chemo is done and while she's in the hospital. I feel like I have the flu or something. Of course, I don't. It has to do with everything going on here and how my body responds to it. It's a feeling I'm too familiar with. I'm anxious for the triathlon training to be over, the weekend behind me, and back to being with my girl.

SEPT 20, 2007

Jonnae is running a fever and her blood pressure is low. An alarm on her I.V. stand keeps going off, causing a lot of commotion. Nurses flit in and out for vitals, but she's managing to sleep through what looks to be the beginning of a rough night. Her nose and mouth now have a condition called mucositis. She's had horrible experiences with it in the past, for it causes a great deal of pain.

When she got this before, the pain was so intense she couldn't even drink through a straw. She was on morphine and put on an IV for nourishment. It's horrific to witness. This "shot" at being cured is the pits. I have other choice words I really feel like using, but I won't.

In the morning, I'll pack for the triathlon trip before going to Morehead with Johnny for the sale of our farm. It's too big a financial burden, and much to Johnny's dismay, we are selling it. After the closing, I'll come back to the hospital to spend as much time with Jonnae as I can, before leaving for the triathlon. Her sedation is scheduled for 10:30 a.m. After that she won't be awake too much. I'll head to the airport at noon.

So much is going on, but I continually remind myself, "Embrace the day you've been given!"

SEPT 21, 2007

I knew when I left the hospital it was the last time I would see Jonnae with hair for a while. She loves for me to play with it and with each pass of my hand this morning, it was coming out by the handfuls. It wasn't like we hadn't expected it. She began combing it and surprisingly got a kick out of how fast it accumulated around the comb. She handles everything with such a great attitude.

Upon my return from the sale of the farm, she greeted me with a huge smile on her face and a Mohawk. Even it won't last. She was just being funny and the Mohawk will be gone by tonight or tomorrow. She plans on putting Leukemia/Lymphoma tattoos on her head to kick off the triathlon festivities.

The team had t-shirts made. Everyone on the team, and in my family, is going to wear them on Sunday. They have Team Taylor on the front with Jonnae's picture, and say "Kicking Leuk's Butt!!!" The Team in Training logo is on the back. We are all geared up and ready for this triathlon to take place.

SEPT 24, 2007

I'M BACK! I'm glad the triathlon is behind me and so glad to be home. If it's possible, I think Jonnae is even more so. She made a beautiful card for me with such loving words, telling me how much she loves me and I mean to her. I will treasure it forever. She started crying when she told me how much she missed me. She said, "I am okay. These are happy tears."

She was so excited about my return. I could sense this and heard it in her voice every time I talked to her on the phone while I was away. She took a couple of naps before I got back, in hopes she would be able to stay awake and visit, but she was too exhausted. She asked me to get in bed with her, snuggled up to me, and slept like a baby.

Unfortunately, that sleep didn't last long. She isn't feeling well. Her mouth sores and headaches are worse, and because her counts are staying low, they are giving her Neupogen. It causes her body to ache. I believe they will be putting her on a morphine pump soon. They asked her last night if she wanted one and she opted to increase the pain meds she is already on instead. She, like her momma, wants to forgo the meds. She has a choice in refraining from them now, but eventually she will need them. She's heard about the addiction of morphine and knows when it's time to stop they need to wean you off it. I think that steers her away from using it. At any rate, she has needed to be on the pump before and will need to again. None of us want to see her in more pain.

Speaking of pain, I'm feeling some today, a souvenir from yesterday's event. People who do Olympic distance triathlons, half-Ironman's, and Ironman's, are not of human status. We are completely insane. With the discipline, training, and willpower that came from participating in figure competitions, I realized I did something many people could not. I had no problem admitting it was the hardest thing I had ever done in my life. Those competitions were cake walks compared to yesterday.

I was hoping frequent water stations on the run would help with rehydrating me after the errors I made on my bike, but I was too depleted by the time I got to that point. As soon as I began my run, I had severe cramping just above my knees. The inner, lowest, part of my quads had baseball-size, knotted up muscle. I've never had cramps so intense.

That is when Jonnae surrounded and carried me. I kept thinking of her and drawing on the strength she exemplifies every day. As I trotted (running wasn't an option), I used her perseverance to keep me from stopping to walk. There were A LOT of athletes who succumbed to walking yesterday. I had my moments, but I refused to stay in them. I offered it up for Jonnae.

I chilled a couple of times. I was afraid of what that might mean. I prayed a lot. Turns out Jonnae had been too.

Upon my arrival in Florida, I called Jonnae and told her my start time. I asked her to say a prayer and ring the cowbell for me if she was going to be awake (She was so looking forward to cheering me on at my transitions and ringing a cowbell). She told me she awoke and fell back to sleep. When she woke a second time, she felt bad, so she prayed the Rosary for me from 9 o'clock to 11 o'clock. She's amazing.

Her counts won't come up, her fever won't stay gone, and her mucositis and other side effects have worsened. She'll probably be in the hospital for another week. It's best we stay here and let the hospital staff keep a close watch on her. Her port is also causing some concern. It's been hard to access the last two admittances and now it's wreaking havoc when they push some of her meds through it.

They are doing a dye study today to see if they can find the problem. I don't know what they are going to do. With her counts this low, opening up any part of her is risky. I guess the doctor will tell us more in the morning.

She's on a pain pump. It is controlled, so there is no way she can over use it. The doctors were in to look at her mouth and made the comment that it made their mouths hurt just looking at it. Poor thing.

Her bone marrow Friday didn't produce the results we needed. They said the aspiration they performed when she first relapsed reported 99% leukemia blast cells. This aspiration showed 28%. I thought that sounded like significant improvement, but it wasn't what they were looking for. She is considered a slow respondent, once again. She was classified that way during her first round with Leuk, also.

I'm tired and sore, but for whatever reason not yet ready to call it a night. I've already prepared my comfy (sarcasm) window seat bed. My back is sore, along with the rest of my body. Johnny was ready, and really wanting, to come spend the night with us tonight when he got off work. He had a long day and didn't get off until 10, so he wouldn't have gotten up here before 10:30. She didn't mind. After a weekend without any, she just wants more mom time.

SEPT 25, 2007

Jonnae is having a much better day. Her pain is down and her spirits up. Her counts are still low, but the pain meds are helping her headache. We've also created a paste that is improving the condition of her mouth sores.

She hasn't been out of bed for a few days, so we went for a walk around the floor. Now we are getting ready to watch one of her favorite shows, *Gilmore Girls*. We started watching the series on DVD the first year she had leukemia and enjoy the mother/daughter relationship of the two main characters. They are really close and funny, a lot like us.

It's best to not sweat the small stuff and celebrate the victories; ALL OF THEM. I had been struggling with my triathlon time and how I fell short of my goal. However, I realize I could have quit and didn't. I went for the cause, not for myself. I'm not going to let the enemy of defeat rob me of celebration and joy. He wrestled with me for a bit, but he's lost his grip. All is well with my soul.

SEPT 26, 2007

The doctor awoke us with alarming news this morning. Not the best way to begin a day at the hospital. Jonnae needed platelets and there weren't any; not just here at the hospital, but the entire state.

He said he'd never seen that situation before, where there is a waiting list state wide. It's never been a problem for us to obtain them, so the concern was one we've not experienced before. Worrying about it wasn't going to change it, or fix it. It was to be viewed as an opportunity.

I've read how every minute presents an opportunity for something. Well, I guess this opportunity was about testing my "surrender" muscle. I've got to F.R.O.G. (**F**ully **R**ely **O**n **G**od) with this.

It's difficult for me to come up with questions, on the spot, that won't cause Jonnae to be concerned. As a result, I end up not having answers for my own peace of mind. She can be better at relaxing, and relying on God, than me. After the doctor left, I made a comment about the platelet situation. She said, "No offense mom, but could you just let me go back to sleep?"

Later, our nurse came in and announced that platelets had been acquired. She said she would back shortly to start transfusing them. Jonnae asked if she could take a bath while the platelets were running and the nurse told her to wait until the transfusion was over. We waited for 45 minutes for the nurse to return before I found her at the nurse's station. I said "Didn't you say her platelets were here?" to which she replied, "Well they were. Another patient was more critical, so they were given to them. We've called in another order for Jonnae."

Given the shortage and the way the doctor relayed the news this morning, it was certainly a test for me to remain calm. I approached the resident to express my frustration, "Correct me if I'm wrong, but isn't Jonnae's situation 'critical'?"

He said she would be fine until her counts got down to 10,000 (They are at 19,000).

I said, "So, you are suggesting we wait for them to drop and for her to feel really bad before we do something?"

He was unaware that her platelets had been given to someone else. He told me he would investigate the matter and be in to speak to me. I went back to Jonnae's room. She knew I was fighting the negatives and she pointed to one of her posters and said, "Mom, when all is right with your soul..." In unison we said, "no one can steal your joy."

I understand that the other child was considered more critical. Evidently, the platelets were divinely provided for that child. But as Jonnae's mother, it was hard for me to know platelets had been there and could possibly not be replaced in time for her.

My husband is going to be staying with Jonnae tonight. He is off tomorrow and I need a night in our bed.

It's been a rainy day here (literally and figuratively). However, I'm going to continue to soak up the *Son*. He's still here, even if it's challenging to see Him. ALWAYS!

SEPT 27, 2007

I don't know what I've done to be so blessed. I had anticipated a need to hunt for blessings, only there was no hunting. As I was open to see them, I realized my cup is overflowing.

Jonnae and I were consistent with counting our blessings the first year-and-a-half of her battle with Leuk. It was a practice we did to help us focus on the positive. There truly is good in everything if you know how to find it. Initially, we'd recall and write the blessings at the end of the day. Eventually, we developed a "radar" that honed in on the blessing as it occurred, and we made note of it then. We didn't consider general things like food, clothes, or shelter, and we didn't repeat a blessing that we had already acknowledged.

We've both decided to wake up this daily gratitude ritual, for it's been at rest. Today, I'm thankful for:

> 1.) Rest. I had a good night's sleep for a change.
>
> 2.) My workout at the gym. Even though it would have been easy to lie in bed longer, it felt good as I pushed myself to get up and go. Pumping iron is something I've missed.
>
> 3.) Getting to go to my son's football game. It's been an exciting time at our school (Silver Creek hasn't had football in over 60 years). The boys got beat badly tonight, but with a minute to go in the game Layne had an incredible run. It was over 60 yards and he must have broken through 3 or 4 tackles. He is small, but has the heart of a lion. I was so very thankful to be there to see it. I know he was glad we were there to see it, too.
>
> 4.) Spending time with Johnny at the game, counseling, and dinner. We got to communicate and express our concerns and support of one another. We've needed an opening to do that. I feel more connected to him after tonight.

5.) A *gift* from Jonnae. True to her character, she is still ever the giver. My mom was going to spend the night with her, while Johnny and I spent the evening together. While at dinner, my mom called to report Jonnae was having a CT and MRI tonight, instead of in the morning. Because it wasn't initially scheduled, Jonnae would not be sedated.

I decided to come back to the hospital after dinner. Jonnae wasn't feeling well when I got back and just wanted to go to sleep. I was preparing my bed when she began to cry. She said she opted to do the procedures tonight, thinking that way I could sleep in and get a good night's rest at home instead of coming back early for the tests. She hadn't planned on my coming back and was disappointed that my "comfortable night" was lost. CAN YOU BELIEVE IT? What teenage girl, fighting a battle like she's fighting, would continually put others before herself? My daughter! In her selfless love, she chose comfort for me over comfort for herself. I live with an angel.

SEPT 28, 2007

The latest news is complicated. What it all boils down to is Jonnae has what they call an *infarction*. It has been caused by the "peg" shots and, basically, is a sign that blood could be clotting in her brain. The concern seems to be more with continuing the drug, than the actual infarction. For me, the bigger question is how might eliminating part of the protocol affect the battle with the leukemia?

There isn't a "Plan B" to take its place. The peg shot will just be eliminated. They don't seem to believe the infarct puts her in immediate danger and will do another MRI in four weeks to see if it has dissolved. At least that is how I understand it. I hate being the only one here at times like this. My mom and Johnny think of more questions than I do.

Everything is still a go where the rest of the chemo is concerned. The blood they draw tonight will indicate something more about the infarct and the plan of action. Exactly what, I'm not sure. I believe it is supposed to reveal something about the blood flow in the brain and indicate if the infarct is dissolving.

She is sleeping now. Her stomach was bothering her as soon as she finished lunch and she wanted to sleep through the stomach upset. That was about three hours ago.

Johnny is coming up after work to stay with her tonight. I will relieve him before lunch tomorrow. I'm hoping to get to the gym late tonight and early tomorrow morning. Exercise is my medicine. I need it to keep up through this. It is a big part of my overall health; not just physically, but mentally, emotionally, and spiritually.

"Toughness is in the mind and soul, not the body and muscles!" (Alex Karras, former NFL player and actor).

The tenacity of the human spirit is a source of strength that would benefit many if they knew how to tap into it. Every day we are alive, there's a gift in life. It's a gift easily taken for granted; a gift that we forget to say thanks for. I just want to help people replace the sorrow with gratitude. I want them to embrace their experience. I want them to have strong spirits.

The saying, "It's all good!" used to seem silly to me, but I've used it a lot this week. Every passing minute provides an opportunity to react either positively or negatively. We can choose to be a contribution or a contamination. I want to be a contributor. Life is good. It's all good. The key is to know how to view it as such.

> TOUGHNESS IS IN THE MIND AND SOUL, NOT THE BODY AND MUSCLES!"
> ALEX KARRAS

SEPT 28, 2007

I'm exhausted and ready to sleep in my own bed tonight. Ahh! Before I do, blessings from today:

1.) I'm thankful for the news from Jonnae's MRI today.

It wasn't great, but it wasn't horrific. She rested; she wasn't in pain. She's fighting her fear with faith. I'm grateful.

2.) At 11 a.m. today, Jonnae and I did "laps" around the floor in our pajamas. Even as a teenager, I didn't wear my pajama's past 8 a.m. Jonnae got a kick out of me walking around, in semi-public, in my pajamas and slippers with her (rooster hair and all). For the way silly humor, and those kinds of laughs, brighten our days in the hospital, I give thanks. Her smile is so infectious. It radiates joy from the pit of your soul when you see it.

3.) For the help I get from neighbors with the children at home. Tonight the elementary school had a fall festival. Lydia has been looking forward to it and my friend/neighbor made sure she got to go and have fun. We live in a wonderful neighborhood, generous in love, compassion, and support. We are blessed.

4.) Not only is our neighborhood amazing, but the town is as well. Today the elementary school sent a gift bag home with generous gift cards to several area restaurants and the theatre. Each child received a gift card to the mall, as well. I don't know who all from the school is responsible. Regardless, LOVE surrounds us. It is by these acts of love and kindness that we experience a blessed life, even in the midst of pain and disappointment. Our cup runneth over.

5.) My children surround themselves with good people. My oldest son likes a girl whose parents have insisted on meeting him before letting him spend time with their daughter. It's okay to go against the grain and do what others have stopped doing, when you know it's what is best. It's good to be in the company of people who cherish family and do what's necessary to protect it.

SEPT 29, 2007

According to the neurologist, the spot on Jonnae's MRI is an infection, not an infarct. The radiology report came yesterday, listing the spot could be one of four things. That doesn't help narrow it down much. I guess the infarct was the worst of the four scenarios. They zeroed in on the infarction because it needs the most precaution and has the most risk with her chemo. It's still being decided whether or not to proceed with the peg shots as a part of her chemo.

They will be doing an echo later to see if the infection has gotten to her heart or to her brain. She will remain in the hospital with antibiotics for quite a while. We had resigned to that idea already. The surgeon is coming in to evaluate her port (that is where the infection is believed to have originated) to see if it needs replaced. It seems to be moving around and causing some problems with the chemo administered through the I.V, so there is discussion on what should be done about it.

Jonnae and I have just finished writing in our gratitude journals. It is early, but hey, we have already experienced the blessings to document them, so why not?

1.) I'm grateful for the resurgence of my Body For Life Success Journal. This book has proven to be invaluable to me as I seek to reach my goals. I believe whether in the hospital or not, I need to have goals, accountability, and focus. I worked out this morning and I'm weaker than I anticipated. I sacrificed quite a bit of leanness and muscle for the triathlon, but I'm ready to get it back. The goal of doing so, and the use of this journal, will keep me fired up and out of the junk food.

2.) Jonnae and I walked again today. Although I don't like entering the same blessing twice, it was a different walk and I'm thankful for a different reason. Today Jonnae asked me how many laps we normally do. I haven't kept count before. She said she wanted to do 10; that was around lap 4. Two laps later she said she was already tired but still wanted to do 10. I shared with her how I offer up my reps and sets as prayer offerings when I feel like quitting. She smiled and said "I'll strengthen my 'I will not quit muscle'." We finished the 10 laps, discussing who we were offering each lap up for as we did it. I'm thankful for the way we walk (literally and figuratively) our spiritual journeys together.

3.) I think the chicken I brought today might be old (my stomach hurt after lunch), so I'm stuck without my planned food. I'm thankful for the hospital nourishment room. It isn't much in the way of real nourishment, but it has bailed me out of a pinch a time or two. I don't normally do soups because of the sodium, but the warmth of both the cup and the soup, helped me for a few minutes in this arctic environment (Jonnae keeps her thermostat at 62. You read that right. I've placed a frost bite advisory on the door). I'm thankful for the soup, for it could've been a much worse scenario.

4.) Lydia is having a fun weekend. Thanks to the fall festival at school and a friend coming to get her to spend the night. I'm thankful she has something fun to take her mind off of things.

5.) Jonnae felt much better and was awake most of the day. We've spent a lot of time enjoying each others' company. Yesterday she slept almost the entire day. I tried to stay busy, but that was extremely challenging (I was busy eating some of the two dozen macadamia cookies her aunts sent up). I'm very thankful for her good day and pray we will be blessed with another one tomorrow.

Speaking of eating cookies out of boredom and response to emotions, I'm going to ride the wave of motivation that an upcoming speaking engagement is providing me. I'm going to execute the meal, mindset, and exercise plans in the *BFL Success Journal* just as if I were doing an official BFL challenge.

In a few weeks, I'm speaking to an audience of health-orientated people. If I can incorporate the stairs, exercise balls, resistance bands, and pushup bars into a workout, and resist the McDonald's on the first floor, I'll get back to the way of life that best serves me. Normally a fast food place isn't enticing to me at all. But put an emotional binge eater in a hospital room with limited food choices, late nights wracked with emotion, and suddenly it's the *poisoned apple* and irresistible. I'm not going to succumb to these temptations and obstacles anymore! I passed the "I will not quit" test before and now it's time for me to pass this test as well. As an emotional binge eater, it is continual slacking that could set me in an out of control tail spin. I'm not going to let that happen!

SEPT 30, 2007

Jonnae is sleeping now and I'm back at the hospital with her. Last night I was home, while Johnny stayed with her. My mom relieved him this morning, while I took the children to church.

Of course, the infectious disease doctor came while I wasn't here. That has happened before and always makes it more difficult for me to leave. The doctor agrees with the neurologist and believes that the dark spot on the MRI is an infection, not an infarct. The infection could be coming from anywhere. Her counts are beyond low and they've changed the antibiotic to one that would help the infection in the brain, as well as in the mouth. This isn't the greatest news, but it's good because Jonnae can still get the peg shots that are part of the chemo protocol.

While not thrilled with any of these drugs, taking out a key ingredient of a study that's proven to increase success rates, poses significant risk. Taking the "peg" out of the protocol seemed like taking the sugar out of a brownie recipe, and we know that wouldn't work (Of course, a sugar addict having withdrawal would come up with that analogy).

On a different, more personal note, I continue to be challenged with my own issues. Workout and eats were 100% until midnight, when I got home from the hospital. It's beyond frustrating.

Our community is fabulous. We have food delivered by neighbors and friends every other day. Last night someone brought sloppy joes, scalloped potatoes, and brownies. My kids and husband were home, but they didn't bother to put the food in the fridge. I got home, peeked into the containers, and even though it didn't sound all that appealing, proceeded to heat up a plate of it and consume it at midnight (after I've looked at macadamia cookies all day long and didn't so much as put a crumb to my mouth). I had been to McD's to satisfy my daughter's crazy, horrific cravings and bypassed ordering any of the stuff for myself (that is something I have not been able to do lately). So I workout, I complete my mind set goals, and I've had a healthy day eating chicken with an apple, tomato soup, protein shakes, protein pudding and Essentials. Why on earth blow it at midnight? I was so close.

I have a history of falling at night and that is what I did, I fell. My *knees are skinned up a little*, but I'm back on track. After a long absence from the gym and excessive excuses from the triathlon training, it is done. I'm back in the gym, I've revived my journal, I long for my best self, and midnight falls are not going to cut it.

I saw an advertisement at the gym this morning, *"Drop the excuses, drop the weight."* Words are the most amazing thing–powerful and inspiring. I hate excuses. I don't tolerate them from others; I am through tolerating them from myself. I'm the only thing standing between me and my goals. I can't control what is going on with my daughter. I can't control the opinions of the doctors. I can't make choices for my kids, for my parents, or for anyone, but I can make choices for myself.

I'm more than frustrated, I'm angry! I'm sick of cowering to outside happenings and letting them be excuses for my poor choices. I despise anger and it won't reside in me, regardless of who it is being directed at, including myself. So in order to kick the anger out, I've got to commit to doing better. RECOMMIT! And so, I am.

We all sit on a fence, straddling it for a length of time, before we decide we're uncomfortable enough to get off. I'm off! I'm through. I've had it! Thank God I've got the Tennessee speaking event looming to keep me on track. I really want to look and feel great when I meet this group of very special people. I want to walk tall and with a smile on my face. When I'm not living to my full potential, it's hard for me to do that.

Jonnae is awake and ready to go for a walk. We are looking forward to a girlie mom/daughter night, with facials, pedicures and reality TV. Certainly not quality television, but junk TV is better than junk food.

Some of my blessings from the day:

1.) My legs are so sore. May seem like a silly thing to be grateful for, but I have the use of them and am back to lower body workouts, which means I'll soon be feeling like "me" again. For that, I'm excited and grateful.

2.) I'm thankful for cotton/spandex sportswear. The long days in the hospital call for comfortable and warm clothing. I can layer up to stay warm in this freezing cold room and remain comfortable. It makes the day a bit more bearable.

3.) I'm thankful that oncology is on the 7th floor. On a lower level, I wouldn't get near the leg conditioning. This way I've got little spurts of cardio sprinkled throughout the day. May seem like a stretch, but honestly, this gratitude journal is to account for the little blessings as much as the grander ones.

4.) I met a woman in the nourishment room today whose granddaughter was just diagnosed with leukemia (four days after her 1st birthday). I think I was able to share some powerful words with her. She seemed most appreciative to speak to someone who's been on this path ahead of them. I'm grateful for the opportunity to be a source of strength and hope to others. It's a blessing to be a blessing. I think I was a small one for her today.

5.) I experienced spiritual warmth, in addition to physical warmth today. I am thankful for smiles.

They're contagious and I've been on both the giving and receiving end of them today.

OCT 1, 2007

Jonnae lovingly called me a fitness freak, gym geek, and nutrition nerd today. I guess carrying my suitcase up seven flights of stairs was asking for it. I admit I can be a bit obsessive sometimes.

She is scheduled to have surgery tomorrow. They're taking her port out because it's been giving her, and the nurses, fits. They put it in, about a year and a half ago, to replace her central line. Both the line and the port are so chemo can be administered without sticking her every time she's given intravenous drugs. The port has been shifting, making it difficult to push the drugs through. It's also the first place the infection showed up. The surgical team didn't want to do the procedure because of her low counts. However, the oncology group feels like it's necessary to take it out.

She got the peg shots today (three of them into the leg). That's the chemo they believed caused the infarct, before they determined the spot was actually an infection. As a result of the infection in the heart and brain, she will be required to stay in the hospital longer. It all sounds awful, but believe it or not, she is feeling well and looking more chipper.

My tri team came up for a visit tonight. I'm sure it was shocking for them to see how different she already looks, with full steroid cheeks and a bald head, but they were thrilled to see her and witness how good she's feeling.

After the visit, I went with the team to dinner and ordered a grilled chicken salad. I must admit, with my latest eating habits and lack of good food choices, I was proud of holding true to the lifestyle I prefer. One of the perks of having lived healthily for the length of time I have is that once I recommit, I bounce back rather quickly.

The blessings from the day:

1.) I received one of the most heartwarming messages I've ever gotten. Its content was personal, but through sharing our story, I've been able to help someone who was living in despair, find peace and joy. Inspiration and encouragement are life giving.

2.) Shortly after receiving that message, I got a phone call from a dear friend, sharing more of the same. God is so good!

3.) After experiencing these first two blessings, I got a devotion via email with this verse:

"Do nothing from selfishness or empty conceit, but with humility of mind regard one another as more important than yourselves." Philippians 2:3 (NASB) Now that's what I call a *sign from the Coach*!

4) Johnny and I sat down to pay bills with profit from the sale of the farm; definitely an answered prayer there. Thank you, Lord.

5) A friend brought grilled chicken to the hospital for me today. That played a big part in my having a 100% clean nutrition day. No blowing it at midnight tonight.

OCT 2, 2007

Some of the blessings experienced today:

1.) I met another mom this morning who is new to this floor. Her son is an adorable little boy, early in his fight against cancer. I helped her find some syrup for his pancakes (the nourishment room was out, but we had some in our room). I gave her a banner that reads, F.R.O.G. (Fully Rely On God). She was very open to receiving it. Sometimes you run into parents who are not. Parents deal with this in all kinds of different ways. I'm thankful for every opportunity to spread a little

Sonshine, certainly up here on the 7th floor.

2.) Jonnae had a really good day considering the surgery and sedation. She's sore, but getting around well and still has her appetite. She's been emotional in thanking all of us for what we do for her. Her gentle, loving, sensitive heart is a beautiful thing to witness. I'll never stop being grateful for the angel I have in her.

3.) "If anyone is to be My disciple, let him take up his cross and follow Me." That really struck a chord with me as Jonnae and I prayed the Sorrowful Mysteries of the Rosary today. I'm grateful, as is Jonnae, for the awareness of Christ's sacrifices made for our eternal salvation. The least we can do is carry our cross with the same willingness.

The Rosary is a beautiful prayer, divided into five decades; each decade representing an event of Christ's life. There are four sets of "Mysteries". The Joyful, The Luminous, The Sorrowful, and The Glorious. We are saying the Rosary more than we ever have and found an awesome website with pictures and thoughts for reflection to assist us in praying it. http://www.catholiccompany.com/content/Mysteries-of-the-Rosary.cfm

4.) My sister has joined me in fasting. Since Jonnae's relapse, I have been fasting every Tuesday, as an offering for Jonnae's healing. We got the news of her relapse on a Tuesday. In an attempt to make our prayer *louder*, her gesture is meaningful and loving.

5.) I've been blessed with artistic talent that allows me to bless others. Today, I was drawing penguins to put in a line at the bottom of Jonnae's door (she keeps it so cold in here, I thought it would be funny as an inside joke). There was a family in the waiting room watching me draw. They shared that their three-year-old daughter loves penguins, so I gave two of the penguin drawings to her siblings to color for her. They were really excited and very appreciative. I was reminded of one more way that I am blessed. "It is in giving that you receive." -St Francis of Assisi.

We're on our way down for a second MRI to check on this infection in her brain. Jonnae tried to get out of it because she's sore and doesn't feel like moving. More than that, she knew I was looking forward to *Biggest Loser* and figured we would miss most of it. I've never known anyone so selfless.

OCT 3, 2007

Last night's MRI lasted about 45 minutes. The parent's waiting room had a TV and we were the only ones down there. So, I did get to watch *Biggest Loser* after all. I get emotional watching these contestants. I cry every week. Last night was no exception. I can relate to struggles with food. I've hit 200 with each of my five pregnancies. More psychologically scarring than that, I was called Miss Piggy up until 7th grade. I have a lifetime history of food addiction. That's why I talk about food, and the choices I make, so much. It's my weakness and where I myself *lose the battle*.

I'm starting to feel pretty gnarly. I'll be stopping by the gym before going home for a much needed shower. Then I will head to my son's football game with the rest of my family. I had hoped we would all be together for Nolan's 17th birthday, but that's a hard thing to make happen these days. Hospital stays or not, the kids are getting older. They are more involved in their own extracurricular activities; everyone's agendas don't seem to blend well anymore. Oh, to turn back the clock and embrace what we had when they were small! If we had known the life we took for granted would someday be gone, we would have paid more attention. We've learned the hard way that nothing in life is guaranteed. The future is overrated and the time to be happy and give thanks is NOW.

> IF WE HAD KNOWN THE LIFE WE TOOK FOR GRANTED WOULD SOMEDAY BE GONE, WE WOULD HAVE PAID MORE ATTENTION.

OCT 4, 2007

The neurologist came in yesterday and said the spot they believe to be an infection, doesn't look any worse. Actually, it's a teeny bit better. The inflammation around the spot has improved. He said it doesn't look like an infarct and doesn't appear to be anything from radiation she received before her relapse. They will repeat the MRI in a couple of weeks and keep her on this new antibiotic for about 4 more.

I didn't journal last night because Johnny wanted me to go to bed when he went. I start my gratitude with that being my first acknowledged blessing. Of course, our time is limited these days in any capacity, but intimacy is really scarce. We both needed it. It was great. Enough said.

The father of a young lady, who had a transplant in 2005, surprised us with a visit today. This father/daughter team have been doing amazing things with fundraising and bringing about awareness to leukemia. Their website is www.meghansmountain.com. I think this will be a very positive connection and am anxious to see, with our forces combined, the difference we can make for families dealing with childhood cancer.

We also got a visit from the local director of the Leukemia/ Lymphoma Society. He was in Florida with us for the triathlon and brought a goody bag to Jonnae. He said he feels honored to be a part of Team Taylor. He had leukemia when he was 4, and relapsed when he was 14. That is a scary thought, but a story to draw hope from, also. We are blessed to meet these individuals who have won their fight against Leuk.

We got the first EOB (Explanation of Benefits) from our insurance company. Jonnae's first hospital stay from this relapse (just the bill from the hospital, not the doctors or anesthesia) was over seventy grand. It makes me sick to my stomach when I open bills and EOB's, just thinking about what would happen if they dropped us or if we didn't have coverage. It is a magnificent blessing not to worry about bills on top of everything else. Our deductible and out of pocket expense for her medical care are minimal compared to the grand total.

I finally dropped the excuses and started dropping the pounds. It took me long enough to get off of the fence. I'm grateful for the *tool box* I've acquired. I can't build anything just by having the tools. I need to get them out and put 'em to work. I like to think of myself as an experienced, skilled builder. I had quit using the tools but am working with them again. It feels really good. I'm so blessed.

> 1.) I had some really silly dreams last night, but I dreamed. That's a sign of good sleep. I never remember my dreams for some reason. Silly dreams and good sleep – they're something I'm not taking for granted. Life is good!

> 2.) I'm thankful for sarcasm, humor, and laughter. Jonnae is great at dishing out all three. We were watching a movie today, *Griffin and Phoenix,* and she made some witty remarks while watching it. We both got tickled.

We love romantic comedies and Dermot Mulroney. Ironically, this was a movie about dying with cancer. There was no indication of that on the box. As we watched it I found myself fighting back tears. Jonnae sees me cry during movies all the time, but I wasn't sure how she would respond to me crying this time, considering the movie's subject. The fact that there was sadness, mixed with the humor, didn't affect Jonnae in any negative way. She loved the movie so much, she wanted to know if we could buy it. We really got a kick out of Dermot's character. I don't know if he's ever played a character we didn't really like. Anyway, back to the blessing - my kids crack me up with their humor.

3.) As I was leaving the house to head back to the hospital, Jonnae called with a list of cravings for me to pick up on my way. When on steroids, her food obsession is CRAZY. She eats one meal while talking about the next one; which will usually be only an hour and a half later. In her natural state, she eats like a bird; on steroids she eats like a horse. I'm getting away from the blessing again…normally I despise shopping for groceries, but today was different.

Grocery shopping and being outside blessed me today. I actually enjoyed getting the things on my list, knowing how Jonnae would smile as she indulged in them. I was almost to the hospital when it dawned on me, the blessing of being out in the open. I was in a car, but I didn't feel cramped or cooped up. Our view from the hospital window is the side of the next building, there's no seeing the world. I'm thankful for the view of the sky and feeling of freedom I was blessed with today.

4.) It was my oldest son, Nolan's, 17th birthday today. He was like a kid at Christmas. I don't remember him looking so forward to a birthday before. Even though he knew we wouldn't be home to celebrate today, he was really excited. It was cute watching him get giddy about his birthday present this morning. For the gift of life and how living through the eyes of children enhances it, I'm so thankful. I don't know how or why God chose me to mother these five amazing spirits, but I'm not going to put a question mark where He's put a period. I'm just going to thank Him for trusting and blessing me with them.

OCT 5, 2007

Jonnae's platelet count is down and she needs a transfusion before they can do her spinal tap and chemo. Worse than that is her broken heart. Actually it isn't that grim, I should say her broken stomach. It's heart-wrenching to witness a child obsessed with eating because of one drug, forced to go hours without food because of it's reaction to another drug.

She always eats something big right at midnight, because she knows that's going to be it for awhile. They always have her NPO (*Non Per Os,* a Latin term that means "nothing by mouth") from midnight until after her procedure. For her to go until 8 or 9 o'clock is difficult enough. That was the plan, but we all know how plans change. Platelets hadn't even started by 10:30. She was so upset.

I reminded her of something we do to ease disappointment or frustration. We replace *have to* with *get to*. It can be challenging, but when applied, it's fail proof. Instead of saying, "I have to wait until 5 o'clock tonight to eat," she would say, "I get to eat at 5 o'clock tonight." It takes a situation that's difficult to see the blessing in, and gives you an attitude of gratitude to deal with it. When we first heard of this powerful word exchange, we were able to rattle off several examples of replacing "have to" with "get to". It's been a while since we've done it. Today was the perfect day to reinstate the practice.

> I REMINDED HER OF SOMETHING WE DO TO EASE DISAPPOINTMENT OR FRUSTRATION. WE REPLACE *HAVE TO* WITH *GET TO*.

We watched a cute movie to get her mind off the food situation; now she's sleeping.

Jonnae's spinal tap ended up being around 1:00. She always gets nervous before they begin, worried she won't be asleep when they go into her back. The routine is always the same. She asks me to hand over her Rosary and weaves it between her fingers so she won't lose it while sedated. I position myself at the head of the bed, facing her. Her backside faces the doctor so they can draw the spinal fluid out. She holds my hand, with her free one, and asks me to make sure she's asleep before they start. She always asks me several times.

Today the doctor told her if she thought pleasant thoughts, once she was in la la land, she would probably dream of them. When the doctor suggested the beach, or horseback riding, Jonnae interrupted her with "frosted flakes and a vanilla milkshake." This steroid-induced, food obsession really is silly.

She went to sleep fine and the spinal tap occurred without any complications. She woke up for a few seconds, long enough to ask, "How soon can I eat?" and then fell back asleep. She awoke only 15 minutes later and again asked if she could eat. They said, "Sure but you can't sit up for another 20 minutes or so." She had me fix her some frosted flakes and ate them flat on her back before sending me off for a milkshake and an apple pie (You know it's killing me to watch her eat all of this sugar, right).

Overall, it was a good day for her. She's been tired from the sedation but hasn't slept. She's had a difficult time sleeping at night and we're hoping skipping a nap, or two, will help.

I'm in a very quiet house tonight. Although I get enough of it while at the hospital, I'm going to enjoy a different kind of "me" time and give thanks for some blessings.

Today was a little more challenging in the *blessing hunt* than I've experienced in a while. It's the challenging days that strengthen my "gratitude muscle" the most. With thoughts of what I GET TO do:

> 1.) *I got to* see the sunset tonight. It's been awhile since I've seen the beautiful colors of the sky as the sun goes down. I took it in and acknowledged that it was something to be grateful for today.
>
> 2.) *I got to* go to the gym on my way home tonight. Some might would say *had to,* but to be a member of a gym is a *get to* blessing. I've lived in places where that wasn't an option. We've been in a bind financially where we couldn't afford it. It makes a huge difference for me to *get to* go to the gym (Of course being healthy enough to *get to* go is obviously a blessing also).
>
> 3) Speaking of the gym, I witnessed an individual tonight who provided me with quite a few smiles. I don't know her story and don't think she really needs to share it. She was in a world of her own and quite content that way. At first, it appeared she was trying to do some kind of arm workout, like some might would do on a treadmill or elliptical without moving arms. But the gestures were

a bit different. It wasn't until I stepped off my machine, that I got a better view. She was doing cheers, playing the drums, doing some dance moves, all while listening to her outdated CD player and lovin' every minute of it. It would be impossible to experience cardio near her and stay serious. Her reminder to lighten up was a blessing.

4) This morning, one of our neighbors passed away from mysterious head trauma. The death of someone, be it a neighbor, family member, or friend, reminds us that we are not going to live this earthly life forever. Death is real! In preparation for it, we need to embrace LIFE, LOVE, and LAUGHTER, every chance we get. It isn't always easy, but one can choose it. I'm more than thankful for the people, the lessons, and the experiences that have taught me how to do so.

5) It's late, but no one is here to be bothered by my staying up late. I'm going to draw a bath and unwind with the soothing properties of a candlelit room and soft music. We've not always had a home with a big tub, or pretty bathroom. I don't take advantage of this one nearly enough, but I will tonight. Another blessing.

The blessings weren't so hard to find after all.

OCT 6, 2007

We may get to come home for a few days. The doctor reported, "We deserve it." Jonnae's counts aren't up all that much, but she starts a new block of chemo Friday. We'll be in the hospital for a minimum of a week because of it. They want her to enjoy some time at home, while she's feeling as good as she is.

The first block is what I call the cake walk preparation phase. It's no fun, but it certainly is a lot easier than what comes after it. When she was on steroids for the first time ever, we cracked jokes about her food obsessions. She felt fine, ran fevers, and needed to be watched closely, but overall it wasn't so bad. I believe they put these kids on steroids to fatten them up for the starvation period on its way in the next block. In the second round of chemo, they're nauseous, vomiting, and have no appetite. I'm really dreading it for her, not nearly as bad as she is I'm sure.

I continue to speak of food issues because it's my personal battle separate from, but still affected by, Leuk. I know how easily I will fall to the bottom of the pit, if I don't focus on staying on top. Even with mom's homemade pumpkin pies and all kinds of junk surrounding me today (bagels, donut holes, cereal bars, trail mix, chips, and a myriad of frozen stuff) I've stuck to my plan and ate right. It feels awesome.

My not-so-obvious blessings are as follows:

1.) The sky was the most amazing hue of blue this morning. The entire expanse of the sky was the same amazing, vibrant color. No clouds, no variation, just a huge perfect blanket of blue.

2.) I've been driving my husband's truck for the last couple of weeks. I haven't needed a vehicle at the hospital and there isn't a place to park our high-rise van. When we switch, I drive the car belonging to whoever is replacing me. Now, don't get me wrong, I'm thankful for my van. A lot of people would love to have the "mom mobile." It's been great for the size of our family. But it's kind of a boring ride and doesn't really fit my personality. I feel kind of feisty and cool when I'm driving Johnny's truck. May seem shallow or silly, but I've been lifted a little from getting behind the wheel of a cool ride.

3.) Easily lifted, easily amused--that's me! So easily amused, I'm constantly cracking myself up. Thoughts that I think are hilarious, no one else even thinks are remotely amusing. I just had a flashback of Doogie Howser; thought it was kind of funny that I'm comparing myself to Doogie and his late night journaling and giggled out loud. I told Johnny; he didn't even crack a smile. He and my children, think I'm the biggest geek. Doesn't bother me though; it made me laugh.

4.) Johnny and I played nine holes of golf today. Perfectionists + golf = guaranteed disappointment and frustration. It was certainly a gamble for me to go. I've not enjoyed the game as much as I used to. It's a time consuming game and my heart's not in it. Granted, it can be a good getaway and rather enjoyable experience. Today was like it used to be. It didn't matter if we shot a good score or not, just being together and attempting the game was fun. We had a really good day together.

5.) The love and support of friends and community continually warms my heart. Although it is an obvious blessing, and I've repeatedly given thanks for it, I must acknowledge the planning and heartfelt participation of my beloved friends and neighbors in an annual charity walk for the Leukemia/Lymphoma Society this evening. Last year, Jonnae was feeling great and we were in the homestretch of our fight with Leuk when we participated in the Light the Night Walk. Time changes things.

This fight snaps you to a place impossible to take time for granted. After visiting Jonnae yesterday, my youngest daughter, Lydia, was with my mom. She said, "I wish I had a time capsule." My mom asked why and she said, "I would turn back time and spend every second I could with Jonnae."

We don't have time capsules and we never know what tomorrow will bring. Things can change so quickly. To have reminders to embrace life, because we can so easily forget to do so, is definitely something I'm grateful for. I don't mind being reminded several times a day: Focus on THE BLESSINGS.

OCT 7, 2007

Jonnae is sore today and has dealt with some headaches, but we're still on track to go home for a few days. The next block of chemo is set to begin Friday. She will be here for at least five days for it. Then it's a "wait-and-see" from there. All in all, she's had a good day. I have as well.

Children are such a blessing to be around. No wonder "Jesus loved the little children." They can be the sweetest, most authentic, love-giving spirits. Jonnae has been getting cards from all kinds of elementary and Sunday school classes. Their drawings and writings are so cute. But she got one from this little girl, Whitney, who had us giggling out loud. We don't know her, but her card was priceless:

God saw you needed food, so he gave you McDonald's,
    Dairy Queen and Taco Bell.
God saw you needed drink, so he gave you Mtn Dew, Coke,
    Big Red and Dr. Pepper.
God saw you in the dark, so he gave you Light.
God saw you needed an adorable friend, so he gave you ME.

My sister brought her daughters down from Northern Kentucky to visit. They've not seen Jonnae since her relapse. They are four and eight and had made a video to cheer Jonnae up. It's the funniest thing. They act out skits and sing songs. The funniest part is their reenactment of TLC's *What Not to Wear*. It's a riot. They did a quick little segment from each part of the show, just as it is on tv. Renee really out did herself with converting the house into different stores for the shopping part. Again, priceless. Having children around to keep it real and to keep us young at heart, what a blessing!

We had the charity walk last night with Team FROG. In church this morning, there were posters hanging that children had made to promote RESPECT LIFE. One of the posters had a huge drawing of a frog that said "RRRRRRRespect Life." I am not used to seeing a frog in church, and I accepted it as a little *hug* from God. As I was leaving our pew for communion, I looked down to see a big toy frog in the top of a babie's diaper bag. Two frogs in church after an evening of *F.R.O.G.*-spirited friends and neighbors; I don't believe are coincidences. More blessings.

I failed to plan last night what I was wearing to church or how early I needed to rise in order to get ready for church and pack for the trip back to the hospital. It could have meant trouble, being I haven't dressed up in a while. My outfit practically put itself together on its own this morning. You would have to be me and living my life, to know just how big a blessing that was. Picking out clothes takes me a while. I didn't have time for that this morning. Effortless means blessing.

All five of my children together for Nolan's birthday cake and ice cream at the hospital today - blessing.

I wasn't tempted by the sugar and didn't eat one bite of it - blessing.

Girly things that make me feel pretty: heels, jewelry, nail polish, and dress - blessing.

Earlier in the week, I gave thanks for some of my talents. Today, I give thanks for the talent of others through acting, artwork, music, and written word - blessings.

OCT 9, 2007

Yesterday was an exhausting day. Jonnae was being discharged to come home for a few days and her room wasn't ready for her. When she's home, during chemo especially, she plants herself in bed and drops things all around it (typical teenager, I guess). She had been making cards, so in addition to the empty food containers, daily calendar pages, and dirty clothes, there were stamps, ink pads, scrap papers, and poster boards on the floor. Gift baskets, from the previous hospital stay, were strung about also. No one would know how to go about cleaning this child's room, except her mother. My work was cut out for me.

Mom came to the hospital and waited with Jonnae for the doctors' rounds and discharge. I booked it home to prepare Jonnae's room. I found more than a messy room. The kitchen sink was full of dishes. The sofa was overflowing with laundry that needed to be folded. Unopened mail, piles of hospital bills, and EOB's were all over the table, waiting to be filed.

When we first got word of Jonnae's predicted discharge, I called a cleaning service, but we hadn't heard back from them. Already, I was feeling overwhelmed and exhausted. Just as I was getting started on Jonnae's room, I got a call. Help was on the way.

The cleaning service took care of the downstairs while I got Jonnae's room ready. I was so relieved to have help. Two hours later, I was back at the hospital packing up our things (It's amazing how much we accumulate in a hospital room).

Once home, we waited for VNA (our home health care pharmacy and nurse). Jonnae flushes her central line daily and prefers to give herself her shots, so a lot of supplies are needed. The initial delivery didn't have what she needed for her shot. As a result, her next scheduled dose was going to be late. We were off to a stressful start.

After all the chaos and Jonnae safely in bed, my parents came over. I went to the gym for a much needed workout (my medicine).

On the way home, I stopped to pick up a few movie rentals. When I got home, Jonnae took her temperature. Fevers can happen quickly with low counts, so she takes it several times a day. If at any time it is 101, we are to call the doctor and head to the hospital immediately. Her temp was 100.1. Half an hour later, she retook it and it was up to 100.3.

She started to cry and said, "I hate this!" She was very disheartened with the thought of returning to the hospital so soon. I was as well, but said, "Are you EXPECTING it to go down? I am."

She smiled and we decided to watch a movie until it was time to retake it. An hour later, it was below 100. It was a little after midnight, so she set her alarm to retake it at 4 a.m. Both ready for bed, I handed her the phone and told her to call me on the cell if she needed me through the night (the interference on 2-way walkies makes for a restless night).

1.) For the assistance I got with cleaning the house, I am so grateful.

2.) For the comfort of being home and the rest it provides, I give thanks.

3.) For Jonnae's independent and responsible nature,

thank You, Lord. She seems to enjoy playing nurse to herself and I'm completely confident in her. When it comes to dosages and instruction for her care, my mind doesn't comprehend the information she receives so easily. For this solution to the stress, I give thanks.

5.) I received an email, from one of Nolan's teachers, about a paper he had written. He wanted to let me know, not only had Nolan written a very touching paper, but he is a pleasure to have in class. Nolan doesn't speak to me about his feelings or Jonnae's illness. For the reassurance that her child is handling this experience in his own way and is doing fine, the mother of these amazing children cries out in praise to You, God.

6.) The body is such a miracle. I've been blessed with good health. To honor it and take great care of it isn't always easy. For my awareness of its awesome nature, the tools I've been given, and choosing to protect it, I give You praise.

For the blessings I've received, for those I will encounter today, and for the ones I will be receiving tomorrow, I thank You, Lord. I'm Soaking up your Son, and living in your abundant Love.

OCT 10, 2007

I awakened to another beautiful day and am so thankful for the favor God bestows upon me. I pray that every word I speak and every action performed by me, brings glory, honor, and praise to Him.

I went to my workout this morning fighting the temptation to let it slide for the day. I'm more exhausted than I realized. Preparing Jonnae's room for her return home proved to be another tug of war for me. I still haven't recovered.

FAITH, and believing God's bigger than any mountain, was on one side. The big WHAT IF was on the other. I was cleaning off Jonnae's desk and came across her ponytail holders and hair brushes.

She just recently found the confidence to go without her bandana. She had just started doing things with her hair. Putting those things away, and dealing with the harsh reminder of where we find ourselves in this fight, blindsided me. As I temporarily mourned being at war with Leuk again, I heard a quiet voice suggest this was a practice run for something later. It said she wasn't going to make it. It said I'm going to be putting away more than her hair accessories, once she's gone. I prayed as I continued to clean her room.

God, as my Coach, please get in my face and yell some commands at me. Give me a sign and tell me what to do! If this is the Devil's way of distracting me, Help me to rebuke him.

Was the devil trying to take my eyes off the Coach? God's bigger than Leuk. Doubting, wishing, hoping, and fearing, are not signs of FAITH. I'm confident in God's game plan. I'm not swinging at WHAT IF pitches. I'm keeping my eyes on my Heavenly Coach. After looking back to the Coach, I felt better.

The distraction still wore me down. Normally, I don't need to zealously coax myself into the gym, but I made it! I had a really strong leg workout and 20 minutes on the elliptical.

I've never enjoyed running errands. Things I would have heard myself saying I "have to" do, before, I *got to* do, today. Not anything too exciting - oil changes, returning bike shoes, grocery shopping, and picking up storage boxes for all the supplies that make Jonnae's room look like a pharmacy. With an *attitude of gratitude*, I felt free and exhilarated.

While I was out, Lydia cleaned her room to perfection. This was no small feat. She gets distracted easily when it comes to tasks such as this. She had been working hard and was eager to show me. Her closet, under her bed, dresser tops, and TV stand, were all spotless. I hugged her, praised her, and let her choose two rewards from our "What a Great Kid" coupon book. I'm blessed to have my children stepping up during this time.

I give thanks that the pendulum is swinging back to being proactive with our health. We live in a society that is reactive. Our healthcare is really *sick care*. I was excited to find new healthy drink options, at the grocery, for my taste buds.

Everything's been laced with caffeine, sugar, aspartame, or sodium. Ordinarily water is my choice. But during a 24-hour liquid fast, Essentials, water, and protein shakes don't always cut it. It's apparent we want to do better, but care is needed when it comes to what promises we buy into. I'm thankful for the quality options we are getting, and for a stronger health movement.

OCT 11, 2007

I had hoped Jonnae would feel better while we're home. She's not been downstairs since we've been back and has hardly organized her stuff. Ordinarily she really gets into that. I thought with new materials and new storage bins, she might be excited for a while. She did get up for a couple of hours to meet, and school with, her new homebound teacher. Jonnae really wants to keep up with her class and graduate with honors. She wasn't up to schooling today, but once they got going, she was happy to dive into some work.

During Jonnae's first cancer battle, we made prayer bracelets. In the beginning, it was something that provided therapy for us. We used them as a fundraiser and eventually gave them away, to remind people to pray for her. They had a frog charm hanging from them as a reminder to F.R.O.G. (Fully Rely on God) I pulled the beads back out yesterday and made some while watching another movie with Jonnae. It's odd doing something we thought was a thing of the past.

History had a way of repeating itself often today; first with Jonnae's lethargy, then with the prayer bracelets. It did so again, as we continued to watch the movie, *Gracie.* Our guy, Dermot Mulroney was in this one too. The back cover only spoke of a family with courage. It was about soccer, so I thought the courage was about the fight for this girl to play on the boys' soccer team. It was, but she decided to play in honor of her brother, who was killed about three minutes into the movie. I sat there thinking, "DAMN!" How many movies about death are going to find their way into our home?" We both sat there watching, with an awkward energy to the room. I decided to talk through it.

The subject of the movie brought up my personal history. I played on the boys' soccer team for two years at my school, before we had a girls' team. Just as the boys in the movie, the boys had a hard time accepting me and two other girls on the team. They didn't think we were tough enough. I loved proving to them I was. My first soccer *high* was when one of the boys went flying through the air, landing on the ground with a thud, because I beat him to the ball and was strong with my kick. It was AWESOME and I was psyched. I earned a starting position on the team and eventually had their respect. *Gracie* was a good movie and I enjoyed the reminiscing.

Memories are blessings. I can't say that I want to pull all of them up, but occasionally I find myself remembering things I had completely forgotten, like the victory of my soccer experience. Jonnae didn't know I had played on the boys' soccer team. It was fun sharing with her how much I was like *Gracie*. The reminder of how I have been victorious, in the midst of a tough fight, is something I greatly need right now.

Excitement and pride, born from a child's success, is a blessing. Sharing victory, whether large or small, brings such joy. After intercepting the ball and running an amazing 62 yards, Layne scored a touchdown last night. He was so PUMPED, the whole team was. It was awesome! I give thanks for his heart, his talent, and his spirit.

Nolan shared his English paper with us last night. He had written about his growth through Jonnae's example. It was beautifully written and a blessing to read. For the daily experiences that remind me that our children are incredible individuals, I'm blessed beyond belief.

For media that allows us to relive the captured moments, I am thankful. In *Gracie* the family was watching old films of the father playing soccer when he was young, and of the brother who was killed. That was one of our favorite things to do growing up; get the old projector out and watch home movies. I wish I had done more with the camcorder, but I've always taken lots of pictures. It's a blessing to relive precious moments through recorded history.

Oct 12, 2007

We were at clinic all day yesterday. There is a "hand" wall that covers one side of the waiting room. When a patient completes treatment and is considered a survivor, they get to dip their hand in paint, put it on the wall, and sign their name next to it. They had run out of room and haven't been able to add names for a while. Yesterday when we came in, they had started a second wall. Jonnae began to tear up and said, "I wanted so bad to put my hand print on that wall."

I told her she would be the only one that got to put two hands up there, side by side, for having kicked Leuk's butt, not once, but twice.

She's been thinking about the long stay she'll have in the hospital, following transplant. Sassy (her dog) already seems to have bonded more with the other kids, in her absence. Jonnae feels like Sassy will not even know her when she returns. I was trying to think of a solution, but there really isn't one. I needed to steer her into a different direction--one of acceptance and not one of sadness.

Again, I shared with her the bravery of our soldiers. They're leaving their loved ones, just like she'll be leaving hers. Some of them miss the birth of a child. Some of them leave when the child is small, and upon their return, the child doesn't recognize them. I said, "Can you imagine being a father or mother, anxious to come home to your children, and them not even knowing you? But they accept it, they give the child time to get to know them. The bond is recreated and the love comes back. It will with Sassy, too."

She instantly let go of the tears, stopped with the sadness, and was content to resume her homework.

These things for which I give gratitude may seem trivial, but when you are in the hospital all day (fighting frustration,) you find thanks in the small stuff:

> 1.) We have a $20 co-pay with each clinic visit. Because we were sent to the hospital for an unpredicted platelet transfusion, we were refunded the $20. Obviously, we

would have rather gone home, but Jonnae said, "That's $20 we can spend on pizza."

2.) We normally pay $4 for parking at the clinic. Because we were sent to the hospital, from the clinic, we didn't need to pay for parking today.

3.) My ringtone gives me a lift and reminder every time someone calls (I downloaded it only a few days before Jonnae's relapse). I tell everyone, "Worry is worthless!" It's good to be reminded with this upbeat Zoe Girl tune called "Don't Worry 'bout a Thing."

> **"WORRY IS WORTHLESS!"**

4.) I'm grateful for the sense of smell. I believe aromatherapy works. Some scents immediately give me a different feeling just by my smelling them.

5.) I'm thankful for how fun it is to shop for a gift for someone. When you take the focus off of yourself, to spread some love and give some cheer, it's never a waste of time or money.

OCT 13, 2007

We're at the hospital again today. Jonnae is sleeping off her sedation. It was a long day here yesterday and probably will be again today.

They performed another bone marrow aspiration to see where her counts are. We may need to wait before starting the next block of chemo. Expecting we get good news and aren't late getting home, I'll be leaving for Tennessee tonight. As long as things are still on track for Jonnae, I'm speaking at an annual Body for Life event in Knoxville tomorrow night. Mom will take over for me until I get back.

As usual, Jonnae has been nothing but encouraging and supportive of this decision.

Yesterday, I said, "I'll wait and go Saturday if they keep you here or start your chemo today. The first day or two are predicted to bring on nausea and vomiting."

She said, (with a smile even), "Mom, I am perfectly capable of throwing up in a bucket without needing you beside me. GO! I'll be fine!"

The Divine spirit that shines through this child's eyes when she smiles is impossible to paint with words.

OCT 15, 2007

Jonnae had a non-eventful weekend. Her counts are on the rise. As soon as they are high enough, we'll be able to proceed to the next block of chemo. It's going to be a nasty one, but the sooner we get it over with, the closer we are to victory. She's tired and resting. It hasn't been the mother/daughter day we had anticipated, but we're looking forward to her feeling up to one soon.

Is there anything in life as wonderful as love? I can't imagine it. I have felt so much love over the last few days that I'm overwhelmed with joy and gratitude.

There are blessings large and numerous from the BFL Tennessee event. I'm tempted to try and recount all of them, but I know it's impossible. I will share the least obvious that I thought of while driving home.

> 1.) I take the era in which we live, and the means of transportation we have, for granted. I'm thankful for planes, trains and automobiles. Without them, many of the amazing *family* I met in TN could not have been there. Many countries don't have freedom, or transportation, to travel. We are blessed.

> 2.) I'm thankful for tuna packets and apples. My traveling time was quicker and healthier. Convenient protein on the go is a good thing.

3.) I'm thankful for the pushup bars I won over the weekend. They're a nice addition to my traveling gym for hospital stays.

4.) I'm thankful for the space Johnny's given me today. Without making me feel guilty, he has given me freedom to apply my energy elsewhere. He realizes I need to spend time with Jonnae after being away. His selflessness is a gift I receive with gratitude.

5.) I'm thankful for how much I hated my "free day" today. Body for Life encourages a day that you abandon plans and eat whatever you want. I've only been disciplined with my nutrition for a little over a week. Before I left for TN, Jonnae asked if I would save my free day for Monday and *eat* with her. She gets such a kick out of me eating *her food*. I am thrilled that I've broken away from unhealthy habits. I'm blessed to be back in the groove.

OCT 16, 2007

I'm not flying as high today. It's been a reality check day for Johnny and me. It began this morning with our couple's counseling. Johnny and I deal with things very differently. I misinterpreted the space he gave me, yesterday. Our marriage has been hit pretty hard by Leuk.

Jonnae woke up with a headache this morning. She hasn't had one for quite some time. The undiagnosed spot on her brain requires us to be cautious about everything. The doctor on call decided to have her admitted this afternoon. They will probably do an MRI in the morning.

I felt drained as I packed to come back here. My body suddenly felt heavy. Drumming up the energy to get here was difficult. I did though, and we are here.

Nolan called while on a work break and said we need to talk later. He wouldn't give me any details. I asked if it was school, work, or girl-related. He said it was work and promised he would call me when he got off. I don't know if he quit, got fired, or what. My mind wants to go nuts with it, but worry does no good. It is what it is. I will help him however I can when I have more info.

1.) I'm thankful for the counseling today, even though it was difficult. Trying not to cause more *ripples in the water*, Johnny and I don't communicate our honest feelings at times. Ignoring them doesn't help. The way our sessions *force* us to come out with it and talk through things, is good for us. I'm thankful we've sought help.

2.) I'm thankful the hospital is close. There are families who drive 2-and-3-hours to get here. It takes us less than 30 minutes.

3.) Nolan read his paper about Jonnae's illness to his class. His teacher sent me an email to tell me about it and described it in a way I could visualize and hear Nolan sharing his story. It brought tears to my eyes as I felt his pain, but I know he's been strengthened by writing it out and sharing it. I'm thankful the teacher shared the experience with me.

4.) Nolan was threatened by a coworker who'd been fired. Apparently, the guy went off on the store owner and made a remark to Nolan on the way out. He carries a knife and made reference to "seeing Nolan later." I'm thankful Nolan feels he can call me when things aren't going well; that he knows he can count on me for comfort and protection. I long to know how my children are feeling and don't ever want them thinking they can't confide in me.

5.) I'm thankful for my laptop. A Christmas present from Johnny last year, it's been invaluable as it helps me pass the time. It gives me something to think about other than where we're at with Jonnae's treatment or how hungry I am (Today is Fasting Tuesday. It's been six weeks ago today that she relapsed).

Oct 17, 2007

Jonnae had a really rough day. Her hands had painful spasms. I felt so helpless when she was having the worst of them. I've remained strong through her spiritual, emotional, and mental tough times, but watching her in such physical pain today, I felt myself weakening.

I could have hit something I was so frustrated. The lack of urgency to find something to help her was maddening. I apologized to Jonnae for being so helpless. After the episode, she assured me that I'm not. She said just my being here helps her and it was me massaging her fingers and holding her head to my chest that comforted her. With such heartfelt conviction, she said once more, "You are not helpless!"

She's feeling much better and I am home now. Johnny is staying with her tonight, while I honor a promise. My youngest daughter wants to spend some one-on-one time together. I look like I haven't slept in ages, but we are heading out for some fun. I'll return to the hospital in the morning, before Jonnae's bone marrow aspiration.

Oct 18, 2007

I find it most comforting to realize EVERYTHING is intended for good, just as Joseph replied to his brothers, "What you meant for evil, God intended for good." No one is doing this to Jonnae as an act of hatred, but I still believe it is meant to bring good in some way, somehow, some day.

The results of the bone marrow aspiration haven't come yet. We should get them soon. We thought we only needed higher counts to start the next block of chemo, but that's not the case. The spot on her brain is not an infection after all. After four weeks of antibiotics, other than increased swelling around it, the spot hasn't changed. The infectious disease doctor says they may do a biopsy in the morning. Until after we know what this spot is, we won't be starting the second round of chemo.

I don't understand it. I asked the doctor if it were more important to diagnosis the spot or attack the leukemia. He said we need to know what the spot is before proceeding. It doesn't sound good, but I am not going to give in to fear. It is what it is. There is nothing I can do to change it. I'll continue to proceed one day at a time. I'm braced and ready - disappointed and confused - but ready.

Jonnae is growing increasingly scared. I'm doing what I can to calm her fears, but it's become more challenging. She's afraid the spasms are a prelude to her losing the feeling in her hands. She is also nervous about the biopsy. I anticipate there will be more to fear in the days that lie ahead. I want her ability to find instant comfort in the Word of God and her faith in Him to be strong. My goal for today is to empower her for the battle that lies ahead, with quick and efficient use of faith as a weapon.

We haven't lost a round yet. We've gotten bruised a bit, but we've not lost. Our strategy won't change. We will keep our eyes on the Coach and trust and find comfort in Him. It is the ONLY way. Fighting battles with anger, sadness, worry, retaliation, or anything negative. It is ugly and never leads to peace.

The life we are living is intended for good. All of it. We will continue to learn from it, apply it, be empowered by it, and pass it on. That is how God has intended it. That is how we will win.

OCT 18, 2007

I think clichés are wonderful.

"When the going gets tough, the tough get going!"

I don't know how most people are when the game gets rough, but I know how I am. When the coach starts yelling and the opponents get nasty, I get fired up and become more determined to play hard and win. I'm as competitive as I've ever been. To me, whether anyone else sees it as such, life is a game. I don't play anything to lose. Today's been a difficult day, but the tough competitor in me says, "Go ahead, bring it on!"

I don't know where this test is coming from; if it's a test of faith or one to shake it. It doesn't matter if it's from God or if it's from the enemy. Of one thing I'm certain, we WILL pass it and we will be victors.

Jonnae's had a short fuse today and has had a difficult time sticking to her game plan. As her assistant coach, I've got to be tough and honest with her and shoot it to her straight. If I know she's got more in her, I've got to do what I can to pull it out of her.

The tough round has shaken Jonnae up today. After the *bell rang*, I *sat her down in the corner of the ring* and said, "Look at me! We are keepin' our eyes on the Coach remember? He doesn't want you to fear."

She said "I know mom, but this is my brain; this is scary."

"Yes, this IS YOUR brain and it IS scary. But this is the enemy trying to shake you of your faith. This is a plan that has been laid out by God and I've heard you say you are okay with whatever He has planned. Don't let the enemy tempt you with doubt or fear. That's what's going on here. I know God will take care of you. This is all for good. It may not be what we want, but good will come of this. Be comforted by knowing it is in His hands. We trust Him and we will not let the enemy shake us."

Many don't understand my competitiveness. But most get a kick out of it, whether they understand it or not. I make a game out of just about everything. Not in a way that I have to beat someone else, but in a way that I push myself to rise to the challenge and come out better than I was before.

I don't know where this *game* is going. There are a lot of unexpected blows and the opponent is tough. The Coach may need to get in my face to fire me up, but I will not succumb to fatigue, physical injury, or mental anguish. I am a victor, not a victim. Jonnae is as well. She is feeling better.

The neurologist didn't find anything in his exam and the neurosurgeon doesn't believe the spot is big enough to biopsy. Since her counts have recovered and are high enough, the oncologist now believes we can start her second block of chemo. She is scheduled for a spinal tap in the morning and her *chemo cocktail* will follow.

This news comes after persistent questioning on my part. It would be easier to keep my thoughts to myself, so as to not hurt, offend, or frustrate, anyone. But this is not about me, it is about my daughter, and every patient and family that comes after us. We need information as soon as it is discovered. Healthcare is not *proactive* enough and is too *reactive*. I'm sick of treating, when we should be preventing.

1.) I got to shower today. Good for me, good for those around me. All were blessed.

2.) I forgot to bring my Ageless Xtra to the hospital this morning. It's an all natural cell renewal drink, made by Univera Lifesciences, that sustains my energy. My husband had packed himself one and was heading home, so he gave me his. What a blessing.

3.) My competitive spirit really kicked in today. It drives me to push myself the extra mile. I experience life fully because of it. I am blessed to *creatively* see everything as an opportunity to *win another round in the game of life.*

4.) There are a lot of storms and funnel clouds, possibly tornadoes, swirling around tonight. I'm thankful for the Doppler radar. I'm certain it's saved someone from harm tonight.

5.) We rarely order from them, but mail order catalogues provide us with humor and entertainment. Some give us ideas; others give us a good laugh. Laughter truly is the best medicine; a blessing.

A prayer for tomorrow:

Heavenly Father, I ask you to *get in our face* and yell at us. Repeat the signs over and over. Help us to keep our eyes on You. We want to give this game all we've got and raise our hands in victory with You when the game is over. There are plenty of distractions in the field. Help us to not be fooled by them. Give us strength in mind, body, and soul. May everything we do strengthen Your team and make it difficult for the enemy to *steal* Your players. May every word we speak bring honor, glory and praise to You; our Coach, our Creator, and our Lord. Amen!

OCT 19, 2007

Jonnae was to NPO after midnight, to have an empty stomach for sedation this morning. NPO is always difficult, knowing you can't eat makes you want to. She did so without complaining.

Our wakeup call this morning was the doctor coming in to our dark, quiet room and loudly saying, "Bad news."

Honestly, who would think that's the best way to relay info to a patient and their family? Jonnae laid there and acted as though she were still sleeping (she's good at that and does it a lot).

He came over to the window seat and proceeded to tell me her counts had dropped again and we could not proceed with chemo today. He kind of chuckled and said, "These things happen."

I'm a patient and forgiving person; one that tries not to say, "I would do something differently if I were you." (because we never have a way of really knowing). But this was ridiculous. He said he was going to talk to the neurosurgeon one more time to confirm the spot on her brain was too small to biopsy before giving Jonnae the green light to eat.

I'm ready to seek out the blessings of the day. This thanksgiving exercise is to intensify the strength of my "gratitude muscle." If I can find 20 minutes to exercise, I can find 5 things to be thankful for. It's in identifying the less obvious blessings that the "gratitude muscle" grows stronger.

> 1.) Our mood was as gray as the sky today. Overcast skies may not seem like something to be thankful for, but having them will make me appreciate the next blue one. If the sky were always blue, I wouldn't appreciate it.

For today's gray sky and this revelation, I give thanks.

2.) Johnny called me as he headed into the "woods of no signal." He said, "I just wanted to hear your sweet voice one more time." It may sound like a line, but I know it wasn't. He has voiced his appreciation and supported me this week. I'm blessed to know the authenticity of his words and the love expressed in them.

3.) Jonnae was craving a deer burger today. Mom cooked some and brought her one. Having them in the fridge when I got home kept me from getting into something unhealthy that I would have regretted. That was a blessing.

4.) I didn't get flecks of paint in my eyes as I used the worn out dumbbells at the local Rec Center. I AM thankful for that. It's not good, should you press the dumbbells up above you and chips of paint fall. I'm stretching here, but at least I'm seeking to be positive.

5.) I have nothing scheduled this evening. The last time I was home, I was needed in many capacities. It was exhausting, but I had promises to keep. Tonight no one is here, so I can rest. The house and night are mine. I would rather have company, but I'm thankful for the comfort of home.

Tomorrow, I'll work out early before heading back to the hospital. The last three days did not include a workout; two of those days, I ate poorly. I refuse to make excuses for myself. I'm committed to staying healthy. I will begin again, working out at the hospital at 4 a.m. if necessary. I will continue to work on my healthiest body as a 40th birthday gift to myself.

OCT 20, 2007

The counts weren't up today. Actually, everything is recovering and coming up with the exception of her neutrophils. They have dropped to 555 and affect her ANC. They need to be at least 750. We opted to stay here through Monday. Nothing will transpire today or tomorrow, but her low ANC makes her high risk to germs and infection.

My youngest has a cold, congestion mostly. Nothing really affecting her, but it could be really bad for Jonnae. The chance of Jonnae contracting a cold at home outweighed the freedom of leaving these four walls.

There is still much concern about the lesion on her brain. It's small and the neurosurgeon believes the risks of biopsy outweigh the need to know what it is since it's not changing. It is troublesome dealing with something more than the leukemia relapse, but I refuse to be consumed with *what if's*, doubt, and worry. There's no payoff in those things.

Jonnae is still struggling with this. I've enlisted someone to go by the house and get her scripture posters. I thought of them three times this morning, but still left the house without them. Today, she told me she needs them. She hasn't felt well. The loss of energy and appetite, and her moodiness, are weighing her down.

She promised she'll walk with me after her movie goes off. I know lack of movement is having its affect. My lack of exercise is certainly affecting me. I've always repeated a body in motion stays in motion; a body at rest stays at rest. The longer you stay inactive, the harder it is to get yourself to be active.

I got up at 4:30 a.m. so I could go to the gym, workout, shower, eat breakfast, pack, and be up here before Jonnae's spinal tap. As I headed out the door to head to work out, I was saying my prayer of thanks. I was happy to have finally done it. Then I realized I was going nowhere. Nolan's buddies had crashed here for the night and their cars were blocking me in.

I went back in, packed, showered, and decided I had made the effort. I had really wanted the workout to happen. I've decided I'm definitely ordering the TRX system that attaches to a door and allows you to use your own body weight. It's a solution to the dilemma I keep running into and won't require my leaving her for a workout.

I used the exercise ball, resistance bands, and pushup bars and feel I've done an adequate job today. It's an improvement.

I give thanks for these things today:

> 1.) Johnny knows I've anticipated the release of Joel Osteen's new book, *Become a Better You,* and surprised me with it. What a sweet gift and blessing.

> 2.) I knew I would appreciate the blue sky more. I was right, today's sky was amazing! I've already given thanks for blue skies, so in keeping with "no repeats," I give thanks for my eyesight today. It is something I take for granted. It should be an obvious blessing, but I don't give thanks for it often enough.

> 3.) I was missing my triathlon team this morning and Molly, our speed swimmer and youngest female on the team, called me today. She said she had the "post triathlon blues." When she called her mom and dad looking for comfort, her dad said, "Molly, you need to call Denise." I give thanks for her surprise phone call.

> 4.) I convinced Jonnae to walk with me today. She's not been out of bed for days. Earlier, I had tied a resistance band around my knees to do wide side steps across her room. (Talk about a nice burn in the glutes, wow.) She dared me to do a lap around the floor the same way. There was a family watching from the waiting room. They had strange looks on their faces because they couldn't figure out what I was doing.

Each time we passed in front of the windows, she dared me to do a different move. I did walking lunges one lap, forward jump squats for another and high knees for yet another. It was ridiculously silly (rather embarrassing), but well worth the laughter it gave everyone. Best bonus, I got several laps out of her. For idiotic fun, I give thanks. ("A cheerful heart is good medicine." Proverbs 17:22 NIV)

5.)We found more comfort from the healing wisdom in scripture today.

> "I, YOUR GOD, HAVE A FIRM GRIP ON YOU AND I'M NOT LETTING GO. I'M TELLING YOU, 'DON'T PANIC, I'M RIGHT HERE TO HELP YOU.'" ISAIAH 41:13 MESSAGE

Discernment about worry being worthless:

"Who of you by worrying can add a single hour to his life? Since you cannot do this very thing, why do you worry?" Luke 12:25 NIV

OCT 21, 2007

I'm tired! Not afraid, just tired. It feels like a cross between the flu and what it felt like when I had mono. I'm not sick; it's simply fatigue. I feel like I've had an intense workout and I've done nothing. I've been sleeping with Jonnae until 9 a.m. That is not like me. Normally, the latest I would sleep is 7:30 a.m.

Maybe it's like "sympathy pains." I feel like I'm experiencing Jonnae's symptoms with her. I know part of it is I'm not working out. I know I'm doing a good job given the circumstances, maybe even a great job, but I also know I'm capable of better. It's what we know in our heart that gives us peace. How everyone else views our progress or performance, isn't a measure of contentment.

I've always been my worst critic and I don't expect that will change. I'm not sure I want it to. I know it propels me to do my best.

I feel like a caged bird that can only sing when I have time out of the cage. I realize I get more time out than my daughter does. I'm freer than she is. If it's affecting me this way, it's no wonder she's lethargic, keeping her room dark, and not wanting to do much. I've got to break free from the habits of this past week and help myself so I can help her. I feel like I'm rambling and the only reason I am letting myself do so is to show I'm not always "up and strong." None of us are beyond a slip, a fall, or a need for reflection.

OCT 22, 2007

Being a perfectionist isn't always a good thing. But letting down is not an option for me when it comes to nutrition and exercise. There is a dark hole looming that will consume me, if I give up. I must see the opportunity here and seize it. I must get the tools out and build a bridge that will allow me to get over this hole and move on.

People consume food for comfort and are obese as a result of it. I know from past experiences of stress binging, my letting go defeats me. Bearing down and overcoming adversity propels me to a higher place. This road we are on is *supposed to be* hard. It's choosing the high road that will make us victors and not victims.

> IT'S CHOOSING THE HIGH ROAD THAT WILL MAKE US VICTORS AND NOT VICTIMS.

Jonnae's ANC still isn't up enough to start the next block of chemo. If we didn't have another child at home sick, we wouldn't be here. The doctors would send us home.

Jonnae's spirits are pretty good today. She couldn't sleep last night and turned the TV on and found Joel Osteen. She said she has a new "code phrase" for me. She said she will recall Joel's story and be strengthened if I just say, "Shake it off." I'm all for that!

My acknowledged blessings:

> 1.) I sat behind a man in church whose voice reminded me of Andy Williams. It took me back to memories of my childhood. I used to sing "Raindrops Keep Falling on My Head" when I was little. I made it a point to

let the gentleman know his voice was a blessing to those near him to enjoy it. I even asked him if he had been told he sounded like Andy Williams. Sometimes I don't step out of my comfort zone to compliment a stranger. Isn't that silly? Compliments make me feel so good. Why wouldn't I take the opportunity to brighten someone else's day?

2.) It must have been a day for "Andys." I went to the rec-center to work out and a lady was on the elliptical watching the *Andy Griffith Show*. Not the norm when it comes to working out, but it did cause me to laugh out loud in the middle of a couple of sets.

3.) Jonnae and I received a gift in the mail from a lady who recently completed her first 5K in a race for cancer. It was a beautiful gesture of love.

4.) Gratitude, for complete strangers who've reached out to support Jonnae, can't be expressed in words. This isn't a small blessing like many I've sought to find. My life is full of Light during a time it could easily be consumed with darkness. I will never stop being grateful.

> MY LIFE IS FULL OF LIGHT
> DURING A TIME IT COULD
> EASILY BE CONSUMED
> WITH DARKNESS.

They believe it may be a virus that's responsible for Jonnae's low neutrophil count. It's not likely, but one of us could have carried the virus from the house. Lydia has not been running a fever; her cold symptoms only began Thursday; it's mainly congestion and nothing that over the counter medicine hasn't cured, but our plan for today has changed.

Instead of mom relieving me, I will wait on Johnny. Mom will take Lydia back to their rental and keep her until all cold symptoms are gone. As a precaution, Mom won't be able to visit Jonnae while doing so. If we don't start chemo by Thursday, another bone marrow aspiration will be done. All of us, doctors included, are hoping that won't be the case.

While Jonnae's napping, I'm changing and doing a stairwell workout. I don't want to, but I need to and will be so thankful that I did. I'll feel better, physically and mentally. I said I'd turn the corner today. This is definitely a step in the right direction.

OCT 23, 2007

Johnny *got to* come to Jonnae's room about 11:00 p.m. last night. I *got* to stop (I almost said *had* to) at Wal-Mart around 11:30 to pick up things Jonnae wants me to make and bring back. I got home about 1:30a.m.

I struggled to stay out of the crap food all day. It doesn't seem to get much easier, passing by food that is so bad for me. While at the hospital, with not much to do, food was tempting me, but I made it! Somewhere between eight and nine o'clock is a difficult time for me. I'm fine through the bulk of the day. It's the evenings that get me to cave.

I made it through the day at the hospital and through the store with all the boxes and bags of junk. Even though I was tired and vulnerable, I still made it through victorious. It was challenging, but not horrible. I was so proud of myself heading out to the parking lot. I didn't so much as pick up a dark chocolate candy bar at the register. Whew, I MADE IT! A full 100% day. Awesome!

Then I get home, open the fridge to put the groceries away and, to my dismay, it's loaded with pizza and cheesy bread. ALERT! ALERT! CLOSE THE DOOR!

My mind said "Guess what? You won't be eating tomorrow, it's *Fasting Tuesday!*" All four wheels fell off before I could blink an eye. I ate five pieces of cheesy bread.

Frustrating doesn't come close to describing what it's like to be a binge eater. I guess it was the "Demon of Tired" that socked me, not sure. I didn't stop there. I ate the dark chocolate snack sticks in the cabinet. Like 8 of 'em. This binge battle comes for a while, leaves for a while. I will not quit trying to champion over it.

I made Jonnae's protein muffins and packed all the things she wanted me to bring back to her. Joke was on me. Doctors decided to send her home today. We'll go back Thursday for counts. Depending on the results, they will either start her chemo, do a spinal tap, or do another bone marrow aspiration.

It's been a tiring day. The cold weather and rain, combined with the packing, lack of sleep last night, lack of nutrition today, and overall exhaustion from the last several weeks, have caught up with me. I've allowed myself to rest since we've been home. I'm sore from a good stairwell workout yesterday. I did a 45-minute circuit using 8 flights of stairs.

I did the first round and thought, "I really don't want to be doing this." Then my kids came to mind. I offered up a round trip of the stairs, down and back up, for each one. I start at the top and jump rope, do pushups, or do jump squats every other flight going down to the ground floor. Then I run all the way back up, taking two steps at a time, for a total of 6 "rounds" down and up. That was quite the cardio/lower body workout. My legs were still shaking in the shower, 20 minutes post workout, from fatigue.

Now that we're back home, Jonnae is feeling quite perky. She has played with her dog, Sassy, and a new DS game, ALL day. No napping. The comfort of home is wonderful for both of us. She is beckoning me now for a PB and jelly sandwich. I give thanks for the blessings. Neither rain nor exhaustion keeps them from happening.

Oct 24, 2007

I'm expecting a great day today. Every day provides a fresh start and new opportunity to be victorious, regardless of what may come. It's bound to be better than what I experienced last night.

I was getting ready for bed; so looking forward to falling into it with Johnny. I went up to kiss Jonnae goodnight and asked her if she had taken her evening oral meds. It hadn't dawned on me earlier that they failed to give us a prescription for her new antibiotic when we were discharged. I asked Jonnae if she took it once or twice a day. She had already had one at the hospital, so we would be okay if it was only once. She couldn't recall. That's really odd for her, she usually knows every med, every dose. I called the doctor to inquire. She was supposed to have a second dose. The doctor said it wasn't a big deal; there was nothing we could do about it until morning, anyway.

I said, "You can call it into the 24-hour pharmacy. It IS a big deal! This shouldn't have happened."

I went to the pharmacy, picked it up, and took it up to Jonnae. It was 11:30 p.m. Imagine my dismay, when as I handed her the bottle, I saw they had filled the prescription with the original antibiotic, not the new one. I called the doctor again. She said she called it in right, but would re-call it in. I headed back to the pharmacy to get the right drug.

Yeah! I was angry, but only for a few minutes. That even surprised me. But staying angry wasn't going to change anything. It was what it was. I finally got into bed at 12:45 (2-and- a-half hours after Johnny.)

Yesterdays blessings....

1.) Warmth. The weather is changing. I don't tolerate cold very well. The heat in the car felt so good last night. The fall season has me burning candles, not only for ambiance, but for the added warmth they bring to a room. The heat and soft glow make the home cozy.

Cozy is nice. Many remained cold through the day and night, coziness isn't something they *get to* experience. We can afford to adequately heat our home and stay warm. For that I'm grateful.

2.) Tuesdays are a fasting day I offer for my daughter's healing. Although it's been 7 weeks since her relapse, it seems much longer. I'm made aware of how it feels to be hungry. So many people have that feeling without it being a choice, and for more than one day at a time. Whether it is because they aren't healthy enough to eat solid foods, or because they can't afford any, they go hungry. I don't have to, my family doesn't have to. I'm grateful.

3.) My oldest son came home early from hanging out with his buddies last night. He came in, asked me to watch TV with him, and wanted me to play with his hair. It's something I've done since he was a little boy. I'm blessed to have a teenage boy that's not too cool to be affectionate with his mother. I know that's a blessing. I am grateful.

4.) I got some rest yesterday. Normally if I rest physically, my mind doesn't rest with it. It beats me up for resting and not being productive. Yesterday I was tired enough that even my mind rested. It felt good to just "be." For surrender and renewal, I'm grateful.

5.) Thank God for our insurance. It's obviously a tremendous blessing, but the pharmacy incident last night served as a reminder. The first prescription was close to $200. The new antibiotic would have cost over $1000. It is insane. I am very grateful for our medical insurance.

Based on counts in the morning, Jonnae will either be readmitted and start with her second block of chemo, or they'll do another bone marrow aspiration. She just got out of the bath and is looking pretty fresh. She's had another good day.

What I'm thankful for:

1.) Self love. There was a time I would have thought that strange. Not anymore. I saw a public service announcement last night that reminded me of its blessing. The speaker said, "Many of us spend a lot of time looking for our one true love. Funny thing is we are born with them. Our one true love is ourself. It isn't until we love ourselves that we are really capable of accepting the love of anyone else."

2.) I am thankful that we don't live where hurricanes, earthquakes, or wild fires are a concern. I feel for the people in California experiencing loss because of them today.

3.) Having my dad in town comes with a multitude of perks. He's a retired contractor and lets us know when he sees something needing repair. I love my husband dearly, but a handy man he is not. Nor does he foresee things that could cause a lot of trouble down the road. Dad noticed we have a window needing immediate attention. I'm thankful for my dad for many reasons. Today he's blessed us with his "builder's brain."

4.) Tonight, Johnny and I got to have our snuggle time, plus more. That's always something to be thankful for. Especially when you've had, and will continue to, more time apart than together (Having a seriously ill child is stressful, emotional, and definitely strains the marriage). To reconnect and spend uninterrupted time together is a blessing.

Nolan came home from work and Jonnae came downstairs as we were coming out of the bedroom. Nolan made a couple of "gross" comments and Jonnae just smiled that amazing smile of hers. They knew it was a sign we're getting along. I'm sure they're giving thanks too.

5.) I lay my head down tonight thanking God for another day. As I expect to serve and please Him more, I give thanks for the opportunity to "become a better me."

OCT 25, 2007

Jonnae's neutrophils are still dropping and the jury still out on how long we wait before proceeding with chemo. Everything else is still high enough and holding. It's just these darn white cells that aren't cooperating. The bone marrow results aren't back yet. If her bone marrow shows higher than 5% leukemia blast cells she's relapsed again. If that's the case, we'll be admitted and start chemo tomorrow, regardless of the neutrophils.

I expected to be frustrated if the neutrophils were still down, but I'm not. Again that's somewhat surprising to me. The last few times they've checked, I've gotten really upset. But I realize this is all in God's hands, not mine, just as everything is. Acceptance of that makes for a very peaceful existence.

I must admit, I'm not always ready to turn it over to God. But ultimately, I want to live in peace. This morning that's what I've done, and it was all a matter of choice. Earlier, Jonnae heard me tell someone, "to let go and let God."

She said, "Mom, I've never heard that. I'm going to remember it."

I find it hard to believe she hasn't. Sometimes we hear something repetitively but don't really "hear" it until the time is right for us.

There's always something new to learn. Once life is embraced as a learning experience and loved for being so, peace, joy and happiness are easy to hold on to. I'm not exactly happy about the way I'm being taught these days. But for the lessons that have come, and the ones I'll still get, I'm grateful.

> I'M NOT EXACTLY HAPPY ABOUT THE WAY I'M BEING TAUGHT THESE DAYS. BUT FOR THE LESSONS THAT HAVE COME, AND THE ONES I'LL STILL GET, I'M GRATEFUL.

I've written of my failings and the temptations I've lost to, but I know they are only temporary. The game of life isn't won or lost in a week. I'm only "catching my breath" before I become the stronger contender and take over the lead.

Jonnae's bone marrow results were good. She's at 1% and still considered to be on her way to remission. Monday we will get her CBC done again and see where her neutrophil count is. Hopefully we will proceed with the second block of chemo. For now, we will focus on the positive. She is feeling well and will enjoy the weekend at home.

The doctor encouraged me to make some calls and make our decision about where we want to go for the transplant. I didn't know where to begin. I have a starting point now. Based on the recommendation of this group, I'm checking out Children's in Cincinnati. I'm praying for direction and will follow my gut. I've learned to trust that inner voice that's not mine, but God's. I've often doubted it, and later in hindsight, realized I should have been quicker to listen. It's called faith.

Blessings from the day:

1.) We didn't hit traffic on Kennedy Bridge this morning. It was rush hour and we got *hit with God's favor* instead of one of those crazy drivers in a hurry to get to work. Indeed a blessing.

2.) Jonnae's sedation and procedure went amazingly well today. She was fast to sleep, fast to wake up, and had no tears. The last two times, they've used a different drug on her. The "cocktail" they've used for two years, can potentially cause headache. They don't want to chance it with the spot on her brain. The old drug took awhile to wear off, left her feeling weepy, groggy, and she hated it. This new drug works much faster and wears off much faster. It's a lot better. It's nerve-wracking to try something new, but it's worth trying. For the success of it, I'm grateful.

3.) I'm thankful the doctors are understanding and supportive of our want to go elsewhere for transplant. I expect they'll do whatever they can to get us someplace we're comfortable and confident. That's a blessing.

4.) Jonnae wanted an Arby's sandwich and Wendy's baked potato on the way home. Even though I can't stand drive-thru food, the aroma can be enticing. No junk for me today! For not letting the temptation master me, I'm grateful.

5.) Nolan's high school open house was tonight. All of his teachers commented on what a pleasure he is in class and how well he's handling himself with everything that's going on at home. They discussed how helpful he is with other students, as well as how respectful he is of the teachers. I'm blessed with an awesome teenage boy. We had fun goofing off in the car on the way there. It was a good night for us and for that I'm thankful.

With my blessing cup spilling over, I can't possibly give as much as I've received. I thank God for His awesome goodness. His love is everlasting. Amazing!

Oct. 27, 2007

Things are uneventful and quiet. Two of our children are at my parent's rental. Lydia's only symptom is a cough, but that warrants keeping her away from Jonnae. Austin is ready to move in and live with them. He's always preferred being a loner. It comes as no surprise to me that he's volunteered to keep Lydia company and in no hurry to return home.

Layne is active with sports and his social schedule. Nolan is busy either working, or running around with his group of friends. Jonnae and I pretty much have the house to ourselves throughout the day. She is staying busy with the Nintendo DS, homework, and occasional cleaning of her room. It amazes me how an inactive child can trash her room so quickly.

Focus on the blessings:

1.) Yesterday I talked to a friend I've not heard from in a while. She said it feels like she's talked to me because of my blogging. She's always been only a phone call or few steps away (we bum bread, cheese, ketchup, sugar, you name it, off of one another regularly.) For the friend I have in her, I'm grateful.

2) I'm very thankful for blogging because it allows friends to stay updated without a call to each of them. This is a difficult thing to understand, much less explain. I'm a social person and love being around people, but during a time such as this it is difficult and draining to be around people, even close friends. Everyone is loving, supportive, and naturally feel the first thing they need to talk about is Jonnae. I understand their intention and appreciate it COMPLETELY. But it exhausts me to repeat things. I make it worse by not simply getting to the point. I give lots of details. Blogging updates everyone, while easing the load for me. It's a blessing in many ways.

3.) I spoke with a "new" friend who was gracious with her comments on how I inspire her with my *attitude of gratitude*. I've been able to lift her spirits as she's going through a really tough time. I'm blessed to know God is my protection and strength. He lifts me so I can lift others. What a blessing.

4.) Johnny and I spent the evening watching a movie.

We had fun doing nothing but enjoying each others' company. Things have been great between us. He's been loving, supportive, and understanding. What a blessing.

5.) Had I not been blessed with an education, I wouldn't be able to read. The written works of others have inspired and taught me, allowing me to be a better encourager and teacher. For the blessings I've known and will continue to experience through written word, I am blessed.

OCT 29, 2007

We just can't talk Jonnae's neutrophils into cooperating. All other counts are up and holding steady. If they still aren't up by Thursday, another bone marrow aspiration will be performed to confirm leukemia is still in remission. If they come up we will be admitted on Friday to proceed with chemo. The doctor is calling Children's in Cincinnati to see if they will accept Jonnae as a patient for transplant. If so, we will go up, check out the facility, meet with the BMT group and see if we're comfortable transferring her to be in their care for transplant.

In the meantime she is feeling good.

Dear Heavenly Father,

We pass the homeless, covered in newspapers, as we drive to the hospital in the mornings. Thank you for blessing us with a warm home, soft bed, and cozy blankets. We take for granted how we lay our heads down at night.

I accomplished much today and feel good about being more productive than I've been. For the rediscovered motivation and commitment I've found to live my day in a way that is pleasing to me, and most importantly to You, I give thanks.

I've received some lovely emails and cards. Sometimes I question if I'm leading others to know your love, the way I long to. It is a blessing to me Lord, to know that others are being blessed. I thank You for choosing me to be Your messenger and for communicating through the words of others, that I'm "delivering the GIFT." You won't allow for me to give more than I'm receiving, no matter how hard I try. You are so gracious and loving. Thank you.

My youngest daughter is well enough to return home from my parent's rental tomorrow. For her returned health and for the opportunity I will have tomorrow to embrace her and to show her how much I've missed her, I thank You. May I be able to express to my children, as much as I love them, it cannot compare to the love You have for them, as their Heavenly Father. What an awesome realization that is. This daughter thanks you.

All is good with my soul. May I spread and share your goodness with all those I meet. Amen.

OCT 30, 2007

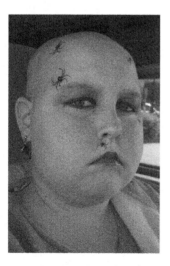

It's another fasting Tuesday and I already want to eat. I've decided to PRAY every time I find myself longing for food. That is what you are supposed to do when you fast, but I haven't been in the habit of doing it. The girls and I have had so much fun today. We tattooed (temporary of course) spiders all over Jonnae's head this morning. She has one crawling out of her nose and one crawling into her ear. There's a cob web, with a spider on it, behind the other ear. Her attitude is incredible. I'm so proud of her.

She had a hard time not smiling for this picture, but thought she should look "spooky."

Nov 1, 2007

I know I'm not the only one in the midst of a season I would like to leave behind. Life is going to have periods that are harsh. If we keep the right attitude in the "winter," we'll flourish come "spring."

> IF WE KEEP THE RIGHT ATTITUDE IN THE "WINTER", WE'LL FLOURISH COME "SPRING."

The season's not over, but I did feel a large load being lifted yesterday. We met the staff and head doctor in Cincinnati. They were fabulous and the hospital was impressive. Oh, what a blessing.

The doctor in Cincinnati believes the antibiotics that Jonnae's been on for the infection in her brain are responsible for her counts not coming up. It makes complete sense. It sure would have been nice to know that sooner. We give thanks for knowing it now.

For holidays, I give thanks (I wish the retail and marketing didn't get so carried away with them). They evoke fun, feelings, and memories that are blessings. Everyone at the hospital was dressed in all kinds of costumes. Made me wish I had taken advantage of the chance to get silly myself. Jonnae fit right in. Her spiders have been a huge hit everywhere we've gone.

I met the mother of a child who is post transplant. They are staying at one of the lodging options we may have in Cincinnati. She was singing the praises of the staff and hospital. It was nice to talk to someone who can tell us what's ahead.

The devil has *been at my door all morning*! I keep trying to close it, but his foot is wedged there. While I'm exhausted, he's feeling frisky.

Yesterday's trip gave us a really good sense of how hard this is going to be, on both me and Jonnae. The doctor went through a pretty descriptive account of the 8-day prep phase, and then the transplant. It's going to be brutal for her.

We're both going to be very uncomfortable and feel completely isolated. The hospital experience is going to be majorly different for us. I won't be able to eat, use the bathroom, or shower in her room. I've got some real prepping to do. I'm trying to muster up the tenacity to stand strong and push through, but I need to do something different than I've been doing. I'm just not sure what.

Once she is discharged, Jonnae will need to stay in a place near the hospital for about three months. Wherever we stay, she'll be kept away from other people. We checked the Ronald McDonald House and a nearby hotel that many hospital families use. The hotel is our first preference. It's perfect in many ways. It's roomy enough, feels homey, and has a kitchenette. They provide a shuttle anywhere within a 5-mile radius. Affordability for us is the only issue. Our insurance will not cover the post-inpatient accommodations we are going to need.

I started crying on the phone with the insurance company. I felt bad for doing so, but I'm not up for fighting the emotions today. Every little thing is a test for me today. I'm keeping my eyes on the Coach and counting our blessings, for I know they are abundant. I know it's just a phase, but I'm so tired. The devil's trying to have his way with me; scoring a few points while he can, but he's not going to win. Everything will work itself out.

Jonnae just had another bone marrow aspiration. This will be routine, every week, until her counts come up; unless she relapses. The last thing she said, before the anesthesia knocked her completely out, was she's not used to seeing me like this and I better have a more positive attitude when she wakes up. She also let me know she wants Taco Bell on the way home and wants stir fry tonight. "Sound good?" she asked.

I've got to patch my heart and get my head on straight before she wakes up.

NOVEMBER 2, 2007

I went to bed early last night. I fought a different kind of fight yesterday. I was completely worn out. I like to fight a good fight and it wasn't within my grasp yesterday. I didn't feel much like myself. I fought tears. I fought anger. I fought temptation to eat poor foods. I fought self pity. I held my own, but my normal strategies seemed to be out of order.

A good night's sleep certainly helped. I've awakened ready to tackle the day. I'm heading to the gym and actually excited about defeating whatever challenger steps up to play the game of life with me today.

> 1.) I'm thankful for "I will go before you and make the crooked places straight..." (Isaiah 45:2 NKJV)

> I'm encouraged today because I've been reminded that God is going before us. He's preparing a way. He's making our crooked places straight. God has equipped us for this journey. We will have everything we need. I know it! I can feel it! Today's going to be better than yesterday. For this I'm very thankful.

> 2.) Our children are self-sufficient in many areas. Since Jonnae's initial diagnosis, they've been able to take care of simple needs, making their lunches and doing their laundry. They are kids and can fall behind on chores, but when push comes to shove, they know what to do and how to do it. When I can't be home to take care of them, it's a blessing to know they can do a lot to take care of themselves!

> 3.) I'm thankful that Jonnae's homebound teacher is spending a lot of time with her. I've heard parents from different school systems complain they only get a couple hours a week. When Jonnae's taught at home, adequate time is spent with her. This new teacher is ready to spend 3 or 4 hours each visit. After a full day at school, that makes for a long day for her. For her compassion and service, I'm thankful.

If the path looks crooked, it's not going to stay that way. God's bestows His favor upon those who have FAITH.

Nov 3, 2007

I've often compared my spirit to a Mylar helium balloon. Both are durable and will last forever. Time deflates them, but they can be renewed; all they need is a fresh supply to keep them "up."

It's no secret how they stay high on life. When they're filled with the *right stuff*, they soar. When they aren't getting what they need, they droop.

Just as a balloon can't fill itself up, sometimes we need to look outside ourselves for help. We can use the words, stories, motivational thoughts, and positive energy of others, to fill us up. Let's seek them out, use them, and be "full" of spirit!

Nov. 4, 2007

Last Wednesday's trip to Cincinnati gave me a whole new insight. With this new knowledge, I will EMBRACE the good days we have left. We are preparing for a very difficult time. I'm going to make the most of the "Lighter" days we have left.

I'm grateful for my husband's concern, although he needn't be for me. I've been quieter around the house, but it doesn't reflect anything is wrong. I'm processing a lot, that's all. My family's not used to me being quiet. Their concern shows their love for me and for their LOVE, I'm blessed and grateful.

I'm on firmer ground tonight, but that's not where I found myself this morning. A song in church brought tears I couldn't stop. I knew it would be best to let it all out and leave it there at the foot of the cross, but I couldn't with the children there.

I didn't feel it coming on, but I wasn't surprised when the emotion overtook me. It's been a difficult week. The reality of what's coming, and its difficulty, has me jumping ahead of where we are. I really need to focus on the moment and take each day as it comes; embracing what I can. This is only a season.

Many mothers have lost a child today, some of them without any warning. I don't know what the future holds, but if it should be that we lose this fight in the end, I've been blessed with today. I've learned to count every day I have with my children as a blessing. For today, I give thanks.

I went to a baby shower for a dear friend of mine today. She's tried to get pregnant for so long. The adoption process has been long also. Many women never experience bearing a child, giving birth, or motherhood through adoption. I have experienced giving birth to five children. I know motherhood, and for all that it's blessed me with, I give thanks.

Today, I spoke with a mother whose child has been treated both here and Cincinnati. Speaking to someone who knows both hospitals, whose situation was similar to ours, was comforting. For the reassurance I have after speaking with her, I am thankful.

I'm thankful for the new recipe that's brewing on the stovetop. For variety in food, I am thankful.

My husband just walked in the door. I'm grateful he's home for the rest of the night. Watching something on TV, while he holds me on the sofa, is going to feel extra nice tonight. For that I give thanks.

Nov. 5, 2007

Much to be thankful for today:

> 1.) Jonnae's neutrophils are coming up. They are 707 and need to be 750. We expect they've increased more. We go to clinic tomorrow morning to check counts and see. Her platelets and hemoglobin are GREAT. Evidently, the antibiotics were indeed to blame for the neutrophils staying low. Thank God, we are moving in the right direction and will start chemo soon.

2.) I called an organization for transplant funding assistance. The representative asked me how I found out about them. I mentioned the friend's name who referred me to them. She actually had worked with her. I'm thankful for the awareness of this program and the much needed assistance. God is so good. I know this is a Divine connection guided by His almighty hand. I praise Him today and always.

3.) I also spoke with the financial consultant at Cincinnati. She assured me things will be okay and we needn't go anywhere else. They'll work with us so we don't need to use credit cards or pay upfront for lodging. After the hotel bills the hospital, they will break down the payments for us so we don't incur interest or need to pay a large sum at once. Jonnae had a big smile on her face when I told her we are going to Cincinnati. We're blessed by the confidence we have in the care they will provide and by how things have come together.

4.) I'm thankful for the control I've taken back with nutrition. I feel like I'm in it again. Last night my neighbor sent over this amazing cake with whipped cream and Heath bar chunks in it. The cake had caramel all through it. It looked unbelievably good. I didn't so much as touch a finger or fork tip to it. Instead, I cooked a pear and sprinkled it with cinnamon.

Tonight Johnny and the children ate Mexican. There was a lot left over and I didn't succumb to it either. I fixed my healthy chili and later ate a cooked apple with a vanilla protein shake. As close to apple pie a la mode as I'm going to get, but it felt so good to be in control and doing the healthy, better thing. I'm in control and loving it. I'm blessed to be right where I am, on the high road.

5.) To get Jonnae out of the house, we took her to the clubhouse for lunch. Afterwards we rode out to the lake.

We took her dog, Sassy, with us and had a good time.
Tonight she's having a couple friends spend the night.
With her counts higher, and the hospital stay just a
couple days away, the timing is right. For her happiness
I give thanks.

Sometimes it's more difficult to stay focused on the blessings than others. The blessings were *louder* today than yesterday. I'm grateful for their volume!

Nov. 6, 2007

Jonnae's counts are finally where they need to be. We start her next round of chemo tomorrow. We have an early admit time and start with day one right away. We will be at the hospital for a minimum of 5 days.

She went to lunch with her two girlfriends who spent the night. With an ANC count of 1000, we don't need to worry about her being out. She is making the most of it today. Her freedom will be gone tomorrow. That may sound sad, but we're not. We're excited to move forward with the plan and be done with the transplant.

I continue to fast on Tuesdays. I got my workout in early this morning (my hamstrings are sore; it was a good one). We're headed to the mall to have a big tattoo airbrushed on Jonnae's head and a t-shirt made to say, "I paid my oncologist big bucks for this haircut."

Nov 7, 2007

It's never easy to admit failure, but I believe in being honest. I can't announce the clean nutritional days and withhold the bad ones. Last night I had a "drug problem." I was *drug* away and enticed with temptation. It's the first time I have not held my fast since Jonnae's relapse, nine weeks ago. We got home about 6 o'clock last night, after running around at the mall. Up until that point, I'd had a couple protein shakes and a meal replacement drink; no food. I was starving, I was tired, and I quit. I had worked the "I will not quit muscle" to failure; not a technique to use with that muscle.

I ate some chili and followed that with a vanilla protein shake and cooked apples (probably enough for three people). That wouldn't have been too bad; at that point it was simply a portion control problem. However, I didn't stop there. I then made it a binge by eating five (you read right) cinnamon rice cakes (not the mini ones). Shameful, I know, but it is what it is. I lost all four wheels within a 30-45 minute period and was so sleepy afterwards. It is crazy how carbs and sugar affect me. I fought the heavy eyes and lethargy for about an hour before I "sobered" up.

We checked into the hospital today and got the *leftovers*. The room we're in is so small, there's no room for a bed for the parent. No recliner either, just a little desk chair. And guess what - NO SHOWER! I always shower at home before we come. The one day I decide to prepare meals instead and plan to shower in her room, she doesn't have one. I will make do with the one down the hall. This is just a test. I choose to pass it and focus on the blessings. It could be worse.

"When tempted, no one should say, 'God is tempting me.' For God cannot be tempted by evil, nor does He tempt anyone; but each one is tempted when, by his own evil desire, he is dragged away and enticed." (James 1:13-14 NIV)

I was drug away and enticed last night, but I broke free from temptation's grip and today is a new day. No more *drug problems* for this lady. I won't be tempted by poor food choices and I won't be tempted to get frustrated with what happens here, today.

Nov 7, 2007

The spinal tap is over. This is the first time Jonnae woke up before they were *out of her back*. She was still too groggy to move, but she was talking in her sleep and cracking the staff up. She asked, "Am I awake because I'm building up a tolerance to the anesthesia?" Only my "little nurse" would think to ask a question like that when she's all looped up and out of it. The anesthesiologist said, "With questions like that, Jonnae will be teaching medicine someday." I said, "No doubt!"

She is awake, alert, has eaten, and is doing homework before her teacher arrives. She is determined to stay with her class and graduate on schedule. We are fortunate that this teacher doesn't mind coming across the river to teach her. It's about a 30-minute drive for her.

I asked a few friends to send Lydia cards, not focusing on Jonnae's illness but rather on how strong Lydia is. When I was sorting Jonnae's cards out of the mail a few weeks ago, Lydia asked if I knew how long it had been since she had gotten something in the mail. She wasn't saying it for me to do something about it, just doing as kids do and stating a fact. I know she feels overlooked. I hate that. She got her first card today. It really did make her feel good. She wanted us all to read it. The gesture had the affect I had anticipated it would. For the lift she got from that card, and its sentiments, I give thanks. I need support in making sure my kids' *"spirit balloons"* stay full.

Jonnae lives in pajamas these days. The steroids have blown her waist out and nothing fits her in both waist and length. Pajamas reign above everything else in comfort. We got her a new pair at her favorite store. I'm thankful she found more than one pair. (I will go back and get the second pair as a Christmas present.) It's impossible to pick them out for her on my own. She is so picky you would not believe. Many shopping trips have ended with her in tears because she can't find what fits her criteria. Yesterday there were no tears, only fun times. I give thanks.

I bought a couple shirts for myself. Shirts that I can be comfortable in and layer when we are in her frigid room.

As we were leaving she said, "Doesn't it feel good?"

I said, "What's that babe?"

She said, "You know! That you can go into a store for Juniors and buy clothes for yourself, that you are hip enough and can fit into it. Doesn't that feel good?"

She had that smile of hers going. She glows with sweetness when she smiles. I'm thankful for that beautiful smile and how it's an instant shot of helium for MY balloon.

Nolan brought his girlfriend over for more ping pong and board game playing with the family. It was actually Jonnae and Lydia playing against them. I'm grateful that he is bringing his friends over more. I've always felt a little sad when they are hanging out everywhere but here. I want them to feel like they have a home to bring their friends to. We don't have the video games, a trampoline, or pool table, which their frequented hangouts do. I hope the trend continues and his friends, be it boys or girls, come around more. For the last couple of nights, we have had *kid company*. It's been nice and I give thanks for it.

This just in - there's a stinkin' clot in Jonnae's line. Chemo won't begin until they clear it out. The line will flush okay when they push something through, it's only when they try to draw fluid back out that there is blockage. I'm not sure why they can't administer the chemo, but they've called the doctor and he isn't comfortable with starting until the clot is gone. They will put a solution in and let it set for two hours and try again. If still no return, another two hours and then I don't know what.

Day one of this block is almost over and the full chemo dose may not happen (It is considered day one because they administered part of the chemo when they did the spinal tap). This is so frustrating. We've waited all this time for her counts to come up so we can move on with this schedule. Had we known it was the antibiotic suppressing her counts, the delay wouldn't have happened. Now, we finally get the green light to go and this happens. How much are we expected to take? How does this affect her overall success? All of this waiting is maddening. I'm trying to be patient, but good grief.

Nov 8, 2007

Last night, Jonnae and I went to sleep around 9 p.m. The plan had been for my husband to come relieve me, but I couldn't leave her, not without knowing if they were going to clear the clot or start chemo.

The nurse awoke me with a "Mom!" and showed me the blood she was drawing from the line. Praise God! The clot is gone. Chemo was administered as she slept. It didn't disrupt her sleep.

Actually it's worn her out. She's slept for the better part of the day. Johnny came up to stay with her around 10:00 a.m. so I could run a few errands before stopping at the gym. I like to work out on an empty stomach, so I hadn't eaten anything. My workout didn't begin until noon. It was late for a workout, late for a first meal, so I grabbed a protein shake out of the gym's cooler on my way out. Of course, once I got home, the fridge had left over food that looked enticing. I passed and chose protein muffins instead.

After I showered, I packed for my return to the hospital, tried a new recipe I found online, and grilled some chicken for a pizza I'll fix at the hospital tomorrow. I also gathered ingredients to make turkey bacon quiche for Jonnae. It wasn't an eventful day, but it was a full day. I'm blessed.

I've lead several people through fitness challenges, in their quest for healthier living. I ran into a former participant this morning at the gym. She was glowing and looks amazing. I'm so proud of her. For seeing her continued progress, as a result of what we began together, I'm blessed.

I've decided with a history of binging when overwhelmed, I need to simplify things right now. I know the fundamentals of eating clean; I just need to get back to them. I know exactly what I need to do, so I am blessed.

I'm thankful Jonnae's body has traded nausea for fatigue. The information we received about this protocol suggested she would be sick the first couple of days. I'm pleasantly surprised and relieved.

We've found a perk in this wing of the hospital. We have the mini fridge to ourselves. I didn't feel at all bad about stocking it with fresh fruit, vegetables, and meat. Normally we're limited in space. Another blessing.

NOV 10, 2007

If life is like a deck of cards, we've been *dealt a difficult hand* and been asked to hold onto it for four years. Recently, the press has been highlighting a local family who's held theirs for over 20. I met a woman this week who will be carrying hers for much longer, as their daughter was born with severe lifelong handicaps. We have been, are, and will continue to be blessed abundantly. That's the way I'm handling the difficulty of Jonnae's illness, and it's affect on us.

I miss being excited. I miss being driven by a purpose other than to just make it through. It's been a different couple of days. Jonnae is tired, wants the room dark and cold, and the TV off. I know she feels like sleeping and doing nothing, but I don't. It makes for a really long day to be wide awake in a cold, dark, room. I'm fighting off the negativism more than usual for me. I've been absorbing the negativity of others and it's fueled my own. I need to deflect it instead.

I'm about to learn more about myself than I've ever known, in the next four months. My character is bound to be strengthened. That part is intriguing and exciting. Knowing how I'm going to obtain it, isn't.

Many books have been written about "not sweating the small stuff" or "living an abundant life." Giving thanks for the small things makes a huge difference in the experience of a day. As I find myself missing these blessings that I've been guilty of taking for granted, I know:

> If I'm able to sit in a comfortable chair while I read or watch television.......I'll give thanks.

If I'm in a room that's lit well enough to read......I'll give thanks.

If I'm able to watch my favorite TV show as a means of relaxing or enjoying my evening.....I'll give thanks.

If I'm in the company of friends or family, able to converse, share thoughts, and laugh........I'll give thanks.

If I'm able to prepare what I want to eat easily, with the right appliances, utensils, ingredients.....I'll give thanks.

If I'm in-between "storms" and coasting in a place of contentment and peace......I'll give thanks.

If I'm able to sleep in a comfortable bed......I'll give thanks.

I'm learning to appreciate my blessings and claim to be present as I experience them.

NOVEMBER 11, 2007

I don't feel as blue today. I hate those days when I struggle to keep my head in the game and eyes on my Coach. Yesterday was one of them. Thankfully the morning brings a fresh mindset and a different perspective.

Jonnae's made it through chemo without getting sick today. She slept through nausea with the help of Benadryl. We should be discharged tomorrow as soon as the MRI is done. We will be home for a couple of weeks, as long as she doesn't run a fever. The chemo will cause her counts to drop. So it's imperative we keep our entire home sanitary and the rest of the family healthy.

She'll get a shot, everyday, while home. They call it "miracle grow." It will boost her counts, and therefore, her immunity. In two weeks, she'll get a high dose of methotrexate in a spinal tap and through her line. This is the drug that causes the really painful mouth sores. This could affect her transplant schedule.

Today I got to go home and get caught up on laundry and housework. I started on a project that has been on the back burner for too long. With five kids (four of them being teenagers) we've veered from the traditional floor plan and have gotten creative with space, in order to designate bedrooms for each of the children. Today I worked on what will be Austin's space. He and Layne are the last two to be sharing a room and it hasn't been working. I should be able to complete his room by tomorrow night, Tuesday at the latest. It felt good to be moving physically and to accomplish something new.

We've made it home. The nurse said we would be discharged by 11:30a.m. We were discharged at 4:00 p.m. The hospital clocks don't run on the same time as real world clocks. It's ridiculous.

> THE HOSPITAL CLOCKS DON'T RUN ON THE SAME TIME AS REAL WORLD CLOCKS.

Jonnae's in bed and has been nauseous the better part of the day. She has no appetite and this is pretty much how it will be for a couple of weeks. We expected this.

When we got home today, several neighborhood boys were playing football in the back yard. Jonnae timed getting out of the car while their backs were to her. She didn't want them to see her bald head. She was upset with herself for being upset. I told her she was feeling what anyone would feel. She didn't feel bad for long, as she turned her attention to Sassy.

I want *"to be running when the sand runs out"* (lyrics from Rascal Flatts). Lately I've been caught just meandering along. I need to pick up the pace and LIVE. Just because we are battling Leuk doesn't mean we shouldn't be creating fun memories, full of love, WITH EVERYONE. Jonnae and I can't be guilty of staying wrapped up in each other. We need to reach out to the rest of the family while we are home and make a lot of love deposits into the family's account. We need to be present in every moment of each day, now more than ever.

I'm thankful we are home and for normally mundane chores I will thoroughly enjoy doing. Funny, things we once resented can become a blessing in different circumstances.

I'm thankful for the American Red Cross and blood drives. I donated blood today; something I'll do more often, considering the way we've been blessed by others doing so. I'm eager to give back.

I'm thankful for our Veterans. I wish I could come up with something more to say than simply "thank you." I dream of the day I'll be able to do things like pay for meals secretively when I see them at restaurants, or donate in a big way to funds that assist them. We'll never be able to repay them, but I'll feel great trying.

I'm thankful for the means I have to exercise, with no access to a gym. My morning workout with the TRX system from Fitness Anywhere was only a fraction of what I'll be able to do. Fitness is a huge part of my life. I would be in a much different frame of mind without it. I'm thankful I don't have to be.

NOVEMBER 13, 2008

Today was my father's 70th birthday. My father has always been a part of my life. The seed of faith he planted took root and continues to grow and bless me in the most amazing ways. He taught me to always set a high bar. He took me to Lexington (an hour and a half drive) every weekend for tennis lessons so that I could pursue my dream to play collegiate tennis. He taught me how to fix things myself, to be independent and strong. He's selfless, loving, and has always wanted the best for me. The gift of him as my father is a blessing beyond measure.

Shortly after Jonnae's relapse, I recorded scripture as my voice mail recording. I wanted to encourage callers to have faith as they left their messages for me. Someone left me a really nice message today.

She didn't indicate what she was referring to for the longest time and then let it be known she was talking about my voice message. It's been a while since I recorded it and since anyone mentioned it. I've been reminded I can still touch others in a positive way, regardless of being confined from the outside world. I've been given the opportunity to display, in difficult circumstances, the change I believe we need in our world. We need more inspiration, encouragement, love, and faith.

Jonnae and I had an intimate, heartfelt conversation today. It is a blessing to be able to speak openly and maturely to my teenage daughter and for her to understand, appreciate, and engage in the conversation. She has been, is, and always will be, a very special girl who blesses me as my daughter and my friend.

Jonnae helped me to realize a blessing today without even being aware she was doing it. For over a year, we have sponsored a boy in a third world country. We were writing him letters today and she wanted to use computer paper and decorate it herself. She didn't want to use stationery or printed paper because the boy doesn't have it for his use when he writes us. One more thing we take for granted. For the use of printed cards and paper, we are blessed.

Jonnae's tentative admit day for Cincinnati is Dec.14, with Dec.21 being the big day for transplant. Initially Jonnae was disappointed with the BMT being 4 days before Christmas, but I told her this could be the year we experience the spirit of Christmas like never before, or ever again. Let's anticipate and expect that this is going to top all Christmases. It is a blessing to finally have a date, even if tentative. We are closer to saying goodbye to Leuk.

My workout and nutrition were good today. Tuesday's aren't about nutrition obviously, but it's been the day it was supposed to be. This may seem trivial to some, but for a binge eater dealing with emotion and stress, it's a victory. It's imperative for me to celebrate what I can.

NOVEMBER 14, 2007

My business colleagues hosted a luncheon today and I spoke about the lessons I'm learning. They can be applied in our business, as well as our personal lives. Our company is going through some growing pains, which has ruffled the feathers of many associates. I would rather exercise my choice to not get frustrated, to have faith, to be supportive, and to use this as an opportunity to better my attitude and strengthen my tenacity. Although there are circumstances in life that we cannot control, we can control our reaction.

I left asking them to focus on what they have, instead of what they don't. I left them with the thought that I'm going home to a teenager fighting for her life; her slick, bald head over a toilet several times a day, confined from the outside world. Her words, her attitude, and the energy of her spirit are better than that of many adults with lesser challenges.

At the end of the day, we can look back at the words we spoke, the energy we put out, and can say we chose to contribute to a positive experience today, not to contaminate it. We speak like victors, not victims. We look to our Coach for the signs and do our best to not get distracted by the game. We may falter, but more times than not, we are standing firm. We are abundantly blessed.

We had a couple of doctor appointments today, the first with Jonnae's radiologist from the first battle with Leuk. He was saddened to hear she had relapsed and needed a transplant. He shed some light on the spot that is on Jonnae's brain and said from the report it seemed as if the spot could be leukemia. He said the oncologist wouldn't normally tell us that. Is it just me, or does it seem ridiculous that they wouldn't tell us, when another doctor might? I'm thankful to know of something else to ask the new group.

The second appointment was for our two sons who are bone marrow matches. Further testing needs to be done. The younger of the two gets sick every time he has blood drawn. Regardless, I had a good time with my kids today. How blessed we are to share laughter and memories. It could be a dark time, if we chose to focus on what's to fear instead of each other.

NOVEMBER 15, 2007

Some days you give thanks all day as the blessings flow about you; circling and propelling you. Today was one of those days.

I had an early morning workout before taking Jonnae to her 8:30 appointment. I fought fatigue fiercely this morning. I was close to getting back into the "jamas" and crawling back into bed for a couple more hours, but I resisted.

Driving home, I sat in silence with God and begged Him to stay close to me today. Normally I know He is near. I don't need to see, or necessarily feel Him, to believe. I'm good at walking blindly in faith. However, as Jonnae's BMT is closer, reality is causing me to tremble. I really needed to feel and see Him today. I prayed for His protection and strong presence today. He responded!

I think the enemy saw that today could be a potential win for him. He decided to send his strongest pitcher to the mound. I report in complete celebration--I hit the ball out of the park. It was a day of victory.

A disappointing pitch came at the clinic this morning. The doctors decided to replace Jonnae's central line, since it's been causing trouble. (I had suggested they do that before we were discharged on Monday. Only then, they responded with, "Why would we do that?")

We were supposed to be there for counts only today. Nothing had changed with her line to make them reevaluate. Nothing has changed since Monday except their decision. I remained calm as I suggested they start listening to parents, and consider their suggestions when they are offered. This was an unnecessary inconvenience and disappointment.

I was proud of Jonnae for taking the news so well. As we waited for her ANC results, I told her if the count was high, we would do whatever her heart desired today "out in the real world."

If they were low, we would still do whatever her heart desired. It would just be at home in "our world." We had a plan A, and a plan B; neither of them included having a line replaced. The doctors were going to do the procedure today, but I asked them to delay it until tomorrow so we could enjoy the day as planned.

We need to be at clinic at 8:00 a.m. for them to check her platelets. She may need to have some transfused before the procedure. Platelets or no platelets, she won't eat or drink anything after midnight tonight, and won't be given any food until 5 or so tomorrow evening. The outpatient surgery is scheduled for 3pm.

That was a rough at bat! But we produced a hit, as we stayed positive. We could feel the Coach smiling down on us, as we felt His strength and presence with us all day.

As we left home this morning, I told Jonnae about my red bracelet. The goal is to see how many days I can keep it on my right hand. If I eat poorly, it will be moved to my left hand and stay until I earn the right to move it back with a clean day.

She wanted to go eat after we left the clinic, but realized her choice of restaurant would not have a good choice for me. I told her it was HER day and I was all for whatever she wanted. I didn't want her to be influenced by what my choice would be. She asked about my bracelet and I told her my being with her and seeing her happy made it a perfect day. She smiled enormously and in the most heartfelt way, said, "I LOVE YOU!"

Her plan included going to see *Martian Child*. We LOVED LOVED LOVED this movie. I highly recommend it. It's a great story. It flew right to the top, as one of our all time favorites. It was just what we needed. I laughed and I cried. I even said, "Awww" out loud, at the child's sweetness, cuteness, and pain. God was close to us all day today.

Jonnae had a sleep over planned for tonight, just one of the reasons the news of tomorrow's procedure was so disappointing for her. She had Happy B-day airbrushed on her head, with a cherry in the middle of it as a surprise. (Her friend's nickname is Cherry.)

The sun's rays were shining in majestic streams through the gray sky on our way home. Jonnae said, "They remind me of Heaven."

God was not just near. He was felt. He was seen. He was heard. And His LOVE was experienced all day today. God's the Coach. All we've gotta do is keep our eyes on Him and we will be on the winning team for eternity.

Nov 17, 2007

I love my Father with all my heart. I trust Him completely. Where is He leading me? What does He have planned for us? Is this a test similar to Abraham's? Is He checking to see if I will willingly hand over my child? I don't dwell on that thought, but certain things happen and cause me to wonder.

It was just the girls and I at home tonight. We decided to watch a movie on pay per view. We spent over half an hour previewing titles we didn't recognize. We were looking for a light hearted comedy and found a couple. We were nearly through searching when we viewed the trailer for *The Ultimate Gift*, based on Jim Stovall's book of the same name. The preview revealed that a wealthy man had died and his grandson had a series of tasks to complete, containing lessons of life, before he got his inheritance. It wasn't a comedy, but in unison, we all said, "That's the one!"

Unbeknownst to us, one of the main characters was a young girl with leukemia. It wasn't revealed until a third of the movie was over. A bone marrow transplant was her only hope for survival. She doesn't fare well and prepares for her final days. The girl's only wish was to have loved ones with her when she died. At the movies end, her mother was out of the hospital and she died in her room alone.

Is it possible to read too much into something that seems so blatantly obvious? Over and over I feel as if I'm being prepared to let her go.

Like in the Tale of Two Cities by Charles Dickens, "These are the best of times, but these are the worst of times."

I've had this thought several times this week. I even expressed it to a friend. So blessed, as I feel my Father's comfort and strength like I've never known it; but so distraught as I live a nightmare. Would you believe they read from a *Tale of Two Cities* and cited this same quote in the movie? *God is on the line; He's phoning me frequently.* I feel like I'm looking at one of those pictures you've got to stare at for a long time before you can begin to make out an image. What is going to be revealed to us?

In this amazing movie, the grandfather says, "Any process worth going through, is going to get tougher before it gets easier. Learning is a gift, even when pain is the teacher." WOW!

> "ANY PROCESS WORTH GOING THROUGH, IS GOING TO GET TOUGHER BEFORE IT GETS EASIER. LEARNING IS A GIFT, EVEN WHEN PAIN IS THE TEACHER."

NOV 18, 2007

Slippery when wet! That's the thought that occurred during my workout, as I continue to struggle with my overall health and fitness. I ignored the warning signs and continued to put the pedal to the metal. I've never been good at slow and steady.

I imagined my body was a car and my soul was the ignition. The rain came, (a short shower of sadness) and made the road slick. I'm supposed to move slowly, but I kept my foot on the pedal, didn't let up, and kept spinning my tires. I knew the car could go; I knew the body could perform. But all I did was burn up the tread on my tires. It stinks.

I ignored the signs and underestimated the importance of simple maintenance. I didn't slow down or even stop for gas and an oil change.

I've run out of gas, my oil change is overdue, and my tires are bald. Now what?

I go back to what I know works. I've got to get my hands on some quality nitro, change the oil, replace the tires, and give myself a little traction. I need to fuel this body with good stuff and stop settling for junk.

I've finally accepted no matter how much I want to drive fast and hard, I need to approach slippery situations differently, and take it slow and easy. The ignition (my soul) is in good shape, but the body needs an overhaul. I'm keeping my eyes on the Coach, (he's also my mechanic) until He tells me it's time to "hit the road".

Nov 19, 2007

My body isn't a car; it's a tow truck. Evidently rain hit everywhere. It wasn't just a gray cloud that had settled over me. My whole family was stuck in the muck. I helped each of them deal with their issues at hand, pulling out what was bothering them, and talking it through.

Jonnae's spending the night with my parents. She's already called, after being gone for only half an hour. I missed her before she even left the house. We are probably too attached to one another. Ridiculous as it seems, we need to prepare to be separated. I can't possibly be with her 24/7 in Cincinnati. For her little escape tonight, I give thanks.

Nov 21, 2007

For some reason, I found myself thinking of the comic strip character, Ziggy, today. As a child he was one of my favorites. I thought he handled mishaps respectably. He didn't complain and was not annoying like Eeyore. I'm thankful, like Ziggy, I roll with the punches.

Jonnae confided in me today that she wanted to pray but didn't think it was working. I shared some of my thoughts with her (no surprise there) and let her know that even though I read scripture and pray daily, even though I listen to Christian music and fight this battle with faith, the ground doesn't always feel solid beneath me. I let her know I have been feeling out of sorts lately too, but that I knew more than ever we needed to cling to the Rock of Our Heavenly Father and not let go.

I told her apparently "spiritual signals" can be like those that weaken with our cell phones. They lose their strength at times, but if we wait it out, they will be strong again. The important thing is to stay on the line and not hang up.

NOV 22, 2007

Don't worry about anything, instead, pray about everything. Tell God what you need, and thank him for all he has done," Philippians 4:6 (NLT).

Exactly what I needed to wake up to this morning, after a restless night of fighting the ongoing battle of *what if?* I know better. I'll be able to find peace, whatever our outcome is with Leuk.

I'm more confused about what to focus on and what my role is right now. Just when I think I've got a clear signal and my Coach is on the line, there's an interference that breaks in. Is it Him or a distraction to keep me from Him? I really believe it's God, but I don't know what to do with it. I want to let go and let God, but part of me keeps fighting it because I don't want what I think He's preparing me for. I want to believe He will change His mind. And then again, maybe it's not Him at all. Maybe it's something that is trying to shake my faith.

Happiness and contentment are not obtained with small waistlines, erased wrinkles, organized homes, successful children, appreciative bosses, or doting husbands. They come when we trust God and despite our circumstances, are thankful. The road that leads to

> HAPPINESS AND CONTENTMENT ARE NOT OBTAINED WITH SMALL WAISTLINES, ERASED WRINKLES, ORGANIZED HOMES, SUCCESSFUL CHILDREN, APPRECIATIVE BOSSES, OR DOTING HUSBANDS.

peace is rough, but it's the road laid out for me.

I can't think of a better day to be practicing prayer, thankfulness, and focusing on the Coach, than today. There is no trying, only doing. Today I don't just wanna give praise, I'm gonna!

NOVEMBER 24, 2007

We spent the first half of our day at the hospital, waiting on, and transfusing the platelets Jonnae needed. Her ANC count was up, so we made some stops on the way home.

We were hoping to find some comfortable sweats for her. She lives in pajamas. Even when we go out, she is in a t-shirt, hoodie, and pajama pants. Shopping for her is challenging. We found one pair.

A lot of people were staring at her tonight. Two little girls were loud with their comments. Jonnae tried to smile through them and shake them off, but she cried on the way home. She caught an entire family gawking at her and expressed they were adults who should have known better. I suggested she might have said, "I've got cancer, you don't need to stare."

Through her tears, she said she didn't want to be rude and that I don't understand. I told her I know I can't understand, but I try to. I explained, "What are you staring at, idiot?" or "Take a picture it will last longer" is rude. Letting others know they are hurting your feelings isn't. It's a needed reminder and lesson. I suggested we get more t-shirts made. Maybe to say something like, "FYI, I'm a girl with cancer."

People constantly refer to Jonnae as a boy. The bald head makes it easy to assume. Even with my awareness as a mother of one hurt by it, I've been guilty of it at the hospital.

Nov 25, 2007

"Don't ask, 'Why?' That's like putting a question mark where God put a period."

I don't know who said it, but it's a quote that's really stuck with me. My question these days isn't why, but "what now?" What do I, as a child who loves and wants more than anything to please my Heavenly Father, do now?

Nov 26, 2007

We spent the morning at clinic, making sure Jonnae's counts were high enough to proceed with her spinal tap and chemo tomorrow. It's her last round before going to Cincinnati for transplant. We were there a while, but Jonnae focused on the good. She enjoyed the babies in the waiting room today; a few happy and one unhappy.

I wasn't surprised that her counts were up, but I was by her reaction. She hadn't anticipated them being so good. When the doc was reporting them, she kept smiling that amazing smile of hers and pumped her fist like "Yes!!!", each time he announced a number. It was so darn cute. Her joy is contagious and I could feel myself being lifted by it. She was ready to *party*, by going out for appetizers, lunch, dessert, and a trip to the mall. We cut the day short for schooling, but she didn't mind that. Honestly, she enjoys school work, too.

I told her today was "fasting Tuesday." I wasn't at peace with the thought of consuming food. She said, "God will understand you letting up, Mom."

I couldn't possibly turn her down. This child gets so much joy from me eating WITH her (that means eating what she's eating). I really can't explain it, but it's a gift of love both ways—her wanting me to be "free" with her; my letting go and just doing it.

We went to the mall and had "I'm irresistible" airbrushed on her head with a myriad of lip smacks all over it. It's really cute, even though they misspelled it.

Jonnae's home school teacher told us Nolan's class wants to give him an iPod for Christmas. How amazing is it that high school kids want to reach out and show their support and compassion in such a way? Sometimes the younger generations get a bad rap. This proves there's a lot of love there. My heart is full of gratitude.

Nov 28, 2007

I wish they sold hospital watches so you knew what time it is when you're here. They don't operate on Eastern Time. Pretty sure it's not Pacific or Standard, either. I've not been able to figure it out and I'm a pretty smart cookie (depending on whom you ask.) Jonnae's spinal was to be at 9:30a.m. At 1:00p.m there was still no sign of the sedation team or doctor. Not sure why the "learning hospital time" manual isn't offered to patients' families, but it should be.

Jonnae's day was mostly peaceful. The spinal tap took a long time. Her spirits have been good overall, but she did have a weak moment when one of the policemen came in with the *Joy Cart*. It's a cart with small games, art kits, books, and DVD's to choose a gift from. This gentleman, in his wanting to help, picked up a Fantastic Four play set and some other little boy toy. She waited for him to leave the room, and burst into tears.

The fact that she was starving was to blame as much as anything. The gender mix up was the final straw. She recovered quickly. She does a great job of keeping her eyes on the Head Coach.

She's nauseated. She ate a roast beef sandwich and some fries as soon as she was allowed to sit up, but I suspect that's all she'll eat. The methotrexate affects her want for food.

Johnny is off tomorrow. My mom will stay with Jonnae, while he and I spend some time together. Not many more of those opportunities left before Jonnae and I leave for Cincy. I'm thankful we'll have the day to make deposits into our *relationship account*. We need to build that up, in preparation for the predicted drought.

November 29, 2007

In two weeks we'll be leaving for transplant. Jonnae's been sleeping a lot. Johnny and mom have pulled a couple shifts and I haven't been with her much the last 24 hours. She's stayed on Benadryl to keep her drowsy through the chemo-induced nausea. The Benadryl always knocks her out. Poor thing can't hold her eyes open for more than a few minutes once they push it through her line. She delayed her last dose so she could see me before her lights went out. The sweetheart's done that before.

Johnny and I enjoyed our day together. He doesn't always see things from my perspective. He doesn't always understand where I'm coming from, nor I him. We've grown into two totally different people. I think that happens with a lot of couples, regardless of whether an illness is present.

We're working on appreciating one another's differences and embracing what we have as a husband and wife who truly love one another. Opposites attract really applies to us. Though they've been painful at times, I'm thankful our differences have strengthened and developed our character.

We've had beautiful posts on the message boards of Jonnae's sites. The world is full of kindness. It's a shame that we don't hear and see more of it daily on the news and television programming. Truly there is a lot of GOOD in the world. The love and compassion that wrap around an individual with cancer outweigh whatever cancer's able to take away. We have much to be thankful for as God is all around us.

Even after a nice day with hubby, and beautiful sentiments sent our way, I found myself in and out of a zombie-like state today. I've compared it to the likes of anesthesia. Your body is capable of moving, you're in a comatose state of mind, and nothing you do seems to produce the effect you desire. I didn't experience this type of paralysis during Jonnae's first battle with Leuk. This is new to me.

I was struggling to come up with more than a couple gratitude moments on the way to Layne's game tonight. As I headed into the school, God said, "Here's one for ya, don't miss it!" An elderly woman was walking up the long corridor to the gym. She had a purse and stadium seat in one hand and a second stadium seat in the other. She was having a difficult time so I asked her if I might help. She hesitated before giving me one of the seats. When the lady at the ticket table asked me how many, I told her two and paid for the woman. She was completely taken back by the gesture. It was the most awesome feeling!

By the way she responded to my gesture, she thought I was a blessing to her. But SHE was a gift TO ME. God gave me the opportunity for a random act of kindness, to show her what we've been shown. I was able to be LOVE! For that opportunity to show kindness, to be Christ-like, and for the electric feeling it gave me, I give thanks. The *paralysis* is gone.

I'm so thankful for having a son that is CRAZY FUN to watch in action. Just like you would need to see Jonnae's smile to know the joy it radiates, you would have to see him in action to understand. He's a livewire, the perfect example of never letting up in a game. Watching him play tonight was good medicine. Every night that I get to witness his amazing spirit on the court or field, I am blessed.

On the way back up to Jonnae, I had Christian music playing. My taste in music sure has changed, but I don't think I'll ever outgrow crankin' it up and belting it out. I'm thankful for the freedom to be a rock star in the privacy of my own car. I'm thankful for the healing properties of music.

November 30, 2007

In the wee morning hours, the lower portion of my sleeper chair fell off its track. My feet kept falling asleep from the way my body was slanted. I woke up with my back stiff and nearly said, "I *have to* sleep on it." Remembering to stay in gratitude, I replaced the *have to*, with *get to*. Out in the cold, some were sleeping on the ground or a floor. While they sought to find rest last night, some were without a blanket and some were all alone. I, on the other hand, was with my daughter, in a building, with warmth from heat and covers. I knew as I wrestled with that bed that I would awake to the blessing of another day. Not everyone slept in peace the way I *got to*. For that I give thanks.

We've been blessed with the gift of LOVE many times today. A friend offered to bring us lunch. Little did she know we would send her on a food scavenger hunt! Jonnae was craving honey mustard pretzels, pizza-flavored Combos, and a sub. She didn't seem to mind.

Another friend presented us with food as an expression of love. I informed her my birthday was going to hit while we are away. I requested a piece of her special cake before we left. She made one and sent it over. The family had eaten all but one piece when I got home. Perfect. That was a blessing.

On the way home tonight, down below the overpass, I could see a man pushing one small child in a stroller while another walked beside him in the dark cold night. I give thanks for the option to get in a car and drive to my destination. It's a blessing anytime, certainly in the winter months.

DECEMBER 1, 2007

We hoped to go home today, but that wish wasn't granted. Jonnae's methotrexate level hasn't come down enough. She had a rough morning. As the methotrexate flushes through her body, it causes pain each time she goes to the bathroom. The pain has been lessened by a barrier cream and she's better now. She's had nausea, but no need for meds. We suspect she will get to go home tomorrow.

Johnny is going to spend tonight with her. I will go to church for early mass and come up afterwards to escort her home. I think I'll wrap the kids' Christmas presents and get the tree out.

At a youth retreat last year, Jonnae was introduced to the *Happy Book*. It's similar to the gratitude journal, only we list what's made us smile or laugh. On a day we're struggling to find our "happy place" we reflect on the running list in the book. It serves up instant smiles.

My husband phoned earlier as I was taking the stairs. He said,

"Are you going up stairs or something?"

I was winded and gasped, "Yeah!" He said, "I need to hang up and talk to you later. Your heavy breathing is turning me on."

That was funny, perfect entry for my *Happy Book*.

I was apprehensive about my parents' temporary move here. I expected history to repeat itself. They aren't shy when it comes to sharing their unsolicited opinion.

I've just recently found peace with my need to meet others' expectations. I've worked hard to free myself from the people pleasing prison. I didn't like the idea of going back into the slammer, even though I'm the one holding the key. I was wrong to think they would make things difficult. I don't know how I, or my family, could go through this without them. They've given up their freedom and thrown themselves into the midst of this battle to fight fulltime. They dropped everything and came to the front line. They've raised me to be who I am. For my parents, what they gave me growing up, and what they give me now, I give thanks.

DECEMBER 2, 2007

Jonnae's report was disappointing again today. She needed to be 1 or less. She was 1.1. It's difficult to tell your daughter to see the glass half-full, when you yourself are seeing it half empty. I held her as she sat with silent tears streaming down her face. I told myself there's a reason; we've dealt with bigger let downs; it's safer for her to be here - than the house. I told myself it's only one more day.

I held her until we could accept things as they were. I knew we wouldn't stay down. Disappointment keeps knocking on our door; we keep adding security locks. Its effects haven't been able to enter or take up residence in our hearts.

> DISAPPOINTMENT KEEPS KNOCKING ON OUR DOOR; WE KEEP ADDING SECURITY LOCKS.

DECEMBER 3, 2007

Jonnae had another difficult night. Mouth sores, symptomatic of mucositis, have appeared. They've hospitalized her twice in the past. May the healing hand of God stop the bacteria in its tracks, not causing her more pain or hindering her transplant.

Now that the reoccurrence is evident, Jonnae's revealed to me she hasn't been very proactive with her oral hygiene. I needed to use tough love on my baby and that's always difficult to do, especially when she already feels so bad.

I've insisted she drink water, use the magic mouthwash, and brush her teeth. She doesn't feel like doing any of it and gets annoyed with my pushing her to do so. It's imperative that we do what we can to keep this in check. I pushed her oral hygiene and hydration, as well as insist she plug into her spiritual resources.

She's not felt like doing a whole lot of anything, including her daily devotions, gratitude, and happy books. It's hard to push her, but this is not the time to *leave anything on the field*. This is the championship game. We must not get complacent and forget what we have with the most powerful source of all - God.

THE SECOND "TRIMESTER"

DECEMBER 4, 2007

After last night's discharge, we went home, packed, and now we're in Cincinnati, preparing for a myriad of tests beginning with a dentist appointment in the morning at 8:15. They're making sure there aren't teeth or gum issues that would be aggravated by chemo or radiation. Then we see the head doctor of bone marrow transplants.

Jonnae has a pulmonary function test at noon. Thursday she has a bone marrow aspiration in the morning and meets with the radiologist. Friday is our busiest day with CT's, Echo, EKG and other tests. All of this is necessary for preparation for her BMT.

Jonnae's mouth is no worse. She has no appetite, but when she eats, she's careful not to irritate her mouth. The magic mouthwash numbs the pain, but then she can't taste the food. Her spirits are still up, though. She's still cutting up and being her feisty little self. She's been ornery, pulling pranks and pillow fighting with Nolan. I'm thankful for her ability to rise above the darkness. Even with the gray skies and cold of winter, her company is warm. Her smile brightens the darkest of days.

I'm nuts about faith, fitness, Og Mandino, health food, and art. I'm also nuts about anything that has to do with positive thinking, dreaming, and goal setting. I have clings for my water bottle; that say things like *Create Your Day*. I'm an artist and love unusual creations. I love taking what others discard, to create something practical, beautiful, or unique. Why not view a day the same way?

I have the power all day, every day, to create something special out of what I've been given; even if others would discard, resent, or be saddened by it. I chose to create a positive day today.

I received my first holiday cards today. They were mostly from an online community created to celebrate the spirit of Julie Whitt. I met her online, while doing a *Body for Life* challenge, and she was one of the most positive people I've ever *met*. She was fighting for her life and I never knew it. Her desire was to lift others, not bring attention to herself.

She didn't make it through her lung transplant. Jonnae's spunk and spirit is much like what I witnessed in Julie.

DECEMBER 5, 2007

I know in my heart *I'll* be fine, but I'm concerned about my family. I'm concerned about Jonnae, Nolan, the kids being home without their mother, and I'm concerned about how the rest of my family is dealing with this whole experience.

The day was full of information, overwhelming decisions, and anticipation. In keeping my eyes on the Coach, I haven't thrown down my bat and stormed away from the plate, but I've wanted to. I'm tired of this pitcher named Leuk! I'm tired of his mean curve ball. I'm ready for some easy ones down the middle.

We were at the dentist office early, got into an exam room early, but still managed to get out of there an hour later than anticipated. I was challenged by the tardiness and fact that we would be behind the rest of the day. Jonnae was challenged with a different pitch. She was being talked to like she was five instead of fifteen. That's a sure way to *strike her out*. I reminded her to *shake it off*, and let her know I was challenged to do the same myself. Her reply was, "Mom, It's hard!" to which I replied again, "But it's doable!" We've had this talk before.

We continued to the oncology group, where Nolan was already being seen (Mom took him). He was having his blood drawn and didn't look too good.

The nurses were trying to keep him from passing out. Mom and I were giving him a hard time (all in good fun). Jonnae felt badly for him and didn't feel like teasing him. Nolan's pretty quick to take advantage of a joke opportunity; Mom and I were just paying him back for when the tables have been turned. He was a good sport about it and cracking his own jokes, even though he felt lousy. I have no doubt he'll continue to provide laughs in this not-so-funny situation.

The pulmonary test wore Jonnae out. As we headed into the pharmacy for Jonnae's mouthwash, I called for a hotel shuttle. The pharmacist informed me it would be $8 because they don't accept our insurance. (The hospital does but their pharmacy doesn't?) I would have paid, but she also said it would be another 20 minutes and our shuttle was already outside with Jonnae and other passengers in it. Because she had already given me the option, I asked the pharmacist to call the prescription into CVS.

After hanging out at the hotel for a while, I went to CVS. Because Jonnae had just filled a mouthwash prescription Monday, (she left it at home) our insurance denied it. Now it was $17. Not a big deal, but enough for me to reach my breaking point. I could not control the tears from falling.

Once back at the hotel, I checked the mirror in the lobby before rejoining Jonnae. She was definitely going to be able to tell I had been crying. She hates to see me cry and knows if I have tears, I'm struggling. More times than not, I overcome the obstacles. For that I'm thankful.

No one can stay upbeat all the time. Certainly, I'm going to be challenged to *create a nice piece of art* every day that we are here. I've worked on an art projects and decided to smear paint all over them and just start over. Or maybe just crumple up paper and begin again. With each new day I get a fresh start. Tonight I just smeared the paint and said forget it, but tomorrow will be something better. For fresh morning starts, I give thanks.

The life of God is in me. I'm created in his likeness and have an amazing ability to clear any hurdle. I cannot do it without Him. I'm keeping my eyes on the Coach. I'm so thankful for that analogy. (God Bless Abby!) When I'm behind with two outs and two strikes in the bottom of the ninth, I can make a comeback. That's the power of God.

DECEMBER 6, 2007

Jonnae's a warrior, no doubt about it. She bit her lower lip and pushed herself through painful tests today. The nurses continually asked if she was alright. Each time she responded with a yes or nod of her head. She laid on the CT table with tears running down her face, but she never made a complaint. Not one!

Even with pain and tears, she kept her sense of humor. We've laughed a lot today. There were more hurdles to clear today than yesterday, but we did it! We have several entries for our *happy books* and much to be thankful for.

The alarm didn't go off this morning. Jonnae had turned my cell phone off (meaning the alarm was turned off with it). I didn't request a wakeup call because it would have woke Jonnae. It would not have been good if we'd been late for our first appointment. I'm thankful for the guardian angel that was responsible for waking me up this morning.

This morning we witnessed babies having bone marrow aspirations. I thanked God for allowing me to be older, wiser, and to have had a normal life for 12 -13 years longer than these parents who are experiencing this journey with babies. It can be viewed in different ways, but I'm thankful that we're experiencing it with Jonnae at 15 years, instead of 15 months.

At the radiologist's office today, we witnessed an elderly woman wearing sunglasses and an odd mask over her face. I gave thanks for the normal features of mine. I don't know her condition, but it must be difficult for her to be out in public, subjective to people staring. I know how it affects Jonnae. I'll never be insensitive to someone going through something similar. For being comfortable in public, I give thanks.

I'm thankful for the shuttle service, complimentary to the guests who stay at this hotel. The employees here are passionate about serving. The drivers, front desk and valet attendants, love their jobs. They genuinely want to make our stay as pleasant as possible. I'm capable of taking care of myself, but now especially, it's a blessing to be taken care of.

If I hadn't all my fingers, or had debilitating arthritis, I wouldn't be able to post these thoughts or pour out my soul on message boards. Encouragement and inspiration are shared both ways and couldn't be, had we not the use of our hands. For the use of my fingers and hands, I give thanks.

A week ago, I was on the giving end of a random act of kindness, a very small gesture that was simple to offer. It gave both me and the recipient a lift. Today we were on the receiving end of an enormous act of kindness. We were impacted by an anonymous donor's amazing gift. It's an act of compassion that will never be matched. I'm uncertain how she found out about us, but she made a very large donation to our transplant fund.

I can only hope that this single mother, who reached out to help us in our time of need, knows that I can't begin to express my gratitude. I will never stop giving thanks for God's divine connection. I'm certain Julie Whitt had a significant hand in this. My online introduction to her has led me to people who no doubt are connected to this miraculous gift in some way. She lives through many, myself and Jonnae included. I cannot stop giving praise for the way we've been blessed.

Our schedule is crazy tomorrow, but we'll not fall victims to it. We'll face the day with thanksgiving, just as we did today. Leuk cannot take away what's been given through Our Father.

DECEMBER 8, 2007

Jonnae's back is still sensitive from yesterday's aspiration, but not causing her near the pain it was. I pushed her around in a wheelchair for most of the day. The tests pretty much ran back-to-back but there were a few breaks to pass time in the gift shop or play games we made up. She wanted to play "name that tune" with us humming different songs. It was pretty funny, (not so easy to do) and good for lots of soul-warming smiles. Those are huge blessings. I will never tire of them or stop giving thanks for them.

When she was called back for tests that didn't permit me to accompany her, I read *The Choice,* by Og Mandino. He always stirs up something within me that can only be described as miraculous. An experience that makes me love life so much I could burst. It's a level of empowerment I'm certain isn't felt by all, and something that I will never have enough of, stop loving, or stop giving thanks for. Mandino is a *messenger* in a league of his own. For the way his work continues to bless me, I give thanks.

I have so much to do to prepare for next week. It's possible Jonnae's admit date will be moved up. We'll find out Monday or Tuesday. The time is near. We give thanks.

DECEMBER 9, 2007

Yesterday, I spent the day cleaning, organizing, and wrapping Christmas presents. I've also begun packing. It's totally different than packing for a local hospital stay. I won't be able to make trips back and forth for things I need or have forgotten. Jonnae spent the day cleaning and packing also.

We've had adequate time to process and prepare for the war ahead. We're armed and ready as much as a mother/daughter team can be. We have awesome troops in the wings to back us and it is time. For peace beyond human understanding, I give thanks.

This next excerpt would be beyond human understanding for some. I'm going to begin an official physical challenge, starting Jonnae's first day of chemo in Cincinnati. I've participated in this type of competition before. I've not been able to activate discipline in both clean eats and active exercise. Unless they had done it, one could not understand the tenacity of spirit that's necessary to complete such a program successfully. If they had, they'd be asking, "What are you thinking?"

This is a time to dig deep and see just what I'm made of. I'm ready to use this war as the ultimate test, and prevail in most extreme conditions. I don't expect anyone to understand. It's a blessing to validate my own actions. I'm no longer reliant on pleasing people to find my joy.

I've learned that true happiness, peace, and joy, come from within, when we validate ourselves. Nobody else knows what my very best is. Only I can know that, through honest communication with my inner self. I've been doing a good job, a really good job, but I know there are places I've not been doing my best. I miss that. Once I regain it, it will lift me to a higher place.

It may seem to be a vanity thing, but it's not about that at all. It's about the choices I'm faced with and if I excuse myself from making the best ones. The only place I truly feel I'm behind is in the care of my physical body. Spiritually, mentally, and emotionally, I'm more able to say I'm doing my best. I owe it to my Creator to take the best care of what He's given me. For self validation and for doing my best to give it back to me, I give thanks.

We received a gas allowance check and long distance phone cards from a financial assistance organization. A lot of expenses are overlooked and not accounted for. This is one of those instances. I'm thankful for the financial support we are receiving from all over. It truly is an amazing thing to witness. It's another blessing that Leuk didn't mean to give us, but did.

I have some Bible studies to complete while in Cincy. I know they'll take me to new heights, as I work to be MY BEST self. For tools to strengthen my spiritual body, I give thanks.

I fell asleep in the family room last night. Jonnae gets a real kick (actually we both do) at how sneaky she can be when she catches me snoozing. I opened my eyes after having dozed a few minutes and she was right in my face. It caused me to leap out of my skin. For laughter in the house, I give thanks.

DECEMBER 9, 2007

We celebrated Christmas with very dear friends tonight. We had a big dinner and the children were lavished with gifts. It certainly was a visit from Santa they weren't too *old* for. We were given a very cool gift based on the movie, The Ultimate Gift. It's a Family Experience Kit and I can't wait to start working on this project. It's one of those things the whole family needs to be involved with, so we won't begin until we get back from Cincinnati.

I'm going through an intense range of emotions. I'm ready to face this thing head on, but know we can't possibly be prepared for what's ahead. I don't know how I'm supposed to prepare myself, much less Jonnae. It's a fine line between how much information is helpful and how much is too much. Sometimes the only thing it does is introduce fear, or doubt, where there was none.

Dear Heavenly Father,

As we prepare to celebrate the birth of your Son, help us celebrate the life we've been blessed with. May we embrace the gift of life, not only during this miraculous season, but throughout the year, too. As we await Jonnae's transplant, and the future it dictates for us, let us stand solidly on the rock of our faith. With every word, action, and deed may we bring glory and honor to you, Father.

Help me to use the time I have with my family wisely before we go. Let me be still and quiet long enough to hear your direction. Show me how to support the daughter I want so much to be healed and the family I'm leaving behind.

When I stumble, let me regain my composure quickly. Strengthen me and give me a heart of peace always. I found myself being harsh with my tone and quick with my tongue today. I need to be more sensitive. Now, more than ever, I want them to know my love for them.

I know You have great things in store for us. Please let my children hear You speaking to them so that they know it, too. Now and always, may we walk as a family in faith.

This I ask in Your sweet Name, Amen.

DECEMBER 11, 2007

Jonnae had a good day yesterday. There are certain daily functions we take for granted when we are healthy. This isn't the first time we've celebrated one of those *everyday occurrences* of Mother Nature. We've made much light of it at Jonnae's expense. She's always a good sport about it. For progress yesterday, and the relief it brought, (figuratively and literally,) I give thanks.

We're still scheduled for the transplant with no poor test results. I'll be talking to the entire group today, on a conference call, to get the latest plan and confirm our admittance day.

We celebrated our family Christmas last night. We had a great night; lots of love in this house. I think the children were happy with their gifts. Nolan might have been disappointed, but he has more surprises coming. He's good about keeping his head up on the outside, when his heart's low on the inside. I don't think that's the case tonight. I certainly think this is going to be harder on him as Jonnae's donor, than he may suspect. I believe all of us are in for a rude awakening. There's no way to predict what will transpire.

Each of us fights this Leuk War in a different way. Johnny and I don't always appreciate each other's way of acceptance and dealing. This past weekend was an example of that. It could have been a strained evening last night, (actually it did start out to be) if we hadn't just accepted the gift we have in loving one another. For the greatest gift of all--LOVE, I give thanks.

One of the greatest legacies we can leave our children is happy memories. My grandma Metzger used to decorate the Christmas tree on Christmas Eve after everyone had gone to bed. I thought of her several times last night, as I was up way into the morning decorating our tree. I reflected on what a gift she gave with that loving gesture. For all the memories I have of her, and the way she loved in countless small ways, I give thanks. The memory of her is priceless to me today.

For Christmas lights and the spirit they bring with their faint glow, I give thanks. I have fond memories of going out for a drive, as a kid, and as my children were small, just to view the lights. A dear friend of mine came to visit us a few years ago. We drove around rating the houses and their decor. We laughed so much that night, it was a blast. Sylvia's humor always had me in stitches. For the memory of that night and the laughs we've shared, I give thanks.

Not every day leaves behind a lasting memory. For special memories that are revisited this time of year, during a season of love and giving, I say a prayer of gratitude.

The doctor called and Jonnae's tests all came back in her favor, Nolan's, too. They both get an A+.

We report to the fifth floor of the A building tomorrow. I'm waiting on one more phone call to give me our appointment time. I'm hoping it will allow us to leave in the morning, so we can stay here one more night.

My arms feel so heavy. I don't think it's workout related. This morning's routine was not that intense. I've also needed to take a lot of deep breaths today. I think it's because we are heading into the eye of the storm.

DECEMBER 12, 2007

We're in Cincinnati. We left the house at 6:30 a.m., got assigned to our room (the "suite" of the BMT unit - God's favor early today) and have begun unpacking her things. Jonnae is worn out from meeting the support staff, but these intros and info are necessary. She's rolling with it.

We have some *moving pains* to adjust to. I knew I'm not allowed to use her restroom, shower, or eat in her room. I didn't know I'm not even allowed to drink water in here. (My water bottle is attached to the end of my arm at all times.)

They don't have wireless, so my computer won't work here. The dial up is super slow, something else that's going to take getting used to. It's funny how set we get in our ways and how difficult it is to veer from them.

In addition to the other adjustments, there's no oven in the family lounge. Preparing my own food is going to be challenging. I don't think I can eat much more cafeteria cuisine than I already have. I can't workout in the stairwells. (Big let down there, they were great for cardio.) They are off limits to anyone not employed by the hospital. I asked if I was allowed to sweat in her room. Seems like a funny question, but if I can't drink water, how much of a bacteria threat could it be to workout in here? They don't have a problem with me jumping rope or using my traveling gym, so we'll see how that goes. There are major adjustments to get use to here.

So far, Jonnae loves everything about her room. Her spirits are amazing and she's so accepting of the recurring news of how rotten she's going to feel from chemo and radiation.

The randomized draw placed Jonnae in the *controlled* arm of the study. She will not be using the new drug. It's in God's hands, and this may be a blessing. All we can do is take things one day at a time.

I read something earlier that really resonated with me. It's related to how we'll choose to handle each day. We'll not use an *if* way of thinking, focused on things that may or may not happen, but a *how* way of

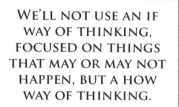

WE'LL NOT USE AN IF WAY OF THINKING, FOCUSED ON THINGS THAT MAY OR MAY NOT HAPPEN, BUT A HOW WAY OF THINKING.

thinking. We'll wait until the *if* happens and then figure out *how* to deal with it.

Jonnae had moments last night where she was struck from surreal to real. She said it hit fast and she didn't know what to feel. I had my own twilight moment earlier, as we were driving up to the hospital. I felt nauseated and shaky; very strange. I was surprised how quickly the feeling came on, and then left, once we got to her room. I understand why I was overcome, but was shocked.

We've enjoyed a few games and taken a couple of walks through the hospital. They encouraged us to get out of the room as much as possible today, before she gets hooked up to her fluids and starts radiation tomorrow. We've brought all kinds of things to do in the room. She brought a pack of colored dry erase markers and was delighted when the nurse told her she could draw on the windows. She had fun decorating her door in festive lettering and colors.

You can tell the nurses are delighted to have a patient who'll cut up and be quick to respond to a conversation they start. Jonnae isn't talkative by nature, but she really does make an effort with her caregivers. I think the nurses *making over her* like they are, is really giving Jonnae a boost. She's got that smile going. I'm continually amazed with her tenacious spirit. You would never know this girl is fighting for her life.

I met a couple mothers who've been here for 28 and 32 days. I picked up a *you have no idea what you're in for* vibe by the way they looked at one another as they were speaking. One suggested I don't ask about particular situations. Evidently there are some complications best to remain uneducated about unless faced with them; backing up my theory that too much information is a bad thing.

The blessings:

Jonnae has the largest room on the floor. After being in tiny rooms our last two hospital stays, I'm thankful the time has come for her to experience God's favor in this way. There are two large windows in the corner with a decent view and ample lighting. It's a blessing to be in this room. We won't take it for granted.

We had a nice trip this morning. No horrible rush hour traffic and I didn't have a hard time staying awake.

I'm not super anxious about the days ahead, but I'm so thankful we're finally here. Nothing altered our schedule. No more waiting. I'm grateful!

A reporter called today. I'm thankful for the opportunity to express gratitude to our amazing community. I have the opportunity, once a week, to see a list of contributors to Jonnae's fund and am blown away that I don't know half of them personally. These generous souls are from all over the country. It continually lifts my spirit to experience the love and support of so many.

Johnny surprised me with a LIVESTRONG ensemble as a birthday present. I felt it appropriate to wear it today. As we left the house this morning, he hugged me and said, "Live strong, baby."

I've been reminded to be strong every time I've seen the words LIVESTRONG on my clothes. There are moments I don't feel strong. They are outnumbered by the moments I feel like I'm ready. I'm thankful for Johnny's expressions of love, support, and understanding these last few days.

Jonnae says she's feeling much better. She said, "I'm not worried anymore. I'm going to nail Leuk. He's on his way outta here."

I pray the confidence stays and we're warriors through even the most difficult times of this war. I'm thankful for her steady strides today. As we go to sleep tonight with anticipation of what's to come, I give thanks for the peace we've experienced today.

DECEMBER 13, 2007

Jonnae's resting before we head back for her second round of radiation. She had a rough night after having an allergic reaction to a drug. I sat in on the doctors' rounds this morning and apparently it's not too concerning. This drug is used primarily for those patients who are part of a new study. She's not, so they are cutting the drug out of her protocol.

I had a better night's sleep than she did. It was my morning that was rough. When they were about to begin her radiation, they led me out of the room and offered me a seat. There was a monitor there, showing Jonnae, and a button to push if I wanted to talk to her. As I looked at the screen, I was slammed with a visual I was not prepared for. She was comfortable enough to close her eyes and just relaxing through the procedure. Her position was no different than the ones she has taken through CAT scans, MRI's or other tests. I've witnessed those, too. But the view was never from above.

Her still body, arms at her side, eyes closed, white blanket covering her all the way to her chest, looked like she was in a coffin. I tried to hold my composure, but lost it as I told the nurse what I saw. I left the area to find my strength. I didn't want Jonnae to pick up on anything that had happened. When it comes to this fight for her life, I don't shed tears often, certainly not in front of her. She's oblivious to what transpired.

We've known we're heading into the eye of the storm. We know we need to be armed and ready like never before. We are doing well for today; a few shaky spots, but overall a day to be thankful for. Her appetite's still good, she's resting well, and no real threats have presented themselves.

Part of the challenge of eating, in addition to it being healthy and doing it outside of her room, is waiting until she's asleep. That way, I'm not shorting us on time spent together during her waking hours. I don't believe the no eating in the room should apply to patients across the board. Jonnae LOVES to eat WITH me. She isn't going to try and eat something she's not supposed to have (she's on a low bacteria diet, no fresh vegetables or food that's not just been prepared). If she's allowed to have food in the room, I don't see what added harm there is in my having food in here, especially if I follow her food restrictions.

Blessings are still abundant regardless of who we are, where we are, and what we're going through. To have a full understanding and appreciation of that is an enormous blessing.

DECEMBER 14, 2007

The side effects from radiation have shown up quickly. Jonnae's head hurts, her nausea is back, and now she has jaw pain. It's all related to radiation. It's mild, but bothersome. We weren't expecting these side effects to show up until next week. She's disappointed to be feeling bad this soon, but still, not one complaint's come out of her mouth.

Finding new things to be thankful for is challenging. Days here are pretty much *cookie cutter days*, but I'll do my best.

I worked out with my Fitness Anywhere TRX system. Thank goodness for this invention. It provides a challenging workout and without access to the stairwells, I know I will turn to this system often. It's quiet, which is another good thing. I try to work out while Jonnae's sleeping, which means jump roping is not an option, it's too noisy. I'm thankful for the alternative this gives me.

I'm thankful for communication with other BMT families. They share only the helpful information, not the scary stuff, and have given me leads to housing options. I will check them out as soon as I can. Most of these families have been here for some time. For the opportunity to talk with others, who know what it's like to be here, I'm thankful.

I'm surrounded by sickness. I pass other parents and sick children all day long. There are so many families dealing with seriously ill children. I will never take for granted having healthy children. I hope every parent who is not in a hospital with their child tonight, realizes the blessing and gives thanks.

One of the mothers in the BMT unit has been here for 16 months. She is from New York and hasn't seen her other two girls for months. I give thanks that our home is close enough that won't be the case for me. I give thanks that we expect to be here for *only* three months. I realize complications could change that, but until something like that occurs, I'm thankful we will be home, with a healthier Jonnae, come spring.

I've had many nurses inquire about my fitness routine. They're interested in the ways I've found to work out in the hospital. Healthy living is a challenge for the patients, their families, and medical staff. I have an opportunity to be an example of what's possible. Health is a choice. I know someone, if not several, will change their lives and become healthier as a result of my example. For being the instrument through which God speaks, I give thanks.

There are no excuses for poor nutrition and lack of exercise. I CAN DO IT! I can reach higher and be happier, healthier, and wiser. IT'S ALL MY CHOICE. I choose to stay IN CONTROL and live my best life now. Leuk can change what I do to get there, but it can't take it away.

As I'm made aware of the blessings I know in the present, I realize how many I looked over in the past. As I think of those things, I'm making a mental note so I will not let them go unnoticed in the future.

> If I'm able to go outside or move about freely in more than a single room, I will give thanks.

> If I've eaten my meals as I was hungry or as planned, I will give thanks.

> If I have company, or am not *forced* to eat in solitude, I will give thanks.

> If I'm able to turn on a light, television, music, or speak out loud, I will give thanks.

If I'm crawling into a comfortable bed, I will give thanks.

This morning, Jonnae rated her jaw pain a "4," on a scale of one to ten. It improved as the day went on. We've watched several episodes of *Gilmore Girls* and made five or so scripture posters for her room. I'm thankful for a much better day today.

Jonnae hasn't napped much. She's eaten fairly well and we've had many more smiles today. That's always something to be grateful for.

Yesterday, the radiation nurse asked what kind of things Jonnae liked. She doesn't ever ask for much. What she did want, she got for Christmas. I was pretty fresh out of ideas. I mentioned we have fun decorating her head and the scrapbooking department had some rhinestone words that stick well to it. The nurse had picked some up and gave them to her with a holiday CD, today.

The Child Life department stopped by to give us a little Christmas tree with decorations. It was a small project, but a nice festive one. I'm thankful for the gifts Jonnae received today. It's a challenge being in the hospital any time, certainly at Christmas. Small tokens of compassion and love are what the holiday season is all about. They are great spirit-boosters.

Jonnae and I are feeling a little *disconnected:* not being able to eat together, drink hot chocolate together, or lay in bed together. Those are things we've always treasured. It's sad that we can't do them now, especially when it means so much. She said even with me in the room, she feels lonely. We bond in so many little ways.

DECEMBER 15, 2007

Today was the last day of Jonnae's radiation. Quite the jokester and cutting up with the transport team, radiation team, and the staff here at the hospital, she was in rare form. Her cutest comment was to the transport and radiation teams, as we arrived for her radiation treatment this morning. They asked if she wanted them to wheel the gurney she was on into the radiation room or if she wanted to walk.

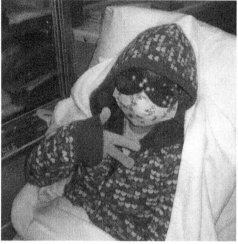

She said, "I'll walk! At the hospital they're keeping me caged and muzzled." It was cute how she said it. We all laughed at her humor. If only the entire stay could be repeats of today. For now, I will relish the thought of today before she the radiation wipes her completely out.

Last night, I asked for an extra mattress cover for the pullout bed. They were quick to respond. With a softer mattress, Jonnae's extra velour pillowcase, and a fleece blanket, I was in comfort heaven as I lay down to go to sleep. Those soft textures and surfaces made all the difference in the world. I'm thankful for comfort. It's something to behold as a treasure, here or anywhere.

This hospital complex has 4 buildings. It's 1/4 of a mile from building A to building D. There is a wide corridor that connects all 4. It's busy during the day, but empty early in the morning. I scoped it out yesterday and went down at 6 a.m. with my jump rope and pushup grips. I'd seen an area for small children with a bench I could use for step ups. I developed a good cardio circuit and only a few passersby gave me strange looks.

The feeling of accomplishment that comes from dragging yourself out of bed to workout, in addition to the adrenaline it provides, is always the perfect way to start the day. Today was super exhilarating. Some nurses stopped me on my way back to Jonnae's room to ask where the fitness room was. It opened the door for me to talk about the choices we can make for a healthier lifestyle, even while confined to a hospital.

The only thing better than Jonnae's sweet smile is it being followed by her sweet giggles. She loves *Gilmore Girls* (Actually, we both do). She laughed so much while watching it today. Her giggles made me laugh as much as the humor of the show. I'm thankful for the very special mother/daughter relationship we share. We have it because of this battle. I'll never be thankful for Leuk, but I'll always be grateful for the relationship we have because of it. There's something good in everything

I'LL NEVER BE THANKFUL FOR LEUK, BUT I'LL ALWAYS BE GRATEFUL FOR THE RELATIONSHIP WE HAVE BECAUSE OF IT. THERE'S SOMETHING GOOD IN EVERYTHING BAD.

bad. This is one instance where I don't need to look hard to find it. That's pretty amazing?

We've laughed A LOT today! I'm easily amused by my own humor and most of the time I'm the only one laughing at my jokes. Jonnae made it clear she wasn't laughing at my jokes, but only laughing at what a geek I am for thinking they're funny when no one else does. That got one of those deep down giggles and that unbelievable smile out of her. Something worth being a geek 24/7. For more shared laughter today, I'm thankful.

In high school and college, I created collages out of pictures and words cut from magazines. I've also done it with different groups I've led as an adult. It's artistic, it's therapeutic, and it tells a story. In the midst of this war, it's going to be vital to keep Jonnae focused on her future.

I've talked her into creating a dreamboard. There are going to be tough days where it will be easy to get *stuck in the yuck* of the day. She needs to have a visual of the future she's fighting for. It's going to be challenging, because she can't handle magazines. I will help locate pictures or words and cut them out for her. I know this board is going to be a powerful tool. I'm thankful for what this board will be for her.

Speaking of futures and dreams, I have plenty of my own. Something I've determined: I'm not going to stuff them in a dark place to be forgotten. The visions I have aren't mine alone. They were placed there by God. The seeds He's planted within me are meant to flourish. I'm going to actively pursue every one of them. Mandino poses this question, "I wonder how many birds die in cages believing that the cage's ceiling is the real sky?"

We're all guilty of placing limitations on what we believe we can obtain. I believe I can obtain whatever it is I desire. I believe the sky is limitless and too many of us stop believing we can fly. The dream is a powerful thing. Jonnae doesn't want to dream, she wants her future. She wants the dream to be reality and it can be. The key is BELIEVING.

DECEMBER 16, 2007

It's day minus five. That's how they count down to the big day here. It was a scary start this morning, but a good day followed.

I was in the family lounge when an alarm sounded and code blue room 524 came over the intercom. The doctors and nurses were all scurrying to the room. I saw them escort the crying mother away from the room and her child. It was heartbreaking. A couple of the other BMT moms came straight to the lounge. Evidently this happens often. The parents come to the lounge to find out what's happened. I don't think one can be prepared for all that occurs here.

Jonnae slept through the commotion. The patient was a 9-month-old baby boy. He seizured from one of the chemo drugs. They were able to get him on the defibrillator and take him to ICU. One of the moms in the lounge told me her daughter had done the same thing. The first thing she told me when she came in was, "Code blue doesn't always mean they've lost one." She was reading my mind. I guess it's easy to do when there's a *newbie* here. I thought I was ready for this, but there have already been two devastating instances, in three days, that have proven I'm not. I'll continue to press forward as a *warrior* and lead my daughter to do the same, but it isn't going to be steady every step of the way.

One of Jonnae's chemo drugs excretes through the skin. She's required to take 2 - 3 showers a day so it doesn't burn her. It's a wicked thing, this chemo. It's mind-blowing and scary to think of how they come up with these cures.

Today, Lydia came up with Johnny to visit. Yesterday, I asked the nurses about it and they said as long as she checked in at the desk, and they took her temperature, Lydia would be able to come in. Initially, I was told Jonnae wouldn't be allowed visitors, especially any under the age of 14, so I was surprised. Well, after we all got excited about our little family reunion, and Lydia and Johnny made the trip up here, the nurse at the desk informed us no children were allowed in the entire hospital. A "flu season lockdown" went into effect today. It was another heartbreaking moment. Lydia, nor I, could stop the tears. Jonnae, of course, was upset, too.

Johnny came in to visit with Jonnae, while I left with Lydia. Later Johnny, Lydia, and I went to the cafeteria for brunch. The visit was cut short, as they left shortly after. Not quite what we had hoped for, but I did get to see her, and my hubby too, so I'm still grateful for that. I miss my family so much already. It's going to be a long haul, but we we'll make it, as many already have and many more will. This experience is profoundly changing our lives and how we'll view the gifts in it, forever!

Our favorite scriptures, promoting faith and rebuking fear, are finally hanging all over the room. I'm thankful they're up in plain view and will help us to keep our eyes on the Coach! The game's about to get *noisy* and the view could get distorted quickly. We're *arming ourselves,* with everything we can. I'm thankful for the shield of strength God's Word provides.

Johnny brought me several things I had requested. A couple of the items I had forgotten, while most were needs as a result of our being here. Hand salve and moisture gloves have become a real necessity. This filtered air, along with increased hand washing and sanitizer, has cracked the skin on my knuckles and made them so sore.

The evening view from our window is reminiscent of a Christmas card. It's a much nicer view than a brick wall. I'm thankful for the white snow, for the eyes I have to see it, and for the way it's bringing our Christmas cards to life. God is good. God's people are good. Life is good.

Lydia brought Jonnae and me gifts from "Santa's Workshop."It's amazing how much thought she put into them. She gave me a snow globe with penguins in and around it.

She said, "Do you know why I picked penguins? Remember the penguin family you made at the hospital?"

I hadn't, and was immediately reminded of how precious my thoughtful, loving children are. Any moment I have, any memory that is made with these *God-given* angels, is such a blessing. I humbly offer up a prayer of thanksgiving for God choosing me as their mother.

Leukemia is a horrific disease, but there are children fighting something even worse. There are many diseases far away from hope of a normal life. They are bidding for time, hardly a cure. I'm thankful we are close to a cure. At least we have options we know have worked. No matter how bad we think our troubles are, there is someone who would trade spots with us in a heartbeat. There is someone who'd take the hardships we have and sing a song of praise. I'll not make the mistake of focusing on what I don't have. I'll focus on what I do. We have hope, we have faith, we have belief, and we have a future. We are BLESSED!

> I'LL NOT MAKE THE MISTAKE OF FOCUSING ON WHAT I DON'T HAVE. I'LL FOCUS ON WHAT I DO.

DECEMBER 17, 2007

Surprise!!! It's me! THE REAL DEAL! Can you believe it?!?! Just wanted to let you know I'm doing fine. It's day minus 4! Woo hoo! Almost there. Good news is I'm going to kick Leuk's butt, I just have a couple bumps in the road before I get there. I know that with all your prayers and keeping my eye on the Coach, I'm going to be just fine. Not only fine but GREAT! I have scripture posters and a dream board to keep me motivated. Thank you for all of your words of encouragement and prayers. You have no idea how much they mean to me.

Dad, just wanted to tell you how much I love you. I can always

know that when I'm feeling down you will be there to help lift me up
whether it's by giving me words of encouragement or just by being
your goofy self and making me laugh. I love you, Dad, and I can't
say that enough. I love you! I love you! I love you! Can't wait to see
you when you come up Thursday!

    Blessings,

    Jonnae

Jonnae feels really good today and I got a great night's sleep last night. It's been a good day for us. It was extremely difficult leaving her to go to a hotel. I don't know how many times the little voice in my head asked, "Are you sure you want to do this?" I nearly changed my mind several times, but knew I needed a shot at some uninterrupted sleep. She was out like a light, and very comfortable, before I left. I'm thankful for both of our good night's rest.

The Ronald McDonald House called with an available room for me today. That's going to be a much better solution for me at this point. I don't like leaving Jonnae for any length of time. I'd rather be right here on the corner, right next to the hospital, than anywhere else. I will go get my things at the hotel tonight and check into the RM house tomorrow. I'm so thankful for this establishment and the volunteers that make it possible. It'll be a great blessing.

I had a decent workout before checking out of the hotel this morning, considering there wasn't a single dumbbell in the place. The universal machine was better than nothing. Since arriving, I've only missed one day of working out and I haven't missed a beat nutritionally. I've rebuked the little voice that's said, "Go ahead, just this once." Determination and perseverance are powerful tools. They aren't hard to utilize when I've committed to using them.

My sister and her family ran by to drop off some items we've been wanting. I have no idea where a grocery store is and still suffer from separation anxiety. I have a hard time leaving Jonnae for anything. I'm thankful for the visit and joy their little hugs provided.

DECEMBER 18, 2007

Jonnae started throwing up today. It's the weirdest thing. She gets hiccups that don't go away. It leads to her throwing up. The hiccups are aggravating her more than the getting sick. She felt so much better after throwing up that she was laughing as she gave me and the nurse a thorough description of what part of her breakfast she could identify in the bucket. I was sending up prayers of thanks as she was laughing and making jokes about it instead of crying.

The hospital technicians tested all code blue alarms in the BMT wing today. The code blue I witnessed Sunday won't be the last one I hear or see. With the boy's fading condition down the hall, and his family all here from Florida and Mississippi awaiting the worst, I'm almost prepared for it to happen today. I feel especially bad for the mom today. She was required to leave last night, as she's apparently come down with the flu. I can't imagine being forced to leave my child at a time like this.

I am so thankful I'm able to be in the room with Jonnae to rub her back, clean her face, and comfort her as much as I can. We both hate not being able to eat together or watch *Gilmore Girls* over a cup of hot chocolate. She shed tears when I left to have dinner in the family lounge last night. She said even though I'm in the room most of the time, she's lonely when I leave to eat. (That child loves to watch me eat, even when she's not.) I'm grateful I'm able to be here with her at all. There are moms too sick to be with their children. There are moms who must send their child away for medical care and can't afford to be with them. Johnny and I watched a show, a few weeks ago, where a child from another country came to the states to have a tumor removed from her face. Her family had no funds to come with her. I can't imagine. And by the grace of God I don't have to.

The hospital is in a really rough part of town. More than once, we've been told not to walk outside at night. The area is desolate, yet there are groups of people out in the cold, dark night. In the morning, they are gathering at the bus stops, again waiting in the cold. I'm privileged to have never lived in the conditions they are. I'm privileged to be able to go to my car and leave when I'm ready, not having to wait out in the cold air. No matter how hard things get here, no matter what the outcome is, I will always be grateful for the multitude of blessings I've known, know, and will always know.

We watched the *Biggest Loser* Finale tonight. I've never been as large as the competitors, but I can relate to their pain, the rejection, and the humiliation from being heavy. (I was made fun of in grade school for being an overweight kid.)

I know the feeling of the victory from fighting the uphill struggle to obtain a healthy body and self image. I'm thankful I know what I know. I'm thankful I've walked in those shoes and they're no longer mine. Twice already, pizza has been sent up here for the parents and families of the patients in the BMT unit. It's there all day to walk by, smell, and see. I've bypassed it for tuna both times. I've forgone the cookies, the candy, and all the junk that's sitting around. It's not easy, but victory is sweet. I give thanks for choosing to be a victor.

I had the opportunity to share a meal replacement drink with another family today. These have been a significant source of nutrition for Jonnae. This family is really concerned about their boy's lack of protein intake. The mom was thrilled to hear about Essentials, so I gave the boy some to try. He likes the taste and drank three today. I don't care how it is I've impacted someone, so long as I've blessed them in some way.

I feel restricted on one hand because we're confined to a hospital, but on the other hand, I know it's because we're experiencing what we are, I'm able to reach so many. There is nothing like being able to give. There is nothing like being a blessing to another.

DECEMBER 19, 2007

Jonnae's not feeling well. She's pale, weak in the eyes, and has dark circles under them. She came out of the restroom today and said,

"Do you think I look different? I think I look different."

I told her she looked like people do when they are sick and I could tell she wasn't feeling good. She hasn't played her DS any today. That's a sign she's not feeling well. The eating is *over.* The doctors say she will not eat now for weeks. The chemo has destroyed her appetite and tasting ability. They'll start her on a feeding tube Saturday, after the bone marrow transplant.

After she got sick earlier, I told her it was going to be a little harder each day for a while. She looked at me matter of fact like, not discouraged at all, and said, 'It's gotta get worse before it can get better." I know how unbelievably strong this child is, yet every now and then, I expect to hear something not so mature and bold come out of her mouth.

This came to me on my walk over from the RMH this morning:

"'I am the Lord's servant,' Mary answered 'May it be to me as you have said.' Then the angel left her." Luke 1:38 (NIV)

Mary was so accepting of her *calling.* There's no doubt it was a glorious assignment. However, it came with tremendous personal cost. Jewish law demanded women to be stoned to death if they became pregnant out of wed-lock. Even though Joseph came to her rescue, there were whispers and judgment for the rest of her life.

Worse than that, she witnessed her son's pain and death at the crucifixion. His birth and death were far from glorious, yet she stood firmly in faith and love for our Father. Jonnae and I want to do the same.

Mary was a willing servant because she was well acquainted with the greatness of God. As our Creator, He has a plan for each of us, just as He did for Mary. He's created us with a purpose in mind and good to come from it. This assignment we've been given in dealing with Leuk is not about suffering, it's about learning, knowing, and teaching. It's about the gift of life and the magnificent power of LOVE. True suffering comes when we fall out of alignment with God's vision for us. Serving Him is priceless and we will not be knocked off course by anything of the world.

I got an email today inviting me to come out to Kansas for a Body for Life Champions Weekend in late June. They want me to be one of their guest speakers. I LOVE sharing my life experiences and how they've empowered both me and Jonnae. I'm passionate about motivational speaking. The Knoxville event this past October is one I shall never forget. This particular community of people is an amazing group of loving, compassionate people. I'm blessed to have this event to look forward to.

I came back from a late lunch and Jonnae said the doctor had been in with some news. I said, "What news? Is it good or bad?"

Jonnae said, "Just news," and smiled as she ripped the sheet back to reveal envelopes. We had mail! She was so cute, her and her sneaky little self.

She's sleeping peacefully now. I'm going to make sure she is comfortable for the night before I call an escort to go back to the RMH tonight. I hate to leave her, but I need the rest. I am thankful for the opportunity to get some tonight.

DECEMBER 20, 2007

I ended up staying with Jonnae last night. I awoke early so I could run over to the RMH for a workout, breakfast, and shower before coming back to the hospital.

Jonnae's day didn't start off as good. Her stomach's hurting (mucositis in the gut) and her throat's sore. Her tongue is completely white now. The mucositis pain she's all too familiar with, has arrived. The RN said we can expect next week to really "suck" (those were his exact words.) We knew this was coming. They're going to place a feeding tube before the mucositis gets any worse. It'll keep her stomach minutely active and provide a way for her to take oral meds without swallowing.

Friends of the family came today to play Santa to the children. The hospital rules prevented them from wearing costumes but I'm certain the children were lifted by their cheerful spirits. A Child Life coordinator escorted them around so the right precautions were taken. We are thankful for their love, friendship, and the laughter that is always had when they are present.

My *soul sister* (that's what we call each other) also brought me birthday presents. She gave me the plushest blanket I've ever felt, silky pajamas, fuzzy slippers, and a basket of creams and balms for my dry skin. I can hardly wait to indulge in them and experience the comfort and restful sleep they'll provide. I'm thankful for "Oneie's" gifts, but mostly for our indescribable connection. Friendship is awesome, but this spiritual union goes beyond that. I give thanks for her.

I've missed all my children, but today it was evident how much I miss Nolan. He had me laughing with his wit the moment he walked in today. He's such an awesome kid. He's accepting this donor role maturely and respectably. The nursing staff really enjoys him too. He's not shy with his humor. He's bound to be a breath of fresh air for them. He is sure to provide laughs in the midst of the seriousness and anxiety. He is a blessing in many ways; a gift every day.

Jonnae's morning was rough, but before day's end, she was feeling better. Tomorrow's the big day and she fell asleep tonight without much anxiety. We've had ample time to prepare for this transplant and it is time. I'm thankful for her improved condition and for the light that's bound to appear at the end of the tunnel.

DECEMBER 21, 2007

Well, the big day came and is nearly over. Everyone is doing well. Nolan's in a room, on the other side of the wing, and recovering fine. Jonnae's still receiving her new marrow cells. They'll run until about 1 a.m. She's had a good day. Now we play "wait and see" and pray the marrow's received well by her body, with no complications. The road is far from over, but we are certainly off to a really good start.

I'm beat, but my blessing cup is full. I don't love what I've witnessed with Jonnae's pain and suffering. I don't love how much time we've spent in the hospital. I don't love the toll Leukemia's taken on our family and what my children have been asked to endure, but I certainly love life and the people who are in ours. We're blessed. So blessed!

Today we were surprised by some visitors from Wal-Mart; store managers that Johnny's worked with. They're ready to help however they can. It's pretty special that they took time to leave their stores, with only a few days left until Christmas. It was special to me, so I know it was for Johnny. Everyone has been so amazingly supportive. God is evident in so many people. I'm humbled and give thanks.

Nolan's baseball coach also surprised us today. We'd been in Jonnae's room waiting for the hospital staff to call us when Nolan was in recovery. We found his coach sitting in the waiting room. He actually ended up spending quite a bit of time with Nolan, as Johnny and I were called back to Jonnae's room for the start of her transplant. It meant a lot to Johnny and me. I know it meant a lot to Nolan.

All of us coming together as one community, one family, to fight the leukemia war together, is an incredible experience. My life will never be the same. I'll never forget where we've been and who was there to share it with us, the good and the bad. There will never be a day that go by that I don't realize how blessed I am. Love is the greatest gift anyone can ever receive. We are the recipients of it over and over again. How can we not feel blessed and sing God's praise?

I witness families who aren't as fortunate as we are. I see families who aren't *plugged in;* who aren't able to see our Heavenly Father, the Coach, much less keep their eyes on Him. I see families who are in financial distress, not knowing if help is going to show up. I see families who are separated as they fight this horrific battle and I realize over and over again how much I have to be thankful for.

We've seen more than our share of hospitals, but I'm finding myself in *awareness overload* as I'm surrounded by sickness in every form. Someone who's finding it hard to be thankful needs to walk the halls of a pediatric hospital. It won't take long to embrace the gift of life outside of it. It's a shame it took being in the eye of this storm for me to see it. I wish it could have been revealed to me differently , but it hasn't, so I will keep this 20/20 vision and live with thanksgiving for all that I have that is good. Once life is embraced with a heart of gratitude, there's no other way to live it.

> ONCE LIFE IS
> EMBRACED WITH A
> HEART OF GRATITUDE,
> THERE'S NO OTHER
> WAY TO LIVE IT.

I now have two children who like cracking jokes while they're throwing up. The medical team told Nolan he would feel like he had fallen on ice after they had drawn his marrow. The first thing he said when he came to, as he was getting sick into a bucket, was, "What kind of ice were they falling on? It feels like Barry Bonds took a bat to my butt." It's crazy how much I've laughed today. What an amazing thing to be able to say. He was non-stop wit and I'm so very proud of him. He may be 6 foot tall and 17, but he'll always be *my baby* and he's proven to be a hero as well. He's doing great. I say a prayer of thanks.

Jonnae's had a much better day today. She was feeling sick earlier, but she's played the Wii, watched a movie, and drank some of her meal replacement drink. She hasn't done any of those things in three days. I wish the entire transplant experience could be like today. I dread the worsening of the mucositis and the shock her body is going to go through, but for now, I give thanks.

I suspected this Christmas would display the sacred spirit of the season like never before. I couldn't have been more right. I feel just like Mary must have, scared but excited. Ready to say, "Yes!" knowing He has a plan and a purpose for what's occurring. My prayer is for everyone to know the same peace; as they LIVE, not merely exist.

DECEMBER 22, 2007

Yesterday was Nolan's bad day and Jonnae's good. Today proved to be the reverse. Jonnae started throwing up just as we were getting ready for bed last night. Her sickness continued through the night. At one point they even came in to do a chest x-ray. Her vitals were changing and they could hear crackling in her lungs. They said it wasn't uncommon and was because of the excessive fluid that had been pumped into her.

She was very uncomfortable and put on oxygen for a while. Finding rest was impossible. Today, her vomiting has been so violent that blood has come from both her nose and mouth. She's amazing as she takes it all in stride. She just sits with her head over a bucket, bracing it with one hand and wiping her nose and mouth with a cloth in the other. Her face is very swollen and she looks so tired. Her eyes are bloodshot, with dark circles beneath them. Her dry parched lips are caked with blood. We took a picture of her and Nolan before he left and her smile was so pitiful. She's trying so hard to put on a happy face, but the spark that's usually in her eye, and the spirit that normally penetrates through you from her soul, is absent today. It's heartbreaking.

They put a feeding tube in place today. It was difficult to watch and once again, she amazed us all with her bravery. The nurse told Jonnae she was her new hero. She said she would need to be put to sleep to have that tube fed through mucositis pain and vomiting.

They fed the tube in through her nose. From there it's supposed to go down her throat and into her stomach. The nurse told her to swallow some sips of water as she fed it through. Only Jonnae's stomach is too irritated. While the nurse was feeding the tube down her throat, the water was making her throw up. The tube curled up and came out through her mouth. They continued feeding it through her nose and out her mouth until it was all the way out so they could try again. The second time was successful.

Johnny says I paint a prettier picture than what is actually happening here and attributes it to my being upbeat and positive. I haven't done that today, for sure. My attitude comes from an understanding and acceptance that some may not comprehend. That's okay. The best way to explain it is others might feel like jerking their hand out of Our Father's when I choose to grip tight.

More remarkable news of LOVE and compassion was reported today. Our boys' football team held a road block today to raise money for our transplant fund. Words cannot express the multitude of emotions and feelings that have resulted from today. It's exhausting, yet amazing. We're so grateful.

One of the roadblock organizers told me that before Layne began working the event, he ran into the local grocery to buy candy canes, with his own money, to give to the donors passing through. It brought tears to my eyes. I'm so blessed with my children. I stay in a state of gratitude for having such amazing kids. I know I'm biased, but I'm told often that my kids are "a joy" or "polite" or "impressive." Those are the words a reporter used to describe Layne after an interview with him today, "an impressive young man." I'm so blessed.

Nolan rested well last night and was anxious to "blow this joint." As we walked him out this morning, he commented on how depressing this place is. Our perspective of life has forever been changed because of the suffering we've seen here. He's going to a girls' basketball game tonight. It's safe to say, he's recovered well. He's walking stiff and you can tell he's trying to cater to the pain in his lower back. I suspect each day he'll feel less discomfort.

Jonnae surprised us when she said she felt well enough to play some Wii tonight. Now she's resting comfortably. I pray that the night is peaceful for her.

DECEMBER 23, 2007

Jonnae's numbers are where the doctors expect them to be. Her blood pressure has gotten high a couple of times, but they aren't alarmed. They're cutting back on one of her meds to counteract that.

She's had some nausea and is sleeping more than usual, but she's been through so much. She only had one bout with vomiting and it was very mild compared to what she's had the last couple of days. She played more Wii and actually may have exerted too much energy doing so. After she quit playing, she went to sleep and has been resting ever since.

Her eyes are still very weak, but her spirits are good. Her throat has not been too bad but she is using the pain pump more often. In comparison to what we've known in the past, we'll take a day like today everyday if we can.

Johnny's on his way back home. He was scheduled to work today but got a text from his management telling him to spend the day with us. I'm very thankful for that. I miss his support, his company, and everything a wife misses when she's not with her husband. I'm grateful for the time we have together, even if it's limited to the hospital.

This morning I woke up in Johnny's arms, got to work out early and watched Joel Osteen before coming back to the hospital. I'm thankful for everyday that I get to start out that way. It was an awesome way to begin the day.

There's a boy here who flew through his bone marrow transplant like it was nothing. They were gone for only ten days before he started running a fever that was accompanied with headaches. Turns out it was toxoplasma and he rapidly went downhill. He is seven-years-old and has reverted back to being like a baby. He can't eat, drink, or talk, and he goes to the bathroom on himself and doesn't even know it.

I've seen children affected by this horrible disease. I don't think it's reversible; yet again, a circumstance worse than ours. That mother would gladly trade places with me.

Things like traffic, holiday stress, gossip, bills, job issues, personality conflicts, and those things that aren't truly "life taking" won't take a way my life and joy anymore. What I used to complain about pales tremendously to what I now know is a "tough day."

Tomorrow's Christmas Eve. WOW. As we experience the spirit of LOVE like never before I feel the presence of our precious Savior. What an incredible gift!

DECEMBER 24, 2007

It's 10 p.m. and I'm about to turn in. I don't recall ever being in bed on Christmas Eve before midnight. Growing up we always went to Midnight Mass. In more recent years, we've been at my father-in-law's when the clock strikes twelve.

Johnny and the other children are home celebrating Christmas in the tradition we normally would. I'm sure it's difficult, as they miss us being with them, but I pray they're lifted by the family surrounding them. Nolan and Austin are going to stay in Corbin a few extra days and Johnny will come back tomorrow night with Layne and Lydia. (Nolan is still sore, a little tired, but recovering quite nicely.) My parents stopped by tonight and are at the Ronald McDonald House. They'll be spending Christmas morning here before heading to my sister's. This isn't a normal Christmas for anyone, but I'm thankful for their visit tonight. I know this is difficult for them, but they carry the burden with strength and are a blessing to me and my family.

If I were to let my mind stay focused on where "WE" are tonight, I'd probably be sad. But I choose to draw encouragement and peace as I think about where Mary and Joseph were years and years ago, as they were dealing with their own uncertainty. Many have said our circumstances are unfair. Granted, I wish they were different. But if God's own son and the young woman he chose to mother His child endured suffering and sacrifice, who am I (who are we?) to question the destiny He has designed for us? Is it that hard to comprehend? I should hope it wouldn't be.

There's nothing worse than watching your child suffer in the magnitude which I've witnessed. Jonnae's been in a lot of pain today and we've been forewarned that each day is going to be worse, until we hit day +12 or 14. We are at day +3. I can't imagine trying to fight it with resentment, worry, anger, or anything other than acceptance. I'm blessed to know God the way I do. I'm not going up and down the hallways cheering. I'm just choosing to submit to His plan, with acceptance and faith. I believe whatever pain and sacrifice we offer up here, He'll make up for when we meet Him face to face. For the promise of eternity, I'm so very blessed.

Father, I pray for the world to experience, in the most magnified way, the love you've shown us. How proud and happy you must be, to see Your Light shining brightly through so many people. I pray they feel the warmth of Your light, as it burns so brightly through them as they help care for me and my family. May it carry them through the Christmas season with happiness and great joy. Our Christmas is blessed because of them, because of You. Thank you Lord. Amen

DECEMBER 25, 2007

Jonnae's pain has increased enough that's she's now on a continuous drip with the pain pump. Her throat is extremely sore and she's slept off and on all day.

I slept here with Jonnae last night. On nights I stay here, I get up early enough to leave, get a workout in, shower, and eat before returning. Being used to this routine, Jonnae set her clock to wake her at 8:30, the time her mammaw and pappaw told her I was born, so she could call me and wish me an *official* Happy Birthday. I came back to find her sitting up in bed, with a birthday cake for me. She had called my sister, about thirty minutes before her bone marrow transfusion started, to make sure I had a birthday cake for my 40th. In true *Jonnae fashion*, she was thinking of someone besides herself, even before one of, if not THE most important moments of her life. I'm a mother, tremendously blessed.

Previous days have gone by rather quickly, but today's been a long one. I had anticipated every one of them being slow to pass. These sedentary hospital days really go *against the grain* for me. I don't like sitting still or being unproductive. I've come up with all kinds of projects to keep me occupied. Today, I updated workout journals, clipping and putting workout routines from my Oxygen magazines into personal notebooks. I actually found quite a few things I can do when a fitness room isn't provided.

We've been visited by the Child Life coordinator many times today, as she's delivered gifts from several "alumni" families who know what it's like to be a holiday resident here. One family has provided Christmas gifts to the children every year since their daughter finished her chemo here, 15 years ago. Through her dad's work, and supporters of Texas Roadhouse, they've been able to gift many children. They brought Jonnae an iPod Touch.

She was emotional in receiving it and told me through tears, "It's a really nice gift. Someone else should have gotten it."

I told her if God didn't mean for her to have it, it wouldn't have come through her door. She shouldn't feel bad about it. She deserves it.

I know where she's coming from. I'm so humbled as we receive the financial support we do, knowing there are many families who aren't getting the blessings we're experiencing. Then I figure it's another lesson God's trying to teach me. There's nothing wrong with saying, "We need help," and then receiving it. I'm learning how to *receive*. In that too, there is a blessing.

A different group of "alumni" families coordinated a donation of Aerobeds, memory foam pillows, and fleece blankets, to give the BMT parents. I will try out the bed tonight, for I won't be leaving Jonnae so soon after she's gotten sick. I think she's going to be okay for the night, but I want to be with her. It's Christmas and the RMH bed will be there for me tomorrow.

DECEMBER 26, 2007

It's been another well tolerated day. Jonnae's pain pump has kept her comfortable. Her mucositis doesn't appear to be getting worse. We're both pleasantly surprised at this point. We give thanks that another day is done and we're one step closer to getting through this stage of the fight. Her white cell count is practically non-existent. She got platelets this morning because they were down to 7000. That's very low, but expected by the doctors.

Her red cell count is staying high. The doctor seems impressed with Nolan's "power cells" as she calls them. She said Nolan blessed Jonnae twice. She referred to the stem cells as fantastic and the red cell count as a bonus. We sent Nolan a text telling him what the doctor said, to which he replied, "No woman can reject me." Too funny!

I've entertained Jonnae with more Wii activity today. She's says it's more fun to watch me, than to play herself. I get pretty into it and admit it's provided entertainment for me too. I didn't know what all the fuss was when these games came out. I think I have tennis elbow from all the matches I've played today. The game is on loan and there is only one complete system here. They'll probably be coming to get it soon. It's helped to pass the time and I'm thankful.

Jonnae is sleeping soundly now. I don't think there's a day that goes by, I'm not aware of how amazing she is. I was 31, laid up with an Achilles tendon rupture in '98 and feeling sorry for myself for having to endure a cast for the second time in one summer. Here she is going through the horrific side effects of chemo, fighting for her life a second time, and she accepts it with such strength. She's mature beyond her years. At twelve, she knew more than I did near 40. At 15 she blows me away. I couldn't be more grateful for her, for all my children.

As I prepare for bed tonight, I look to the heavens and say, "THANK YOU." If my life as I know it were to end today, my blessings have been abundant. Are the blessings going to dwindle? I don't expect they are, but if they do, how could I not give thanks for what I've been able to witness? These thoughts with the Word of God are my armor and protect me from negativity and the snares of the devil. Thanks be to God!

DECEMBER 27, 2007

The doctors are quite happy with Jonnae's progress. She's looks better and has been more active today (she played the Wii with every hospital staff member who came in). She watched television some, also. Since transplant, she's done neither of those things.

She's been uncomfortable with what they call "red man's disease." It's caused by an antibiotic they've given her to counteract a skin contaminate that could've been introduced to her with Nolan's cells. His blood culture tested positive and they aren't sure if she will pick up on it. They've administered this drug to cover her, just in case. I have a huge problem with administration of drugs for a condition that might not even happen. Far be it from me to question what needs to be done after a transplant, but she was feeling fine until they gave her this drug that she may not need. It's not the first time I've questioned if all of the drugging is necessary, but what do you do when your daughter's life is at stake and they won't research more natural methods?

She wanted to go to sleep earlier than usual, so I've come over to the Ronald McDonald House, thinking I would take a long hot bath.

I'm ready to fall into bed myself. I give thanks for this bedroom that provides a *retreat* from the hospital. I'll always appreciate the blessing of a home. To move freely, to rest, to entertain, to eat where I want, to watch TV, or to just be able to touch the thermostat are blessings I'll not take for granted when I get back home.

I *arm* myself with jewelry every day. I have several bracelets I wear as weapons. They have thoughts, symbols, or special meaning that I draw strength from. I have a bracelet with a frog charm that reminds me to Fully Rely On God. I have one inscribed with spirit, dream, balance, wisdom, and joy. I have one that says "God's Team" and another that says, "There is nothing worth more than this day."

I have an Athlete's For Christ shield of strength that has Philippians 4:13: (WEB) "I can do all things through Christ who strengthens me" and a necklace that has "angel's wings" from completing a challenge dedicated to Julie Whitt. I have a necklace and rings from my husband that remind me of his love. I'm blessed to start my day arming myself with affirmation as I remind myself that life is a gift and I choose to embrace it.

A special BMT family was discharged today. They are still close to the hospital at their "home away from home," where they'll finish out the remainder of their transplant recovery. The mother has blessed me since the first day we arrived. She recognized me as being new and showed me around. Instantly, I felt like I wasn't alone. I have enjoyed her company more than I'd realized. As I signed her son's guestbook today, I was overcome with tears as I felt her absence. I'm blessed to have been here while she was here, also.

My sweet Jonnae called to wish me a good night. She woke up to go to the restroom and take the last of her meds and called to see how my bath went. When I told her the shuttle was late picking me up and that my first journal entry got lost in cyber space, she said, "Well if you don't get one tonight, you're leaving early enough to get one tomorrow night." She's so maternal. Sometimes I feel like we're doing the *Freaky Friday* thing and have reversed roles. I'm blessed to have two daughters who love to look after their mommy.

As I lay my head down to sleep, I thank God for another blessed day. I will awake seeking the treasures of tomorrow, both obvious and hidden. I also pray the world joins me in doing the same.

DECEMBER 28, 2007

We knew it was bound to happen, but were hoping the string of good days would continue and surprise us all. Today was a painful and difficult day. Jonnae's heels are causing extreme pain. It's hard for her to describe, or for the doctors to understand, although they aren't too alarmed and say it is from the prep chemo. A lot of the side effects from the pre-transplant chemo are showing up. We've had good days throughout radiation, chemo, and the transplant. It was easy to think we might coast through this. The body said, "Not so fast!"

Her personal areas and under her arms are swollen. She also has skin discoloration, rashes, tremors, itching, and bizarre heel pain. The pain meds aren't helping with the swelling and tenderness, but they are with the mucositis. Her mouth and throat have gotten worse.

Jonnae had a violent spell of vomiting while the doctor was in visiting. In her "matter of factness," she just kept her head over the bucket, mucus stringing from her mouth, (mucositis makes it impossible to wipe her mouth) and motioned with her other hand as to say, "Go ahead, keep talking."

In her surprise to Jonnae's reaction, the doctor laughed and said, "I can wait to continue the conversation, sweetie. There's no hurry."

She's been very emotional today. We played Outburst, Jr. earlier and she was easily agitated. Who can blame her? The rollercoaster is far from being over. In the family lounge, I hear other BMT moms discussing the different obstacles they've overcome and can't help but wonder if the same is in store for us. We are early in the game and so much left to happen. I continue to keep my eyes on the Coach and ask him to keep a firm grip on both of us, as we battle our way to victory.

Every Friday there's a chat session in the family lounge. Today it was attended by some bitter mothers voicing their anger. I sat and listened for a while before being told the doctor was in our room waiting on me. I'm thankful to be at a place in my life where I realize that if anger, bitterness, hatred, or unforgiveness reside in my heart, there is no room for love, joy, happiness or peace. It took most of my life for me to understand that. But now when it's most valuable, it serves me well. For that I'm eternally grateful.

They bring in cookies, cake, and soft drinks for these sessions. There have been times in my life when I would have pigged out to numb the pain, just like I witnessed everyone doing. I'm thankful I'm in control and making good choices. Sugar highs won't help me acquire anything but added pounds and energy crashes. Neither of which contributes to my life, certainly not here. I've heard family members talking about the weight they've put on since being here. That's not good for physical, mental, or emotional health. I give thanks for the tools I'm using to keep the "temple of my spirit" in top condition.

Jonnae's wearing a shirt that reads, "A blood donor saved my life!" on the front. It looks like a Red Cross shirt. The back of the shirt has a giant cross with the words, "This is the blood of my covenant, which is poured out for many for the forgiveness of sins." Matthew 26:28.

We've witnessed to many with the posters on her walls. Her shirt gave us a fresh opportunity to do more today. I'm thankful to get to speak the glory of God.

Although today has been rough, it's another step forward. As long as we continue to take baby steps, we'll get to our destination. I'm here with her. I'm able to walk beside her, encourage her, and provide the comfort only a mother can, for that I'm blessed.

We'll sleep together (or try to) in her room tonight. She's encouraged me to go to the RMH for a better night's sleep. She's so brave, so selfless. She's a saint. Every moment I have with her, I'm forever in debt to my Heavenly Father for gracing me with her presence. I'll live every last breath I have in praise of God for my blessed life. If everything and everyone were taken away from me, I've been blessed beyond what most have known. He saw me worthy and I am thankful.

DECEMBER 29, 2007

I've tried *not to swing at the high outside pitches* today. I've made a conscious effort to stay focused on the Coach and not be overwhelmed by the action of the *game*. With Jonnae's increased pain, fever, and headache, I've caught myself swinging at balls I should let go. Her fever could be a result of any number of things.

Since there's a family here dealing with toxoplasmosis, and Jonnae's had a questionable lesion on her brain, (not unlike the boy) I caught myself swinging at "*what if.*" That's not my style of play. Predictions of worst case scenarios are pitches that result in strikes every time.

The doctor said she'll have a couple more rough days before we can expect to turn a corner. I've been unable to discuss her fever with a doctor tonight. I imagine there aren't many kids who get by without running one after transplant. The hard part is not knowing the cause of it.

These kids have no way to fight off infection, so it could be anything. They have three antibiotics going now to try and hit whatever it is, until they figure it out. It's still hard for me to accept the administration of so many drugs, many that aren't necessary. How could the liver possibly be able to filter so much?

Jonnae's neutrophils came up a teeny bit today. Not anything significant, but at least a step in the right direction. The staff seems quite pleased with the increase, even if slight.

I went over to the Ronald McDonald House while Jonnae slept. (She has slept more today than any day so far). I met some other families staying there. I've only been to the house very late at night and have always left early in the morning, so I've not met anyone there. It's a great thing to have communication with other moms who have similar stories, or at least know what it's like to be ripped from *normal* life to save their child's.

As I was walking over to the RMH, I thought of different forms of suffering. No one is exempt from trials. Some suffer from much worse than what I know. Everyone is trying to overcome an obstacle of some kind. If they aren't, it won't be long before they are. That's how life is. Be it large or small, extended or short lived, something good can come from bearing a cross. I'm experiencing the heart of God, all over the place, with this one.

I dropped Jonnae's camera last week. I bent over to pick up her dream board and it fell out of my pocket. I was correct in thinking she would be really upset with me. She used her birthday money to order a pink Easy Share Kodak camera and matching camera case. She was quick to forgive me, but let me know if and when she got a replacement, I was not to touch it. I found one at Amazon.com and it arrived today. I'm thankful for being saved by the online ordering option.

Our legs are a little shaky after today. We could use some good news to keep our footing solid. Tomorrow will bring a fresh dose of stability. For how God blesses us with a new supply every morning, I give thanks.

DECEMBER 30, 2007

It's not just been a good day, it's been a *REALLY* good day! Prayers of thanksgiving are being said tonight.

She was alert as soon as she woke up this morning, about 9 a.m. and has just gone to sleep (It's 8:30 p.m.). She's played the Wii and Outburst, Jr., had special visitors, read email, and watched TV. She even let me put some snowflake tattoos on her head. No vomiting, only nose bleeds and she hasn't mentioned the pain in her heels and mouth. The pain pump is keeping her comfortable.

She's had no fever or headache and her counts are the same. They should start coming up next week. It appears she's slowly "turning the corner." I pray we stay in this trend.

I met a mother on the shuttle to the RMH last night whose 17-year-old son has been in ICU for the last three weeks. He'd been completely healthy, no history or signs of any problems, and just became incoherent. He can't sit up, walk, or talk. I'm praying it's one of those crazy viruses you hear about. The doctors can't figure it out.

Again, I find myself giving thanks that we weren't blindsided with an illness that left us questioning what direction to go. Jonnae's leukemia came on sudden, but the worst of the fight was delayed in a way that allowed us to process where we were and what we needed to do. Some of these families are just thrown into the pit with no diagnosis available, no answers, and a child instantly different than the one they've always known.

Because Jonnae's had a good day and is sleeping very soundly, I'm much more comfortable going to the RMH tonight (Last night it was difficult, but she insisted). I have a much better chance of getting rest away from the beeps and intrusions (I'm not medicated to assist me in sleeping through it). Jonnae, bless her heart, cannot break away from the intrusions, but does seem to sleep through most of it.

DECEMBER 31, 2007

Today wasn't as good as yesterday, but certainly not as bad as the two prior to it. I knew it was going to be interesting when I walked into her room this morning and found her consulting with two pain management doctors. She requested a reduction in her pain pump dosage. I had no idea. This was all instigated by her.

I had to smile, though, for she's just like me. I often refer to her as my "Mini-Me." Four out of five of my children were born natural and I took no pain pills after my Achilles tendon ruptures or ACL repair. None of those things can compare to a bone marrow transplant, but I can relate to the resistance of medicating when I have a choice. After the rounds this morning, the doctors told me they can see that she's the "commander-in-chief" and a take-charge patient.

Thankfully, she hasn't paid any consequences for having reduced the pain meds. Her mouth is getting better and the soreness she's experiencing in her heels and hands has to do with engraftment. The pain pump wasn't helping with those things, anyway. Under her arms, her heels, and the palms of her hands are causing the most pain. Hopefully that isn't going to last much longer. She got sick once, early this morning, and has taken a few naps, but it's definitely been a good day. Thank God we made it through another one without any complications.

I'm being careful about the time I spend in the family lounge. It can be both good and bad. I benefit from the families who are strong, but am weakened by the ones who are angry, bitter, or negative. Whether in the hospital or not, I choose to stay away from people who contaminate my spirit and claim my joy with an attitude of gratitude.

As this year comes to an end, I thank God that I can take in air with my own lungs. I thank him that I can swing my feet to the floor and stand on my own strength. I can walk, jump, lunge, squat, sit, and run. What a blessing! I can see everything around me. I can taste food, digest it, and keep it down. I can hear. I can touch, grip, and hold things in my hands without pain. I can laugh in the midst of leukemia. I give thanks for these blessings and many more that I haven't thought of. Through my daughters suffering, I've been reminded just how much I take for granted. I look forward to the blessings of the New Year, in faith, as I know God will continue to bless me with peace and joy.

JANUARY 1, 2008

HAPPY NEW YEAR!

Jonnae got platelets this morning. Her white cell count and neutrophils are still 0. Her red counts are a little lower, but relatively holding. There are no *alarms* going off. Things are pretty much still going as expected. Her throat seems a little better, but more sores have come up on her mouth. Her heels don't seem to be as painful; hands and under her arms are about the same. She hasn't been sick or vomiting, but the drugs are affecting the control of her bowels and it's very upsetting for her. All in all, we give thanks for another well-tolerated day.

I was blessed to spend much of my day with my three youngest children. They hung out with me at the RMH, while Johnny stayed with Jonnae at the hospital. We shot pool and played some old fashioned arcade bowling. I know they were bored by the end of the day. You can only shoot so much pool before you've had enough, but it was awesome being with them. I think they've already matured and grown up since I've been away. It doesn't seem like that much could change in such a short time, but my "mom instincts" tell me differently. I'm very proud of them and of course, I give thanks for them every day.

Several friends from home came up today to visit and serve dinner at the RMH. It was great to have their company. The meal was really nice and was a big hit with everyone. Most importantly, the love that comes from their friendship was an especially wonderful gift to receive today.

When I entered the RMH this morning, I was greeted by the house manager. She assured me there was nothing I needed to worry about while staying with them. Our stay has been covered for the duration of the time we need a "home." A large donation, on behalf of Jonnae, is being presented to them this Friday. I had not known (nor had Johnny) anything about this donation and am really excited, both for us and the house. I can't imagine not having that bed to fall into when Jonnae's condition permits me to do so. There are a lot of restrictions but it's a huge blessing for us parents with children in the hospital. It was great to start the day with such awesome news. Many families will benefit from this generous donation and for that I give thanks.

JANUARY 2, 2008

Jonnae's counts still aren't moving. They expect something to happen soon. She's running a fever and has been really sleepy the past couple of days. She hates sleeping the days away. The doctors say the fever and fatigue could be a sign of engraftment. That's a good thing. That would mean Nolan's cells are working and multiplying to move her counts up.

Her throat is better; her lips not so much. Overall her pain seems to be staying about the same. She rated it a 4 this morning and the pain team opted to leave her pump alone.

She asked me to do the Wii Fitness Test. She doesn't feel like playing herself (I'm kind of over it, too,) but she said watching me helps her stay awake, so I tested my age. Woo Hoo, I'm 27. I did a *real* work out in her room today because I slept in with the family this morning. She liked helping me count my reps. It was something else that helped keep her awake.

As she observed me struggling to finish some of my reps at the end, she said, "Thanks for being a healthy mom." We discussed how, when she felt better, we would create a plan to help her regain her strength. I think her seeing me push myself, even when it was difficult to finish, was a positive thing for her. I would like to think so anyway. It was one of my "gifts" for the day. Given and received--the best kind.

This morning presented challenges when it came to our finances and how we acquire payment for certain things. The organization in charge of our transplant fund has restrictions that are understandable, but they complicate matters. Although it will be most helpful with our traveling and lodging expenses, the account is difficult to access for some of the other expenses we'll incur while in Cincinnati. Frustration and worry are pointless. All that's necessary to eliminate the problem is to have future contributions sent to an account we've established at our local bank.

JANUARY 3, 2008

Jonnae's day was "unremarkable." That's the word the RN uses when things are staying the same and no alarms are going off. Jonnae's counts are still bottomed out and there are no signs of engraftment yet. We're expecting something to happen soon. She's gotten sick only once today, her lips are still very swollen, and the mouth sores are not healing yet. When the counts start to move everything will begin to improve. She was awake and sitting up in her bed for several hours today. That is improvement over the last couple of days.

When we're faithful to receive His Word, God opens doors for us. They were opening right and left today. This morning, I received great news about the Kansas event in June and tonight I got a phone call about a very generous donation from a company back home. The gift will be deposited into Jonnae's account for use on those expenses not covered by the NTAF fund. I can't wait to meet this group of employees and express my gratitude, along with Jonnae. The work of God is so present in the expression of His compassionate people. I can't help but be thankful for the life God is leading us through and to.

God may not show up when I'm looking for Him, but He's always on time. It's IN HIS TIME ALWAYS. I trust He knows best.

Something I've been blessed with, and have failed to mention, is a gift my daughter, Lydia, experienced Tuesday night. It was as much a blessing to me as it was to her: the gift of "self empowerment." Witnessing the pride she had from knowing she'd done something really difficult, all by herself, was a fabulous gift.

Lydia is built much like I was at her age. Unfortunately, as a result she's experienced the same name calling, bullying, and personal challenge of recognizing her beauty that I did. She's been making a conscious effort to choose healthier options at the table. She was going to "let down" and indulge in a piece of dessert tonight. But when it came time to partake, she chose to forego the sweets. It was an extremely difficult decision for her to stick with, yet she did.

A few hours later she let me know how good she felt about staying away from the temptation. It allowed me to talk more with her about the choice between easy short-term gratification vs. the more disciplined long-term gratification. The boys even chimed in on other ways that instant reward can't hold up to the harder choices and long term blessings they provide. It was a powerful realization that will serve her well. I hope she draws on it continuously as she develops better habits.

"No life is so hard that one can't make it easier by the way one accepts it." (Glasgow) My life has been planned for me years in advance by my Heavenly Father. I accept it, live an abundant life, and choose to stay in gratitude for the blessing of His love.

JANUARY 4, 2008

Today's counts are no different with the exception Jonnae's liver enzymes are high. She went from 90 to 220. They said that is high, but not alarming, as long as there are no VOD(veno occlusive disease) symptoms, such as excessive weight gain or soreness around the liver. I'm not at all comfortable with this news. I've heard VOD isn't something I want to know about. It's horrific to go through. I'm trying hard not to swing at pitches that aren't being thrown.

The opponent has been quite nasty today and it's been more challenging to keep my eyes fixed on the Coach. There's so much *activity in the field with other players*, it's been distracting. A family discharged a week ago, is already back. There's been an erratic change in the son's counts and the doctors are baffled. Another boy in the unit is going through his third transplant this year. The mood is heavy up here and many families are fearful. I will not allow the fear to penetrate my mind or affect my spirit.

My husband, Johnny, is struggling with wicked pitches of his own today. He had a bad dream last night. That, too, is trying to get my attention. My heavenly Coach is not sending me signs to view the *game of life* any differently than I have been. I've had some close calls, but I've not struck out. I'm confident I'll make contact with the ball, before I lie my head down to sleep.

I was able to get out of here today and pick up some groceries and health care items for Jonnae. I felt like I was on a practice run for the TV show, *Amazing Race*. I passed the test and made it to my destination and back without any wrong turns (no GPS for me). I felt pretty accomplished and said my prayer of thanks for a safe journey out and back with no "I'm lost" phone calls.

For the enthusiasm I have about God's love, for the gift of a dream, and for the power I have to manifest the glory of God, I give thanks. Life is the most magnificent gift. Words spoken and written help to make it so. I shall continue to receive them as well as share them.

JANUARY 6, 2008

Jonnae had a restless night. She got sick just before bedtime and needed to use the "blow by." That's when the oxygen mask doesn't need to be attached to her face, but is propped up in front of it. They did a chest x-ray because her heart rate and respiration were off. It only seems to be a concern when she's sleeping. The x-ray showed nothing. Without any inflammation or fluid buildup showing, they've asked her to exercise her lungs periodically by blowing into a small tube. She's had a fever all day, but they aren't worked up about that either. Engraftment is still expected to happen any day. We need some counts to show up.

Jonnae's slept most of the day, but did get up long enough to download some music onto her iPod and watch television with Johnny and me. Her lips look better, but her color hasn't improved. She's still swollen in the face and neck.

Johnny and I had an uncomfortable night here. We both feel the effects of it today. Johnny has a headache that he blames on the restlessness night. He knows to keep away from Jonnae just in case it's something else. It concerns me. I doubt he'll be getting too many more kisses from me. I wouldn't be able to stand being kept away from her because I was sick. I'll take every protective measure to stay healthy.

Even though the sleep was restless and the night not peaceful, having Johnny here has been the blessing I expected it would be. As with many other things I've taken for granted, I will never overlook his support, his love, his company, and having his arms around me. I'm blessed to have a spouse who tries so very hard to give me what I need.

JANUARY 7, 2008

As I came into the wing this morning, the RN greeted me with the news engraftment has begun. PRAISE GOD! This is a big step for Jonnae. It means Nolan's cells have started working and her counts should continue to rise until she is 100%. It's a very miniscule showing of cells, but it's a beginning.

I came in to high-five Jonnae and share the news with her. She was sitting up in bed, her mouth full of fresh blood; her cheeks, gums, and tongue oozing from sores and low platelets. She was just sitting there trying to dab them and keep the mouth dry. It wasn't going to happen.

She kept spitting it out the best she could. When I told her she had begun to engraft, her expression hardly changed. She's so darn cute. Without saying a word, she raised her eyebrows like I wasn't telling her anything she didn't already know. She didn't need the doctors or labs to tell her. She had faith; no concerns or doubts it would eventually happen. I wish you could see her in action. You can't help but smile. Her attitude is "When are you guys just going to follow me, have faith, and relax?"

I smiled and sat on the edge of her bed, replenishing her supply of gauze pads as she continued to wipe her mouth.

She got another platelet transfusion this morning. I asked the doctor about her bloodshot eyes and the red vessels that are showing underneath them and on her eyelids. He said it was from the pressure created when she's getting sick (which she did twice today, rather violently.) With low platelets, the vessels burst. We will see improvement as the counts continue to come up.

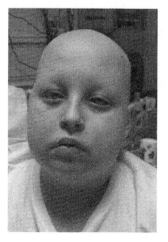

They did a CAT scan today of her head, stomach, and pelvis to make sure her fevers aren't from an infection that's not being detected by the blood cultures. Everything looks good. Her only complaint is that her belly hurts. They have administered Lasix, a drug used to flush out some of the fluid she is retaining. Hopefully she'll get some relief tomorrow. She went up three pounds because of fluid retention, and lost one today with the aid of the Lasix. She's holding that extra fluid in her stomach and face. Those two areas are so puffy, while everything else is as little as ever.

Jonnae receives mail almost on a daily basis. One might think mailing cards is a thing of the past with cell phones, text messaging, and email. Thank goodness some still choose to use this form of communication. It blesses us as we are away from home.

I previously mentioned the one child who's been discharged and was readmitted. He got to go home again today. The patients on the floor seem to be holding their own and there's been no loss of life. That may sound grim, but it's a reality here. I send up a prayer of thanks for another blessed day in the BMT unit.

Jonnae's not in tremendous pain. She doesn't look or feel perky, but the pain team is talking about taking her pain dose down. That is another sign of progress. We are on our way to victory. Praise God!

JANUARY 8, 2008

We've waited patiently for engraftment. It finally comes and Jonnae feels so bad she can't even smile. Forget that her mouth hurts and keeps her from smiling, she feels so rotten she can't even do it with her eyes. She looks at me and I'm thinking, "Come on baby! Let me see the 'light' in your eyes." But there is none.

Her belly was the only thing hurting her until tonight. Her last vomiting episode was so forceful, she may have broken a rib. I've heated up some aromatherapy packs and we're waiting for them to come and do an x-ray. There won't be anything they can do for her, but they want to make sure that's what's causing the pain.

She asked them to take her off the continuous drip of pain meds this morning and leave her on the button for controlled distribution. The rib and lower back pain may require her to ask for more. I was so happy to get her off something. I've heard so much about VOD and am concerned about her stomach. The Lasix is not helping her body to rid any of the fluid. All of the drugs are leading to side effects that require even more drugs. How surprising if the liver would be damaged?

I may sound discouraged, don't misinterpret me. I'm as steady and focused today as I have been through this whole storm. I read today, "The only thing constant

> "THE ONLY THING CONSTANT IN LIFE IS CHANGE."

in life is change." (French Author, François de la Rochefoucauld)

I'm well-equipped in faith. All the changes that come, can't take away what God's got waiting for me. Sometimes the change is easy to handle, sometimes not so much, but if I'm acceptant, knowing that nothing stays the same, I'll not be shaken. Tomorrow I expect the change to be for the better!

Jonnae sat up more today. She's still drinking a lot of water and some of her Essentials. She played some Uno and Outburst and has watched television. With her feeling so bad and uncomfortable, I'm proud of her for forcing herself to stay awake and not sleep through it. It's important for her to be moving about and sitting up. She needs to get off the oxygen and out of the sights of pneumonia. Her fever is consistently 101, and isn't attributed to infection, since her cultures all came back negative. We're hoping it's due to engraftment.

I walked to the fitness center that's a couple blocks away from the hospital. It felt good to lift some *real* weight. I know I speak of working out entirely too much, but its gives me strength when I celebrate some personal victories. Working out is as good as any.

Several times today, I bypassed the cookies in the family room lounge. They seemed to *call out to me* more today than other days, but I didn't cave in. Another victory; I'm thankful!

Being able to laugh, even when the joke's on me, is a blessing. I was in the RMH kitchen when a woman across the counter said to me, "Rough night?"

I was getting ready to head back over to the hospital and this lady thought I was coming into the house after a sleepless night.

I was a bit startled as I replied, "For my daughter? I hope not, I'm heading over now," and she said, "OH! No, I meant YOU look rough."

I chuckled as she said, "Sorry, I can be rude."

I'd had a shower, fixed my hair, and put on makeup. I checked myself once I got to Jonnae's room and honestly thought I looked pretty good, not haggard, like the woman's comment would have one think. I shared the humorous story a couple of times today and chuckled each time. Laughter is such good food for the soul.

Lydia, I know you are faithful in reading the journal and I want you to know that I smile and giggle the entire time I read your posts on the message board. You bless me with your love and sweetness, baby. I miss and love you, too. I give thanks for all of you kids every day, but your posts are loving gifts that I thoroughly enjoy receiving. -Mom

Jonnae started getting sick tonight, as I transcribed her gratitude journal entries for her. I offered to wait and do it later, but she insisted on doing it then. She's been pretty lifeless the last few days, but ready to give thanks all the same. How many would be capable of doing that? What a blessing to learn from her.

Her heart rate and blood pressure went haywire with the last vomiting episode and she's been crying from the pain in her diaphragm and stomach, as well as her eyes. I pray for a restful night's sleep for her and for better changes tomorrow.

JANUARY 9, 2008

I wish I could report that it's been a good day. Jonnae's gained another 2 pounds in fluids and the Lasix hasn't had the effect the doctors hoped. Good news is: as long as no one's pushing on it, her stomach's not as tender.

This morning they did an extensive ultrasound because of her weight gain. Her liver enzymes and bilirubin aren't increasing like they would expect in VOD. The pushing of the probe along her side and stomach had her in tears. It took them a good hour to get the images they needed. She's not aware of the seriousness of the news. Two mothers were quick to tell me upon my arrival that I didn't want to know anything about VOD because it's horrific and terrifying. I suppose that's a good strategy until you're given the news your child has it. Then you're up against your imagination wondering what you're in for. I haven't researched or Googled it yet. I've been waiting for a doctor to come in to discuss her kidneys. In addition to the liver not functioning properly, her urine output has decreased significantly.

I don't see any fight in her eyes. There are no whites left, only dark red blood.

She offered to wear sunglasses if it bothered me to look at her. I told her I could handle the whites of her eyes being red and her belly being distended, but that I missed seeing the spark or fight in her eyes.

I made an attempt to *"fire her up"* for tomorrow's *"game"* and she took it like I thought she wasn't trying hard enough. She cried as she told me she felt better today and thought she had tried harder. Instead of pumping her up, I managed to deflate her. I've tried to hide my tears from her as we've been watching television. I don't know when to push her or when to sit idle and be quiet.

Tomorrow will be a day of new hope, strength, and focus. I'm anxious to experience those new gifts.

JANUARY 10, 2008

Jonnae's kidneys and liver are damaged. The doctors called me into the hallway tonight to discuss dialysis. We will be moved to ICU tomorrow if things don't improve tonight. They said they are between a rock and a hard place. They don't have answers.

Jonnae's not at all concerned. If she is, she isn't showing it. When the BMT coordinator came in to visit us today, Jonnae got quiet. I looked to Jonnae and said, "What are you thinking about, baby?" to which she replied, "I'm thinking about getting out of here in 8 days."

She's hell bent on being out by day +28. When we had our consultation prior to coming here, we were told if everything went well a good estimate for discharge would be day +28.

Jonnae's not asking a lot of questions. After one of the doctors came in and told Jonnae she was very sick and the staff was worried about her, she waited until he left and said, "He kept saying you're getting sicker and I kept thinking, no, I'm getting better and better, every day in every way!" That's a mantra she's repeated daily. She truly believes she's getting better and better every day.

We were evicted from the "penthouse" of the BMT unit today and placed in one of the smaller rooms. As a precautionary measure, a patient can't stay in the same room longer than 30 days. They need to clean the room thoroughly after it's been occupied for that long. It took me all afternoon to move our stuff to our new room. When I made an inquiry about the possibility of moving to a different floor, Jonnae was quick to tell me, "MOM! We are *NOT* going to ICU!"

The vent in this room is DIRECTLY over my sleeper chair in the corner. Jonnae is a hot rod; I'm not. Obviously, I relinquish any control over the thermostat to Jonnae. I went to the RMH to pack my belongings to stay with Jonnae tonight and tomorrow. There's no blanket that could compare to the one I just received for my birthday. I'm about 38 years late for a *blankie* but between my prayers and the blanket, I expect I'll find much comfort as I lay my head down to sleep.

Johnny is coming up tomorrow. There was tension in our phone call tonight. With my inability to give him the answers he was looking for, and my fatigue, I had a tone to my voice that was condescending. It's not how I meant to be and one of the many things I need to work on about myself. I failed to control it tonight. I'm thankful he'll be here tomorrow and that we'll work to hold each other up, not break each other down.

JANUARY 11, 2008

Jonnae's stable today. She was able to head off ICU and dialysis. She's had two ultrasounds and the liver seems to be showing small signs of improvement. She's been able to urinate today, which is a celebrated improvement over yesterday. My baby is still so uncomfortable. The stomach will remain distended and not be quick to overcome. She's rested off and on all day. The high dose of steroids, used to treat the inflammation and fluid retention, is effecting the growth of Nolan's cells. However, doctors are hopeful that it will not affect the overall success of the transplant.

We've hit a major bump in the road to recovery. We're far from being out of danger. All we can do at this point is be patient and take one day at a time.

"'Never will I leave you; never will I forsake you.' So we say with confidence, 'The Lord is my helper; I will not be afraid. What can man do to me?'" Hebrews 13: 5b-6 (NIV)

My cross may seem heavy, but there are crosses that are harder to bear. There's a little boy, a few doors down, who wails all day and all night. He cries loudly, "OH MY GOSH! OH MY GOSH! MAKE IT STOP! HELP ME!" It's heartbreaking! I've never seen his mother in the halls or lounge. She is always in their room.

Jonnae's strength is incredible. It breaks my heart to hear her moaning in her sleep. I can't imagine how it would wrench my heart for her to be conscious and wailing for days on end. I'm thankful for the peace we have in this room. I'm thankful for the peace we know in our hearts. I pray for this boy and his mother to be comforted and for his pain to stop.

Johnny's here now and Jonnae and I are blessed by the gift of him. It's always rough when he first gets here. I don't know what it is, but it's like there's a release that's necessary before we can enjoy one another. The initial communication is unpleasant. Built up tension unleashes itself on the ones we love most and want to hurt the least. It doesn't make sense, but thankfully we get through it.

January 12, 2008

Jonnae's not as stable tonight as she was. Her A.N.C. is up and the blood cells are doing well, but her liver and kidneys are not. The nurse says we are close to dialysis. Jonnae's BUN (blood urea nitrogen) is reaching borderline high levels, indicating renal failure. Labs will be run again later to see where we stand.

I've come to believe the "small quiet voice", often mistaken as one's own, is actually the voice of God. It has to be, because the whisper inside me is not my own. Sometimes it's hard to accept what He's saying. I try to dismiss Him, but He doesn't go away. There are constant signs saying the time is coming we'll be asked to let her go.

In 2005, when Jonnae was first diagnosed, my first thought was of Abraham and the command he received to sacrifice Isaac on the mountain. Because of his faith, he did so. In prayer, I let God know if He wanted her back, I would faithfully release her. I let Him know I would respect His will and give thanks for the blessing I've had in her.

Through her initial chemo treatment, it appeared as if we were being tested and passing in flying colors. We took one day at a time, grew very close to our Father, and thanked Him for all the blessings that came from having accepted this cross. However, since Jonnae's relapse there have been many instances to indicate it's not a test. She will be a sacrifice. Since our arrival in Cincinnati, I hadn't heard the voice and hadn't missed it. With Jonnae's condition worsening, the thought's recurrent. Is He about to take her back? Tears stream down my face as I'm trying to imagine life without her.

I think about Hezekiah's illness in 2 Kings 20: 1-11. When Hezekiah requested for God to spare him, He gave him 15 more years. God has changed His mind before, He could now.

I've kept powerful thoughts and quotes written in a small notebook. The one standing out to me tonight is "When you're down to nothing, God is up to something." I have my eyes on

> "WHEN YOU'RE DOWN TO NOTHING, GOD IS UP TO SOMETHING."

the Coach and my hand in His. I'm not letting go. He is my fortress, my refuge, and I will praise Him in the storm.

JANUARY 13, 2008

Last night's post was sad, but my heart's not as heavy today. Jonnae seems to be stable. She was on the brink of dialysis with counts rising last night. This morning they've dropped enough to keep us hopeful.

If engraftment continues to take place, (that's where Nolan's cells seed and start to replenish) her counts will come up. If her body rids itself of this fluid, healing will begin and her discomfort will cease.

Her night was uneventful and she's resting semi-comfortably. I awoke early, left Johnny in the room with her, and went over to the Ronald McDonald House. I got a workout in, showered, and watched Joel Osteen's service. Since we've been here, this is the way I've opted to start every Sunday, when I can.

Jonnae's had a good day compared to what she's known over the course of the week. Today, she told me her goal is to be out of here by the 19th. That's my girl, forever the optimist! She's been able to use the bathroom, she's eaten her first meal worth commenting about since transplant (two cups of pudding) and continues to drink plenty of water with her Essentials.

She trembles nonstop. Her hands are peeling big sheets of skin, the whites of her eyes are still nearly all blood, and the continual drip of pain meds began again last night. She's feeling less pain but still extremely lethargic.

Jonnae's "kicking me out." She's told me several times today that she prefers me not to be here at night. I'm a *guest* hindering her freedom. She likes watching television or moving about at night but won't because I'm here. Her sleep schedule is way off and she doesn't want to disturb my rest. Therefore, she won't turn on the lights or television or get up and move about.

I can understand her wanting to "be," without consideration of me. While here, I've not been the guest of someone's home for the same reason. There are times when you're just more comfortable being alone. So, I guess I'll be sleeping at the RMH tonight.

We still choose not to fear or fast forward to "what if." We're living in the present, absorbing the glory and blessings available to us tonight and in the morning.

JANUARY 14, 2008

Most of Jonnae's counts improved overnight. The ones that haven't aren't alarming. Her road to recovery is a long one. I was relieved and feeling better after the medical group talked to me during morning rounds this morning.

I left her room to go throw some of our laundry into the machines down the hall. When I returned, the radiologist was in the room with Jonnae performing an ultrasound. One of the arteries in her liver has reversed and is taking blood away from the liver and towards the heart. Not good!

It's confusing and over my head. Sometimes I'm able to comprehend what they're telling me, but other times, I'm not. Bottom line is the liver is not functioning properly. It's very serious. The liver does have the ability to repair and recover; it's a question of whether it will.

Jonnae has been really out of it today, falling asleep midsentence while sitting up, and talking in her sleep.

Last night I ended my entry with "We still choose not to fear, to not fast forward to 'what if.' We're living in the present, absorbing the glory and blessings of life available to us tonight and in the morning."

This morning I opened one of my daily devotions to find: "The past is gone, the future is uncertain. Today is now and I face it head on!"

How I love receiving *phone calls* from God. Later I was reading one of Jonnae's devotionals. He knows how badly I need Him to talk to me, so He *"rang"* me once more: "I have told you these things so that in Me you may have peace. In the world you have suffering. But take courage! I have conquered the world." John 16:33 (HCSB)

A family was admitted on the floor today with two daughters, both with immune-suppressed diseases. They are here for transplants, both of them. I don't need to be told more than once. No matter what troubles we have, there is someone that would trade places with us and considers us blessed. I acknowledge our life as blessed and thank God for His mercy.

JANUARY 15, 2008

It's been a full day; full of confusion, questions, dreams, friendship and love.

The rounds this morning started out favorably when Jonnae's report included her counts are improving. But this BMT experience is a crazy ride. One minute there's cheering because her numbers are good; the next there's concern about her being incoherent. They briefly talked about a CT on her brain and a spinal tap to test her central nervous system. But then decided the alarm may have been pulled too early and a spinal tap too risky. Crazy and maddening!

I miss my girl! She sleeps all the time, doesn't look like herself, and now doesn't even talk or think like herself.

I've been blessed with visitors today. Initially, I didn't think it was a good idea to have them. All I really want is to be with Jonnae. But she's slept so much these last few days it's not necessarily been a good thing to be holed up in the room with her. She's oblivious to whether I'm in the room or not. The visiting proved to be a welcome break.

Sharing company with others who have a grasp of God's great love is awesome. Witnessing others find their way to Him is also. This illness has made it more possible, so for the gifts it's given in the midst of the pain, I must give thanks.

JANUARY 16, 2008

It's been a very, VERY, good day. Everything that needed to go up, went up. Everything that needed to go down, went down. She ate more, drank more, and has spent more time awake. She's been more present during her consciousness and not so out of it.

Yesterday I was wondering if I'd had my last real conversation with my "Mini-Me." It's as though we've become one being. For the last three days, she's been senile. I wondered if I'd "lost" her. I was forced to consider living without her. I didn't *keep company* with "what if" for long, but it's impossible to not *visit* occasionally.

I'm encouraged. Jonnae's engraftment test came back. Her white cells are 100% Nolan's; no more leukemia. Her cells are all strong and healthy, a gift from Nolan and God. After the RN told me the news, he stood there waiting for more of a reaction from me. My dad was here to receive the news with me and was overcome with emotion.

One of the nurses congratulated me as she walked by. My mom called and asked if I wanted to call my brother and sister with the news myself. I chose not to. It's difficult to explain. The parents with children in this unit understand. Johnny described it well when he said, "We've learned to take some off the peaks to even out the valleys. We keep a level playing field."

> JOHNNY DESCRIBED IT WELL WHEN HE SAID, "WE'VE LEARNED TO TAKE SOME OFF THE PEAKS TO EVEN OUT THE VALLEYS. WE KEEP A LEVEL PLAYING FIELD."

It's like a revolving door; news comes in, with more news right behind it. The door never stops moving. Our days here are like the tide of the ocean, they don't stay high or low. They are constantly changing. I'm guarded. We received the awesome news about her engraftment starting one day and she was diagnosed with VOD the next.

I'm not overwhelmed by the bad news, nor am I elated with the good. Too much can change, too much still to overcome, and too much devastation if we don't stay flexible. I am very thankful the engraftment was successful, I just think it's premature to celebrate.

I had another full day of company and am surprised from the resulting fatigue. Keeping conversation "normal," while wondering how my daughter is while I'm out of the room, is exhausting. It's amazing how accustomed to being alone I've become. For the love of my friends who came to visit, I am blessed.

Life is a beautiful experience. What can I do so people realize we waste it with negative emotion? I had many experiences, in my younger years, when I responded with anger, hurt, confusion, anxiety, worry or depression. That's exhausting and there's never any relief. I laid it all down and forgave others, as well as myself. All I can do is offer my personal best. That changes from day to day, but that's all I can do.

JANUARY 17, 2008

Jonnae seems to be out of the woods, as far as renal failure is concerned. That is HUGE! Everything is coming back to expected post transplant levels. Even with the clinical improvements, it'll be several weeks before the fluids move and she experiences relief in her stomach. She's still so very tired, emotional and uncomfortable. She's not ready to come off the oxygen, but she's off the continual pain pump. Thank you, God!

As I do every morning, I began my morning with cardio. I need to take care of myself if I want to take the best care of her. I loathe cardio. I'm only on the machine for four minutes before I'm bored and ready to get off. I've come up with a great way to make sure I finish my session. I make my workout a prayer.

As soon as I feel like I'm about to step off a machine, I start to pray. Only it's not a traditional prayer. For 10 minutes, 12 minutes, 15 minutes, whatever is left of the time I established when I began, I offer it up as a special prayer for someone besides myself. It could be someone I know, a stranger that's just walked in the gym, or someone I've heard or read about. The workout goes from being something physical for me to something very spiritual for someone else. It's an amazing way to start the day.

This works when I pump iron too. In exchange for counting down reps, I chant names of people I've said I would pray for. Quitting the workout would be like quitting on my prayer. This reflection created an epiphany for me. This illness isn't about Jonnae. It isn't about me. It isn't about

> THIS ILLNESS ISN'T ABOUT JONNAE. IT ISN'T ABOUT ME. IT ISN'T ABOUT ANY OF US INDIVIDUALLY, IT'S ABOUT US AS A WHOLE, AS GOD'S PEOPLE. THIS TRIAL HAS HAPPENED TO BRING US TO HIM. I FIND GREAT COMFORT IN THAT.

any of us individually, it's about us as a whole, as God's people. This trial has happened to bring US to Him. I find great comfort in that. I've never been as passionate about anything as I am about serving Our Father. There is nothing that can take that away.

JANUARY 18, 2008

I'm spent. This kind of day is bound to happen periodically. It makes me realize how good the good days are and how fortunate I am to have so many. Jonnae's lab reports continue to impress the docs. This morning, as her report was being read, I saw several eyebrows raised and nods of the head. They indicated the surprise of the doctors and they were pleased. I wish Jonnae's spirits and physical condition would follow her clinical condition. She's still so uncomfortable. Her belly's too large to sit up and it's hindering her breathing. She's irritated by the oxygen mask, too.

She's fallen twice today, once in the bathroom as she was trying to get up from the commode and once as she was trying to turn herself around in bed. She was sitting at the foot of the bed and going to lie down on her stomach. Her arms were braced on the footboard and they gave out. She fell on her face, hitting her cheek on the footboard of the bed. She hasn't fallen before and today's incidents have upset her and me. We both feel so helpless. After she's fallen, she has no strength to get back up. My trying to lift and pull her up hurts her. Both times, it was physically and emotionally exhausting.

Her smile, the sparkle in her eyes, and her sense of humor are still absent. She's so worn out. Exhausted, tired of being tired, and bored with lying around. It strains her eyes to read or watch television. Her hands are still trembling, so she's unable to write or do anything with them, even if she did feel like it. She doesn't have a lot to say, although she's mentioned not remembering much of the hospital stay.

She said it doesn't seem like we've been here for over 30 days. I'm thankful the long days are a blur to her. It's a blessing that she doesn't have any recollection of how difficult this transplant has been.

I started my day off in the same manner I claim each morning. Up by 6, workout, prepare my meals for the day, shower, do my hair and makeup and arrive back to the hospital by 8:30. That's all that's left of "normal" to my life for now.

Johnny's here now. I was looking forward to his arms being around me, but because I'm more exhausted than usual, I appreciate his support and loving embrace even more than I anticipated.

He came bearing cards, posters, and gifts from back home. Included in those goodies was a donation from a family who did two fundraisers. In addition, they offered up their Christmas gift exchange in order to help with our expenses. Is there a greater gift than an act of kindness and love?

JANUARY 19, 2008

Jonnae's counts continue to improve. Her fluids, need for oxygen, discomfort, appetite and spirit, do not. She is not in poor spirit, just doesn't have much "life" to her. She can't stay awake because her days and nights are mixed up. I'm hoping the fluids will start to move soon and we see a little more of her smile. I miss her, but give thanks for another stable day. I'm not taking for granted that she is in fact improving. Slower than we'd like, but she IS improving. What a blessing.

One of the patients a few doors down has made mock prison bars to hang on his door. I think it's great the kid can joke about it. It does get to feeling like a prison here. I'm not a prisoner as much as these children are, but I certainly don't feel free. I'm thankful I've had Johnny's company and we've spent some time out of the room today.

JANUARY 21, 2008

Nearly every morning, I spend time in silence with God before heading back over to the hospital from RMH. Sometimes I hear the still quiet voice pose a question or thought that takes me deep in thought. I refer to it as "an assignment" because I feel like I'm supposed to ponder it more or possibly share it with someone during the day. The thought today was, "Why does society spend so much time working on the wrong things? We work ourselves ragged at work. We work on our homes, cars, hobbies, budgets, wardrobes and golf games. Why aren't we working on ourselves? The one thing that is going to provide true happiness, peace, and joy; the one thing that contributes most to ourselves, our children, and our grandchildren that will not wear out and can be passed down forever, we neglect to work on. Is sense of purpose, our fullest potential, and nurturing our spirit going to come from anything outside ourselves?"

Later, I got a *phone call* from God when I logged on to read my daily devotion. "All of us have strayed away like sheep. We have left God's path to follow our own." Isaiah 53:6 (NLT)

I love being in God's classroom!

JANUARY 21, 2008

I'm no McGyver, but I did get a kick out of my "problem solving" skills this morning. I am in dire need of a haircut and have no scissors. I never think to ask for any at the hospital and am tired of trying to fix my hair at RMH with my bangs hanging in my eyes. I used my fingernail clippers to trim them this morning. Funny, but it got the job done.

I came earlier than usual to the hospital, thinking I would surprise Jonnae and get her up to walk before "curfew" (They want patients and families in their rooms before doctors start rounds at 9 a.m. Normally I get here just before that). She surprised me instead. She was sitting on the side of her bed and had paged the nurse to be her company for a walk. We let the nurse know I'd arrived and Jonnae and I covered more distance than she has up until this point.

She got nauseous after that and they gave her some Benadryl. With or without assistance, Jonnae sleeps a lot. Therefore, I spend much of the day in silence. I got in the habit of "quiet time" before we began this journey with Leuk. The solitude I'm experiencing would be much harder on me, had I not already learned the power that comes from it. It's easier to hear God's voice when we're not distracted by noise. My listening skills still need strengthening, so I'm getting good practice here. That is a blessing.

January 22, 2008

Jonnae continues to tell everyone she's getting out of here on Saturday. Her tenacious spirit makes me smile. The nurse practitioner smiles with me.

When we headed out to walk this morning, close to the 9 o'clock cut off, I said, "They may not let us go for a walk this close to curfew."

She replied quickly, "I'm going. They CAN'T stop me."

She's acquired quite the backbone (and voice) lately. It's fun to witness. This is a side she's not always shown or even had. She's always been strong spiritually. It's great to see her strong mentally, too.

We'll be staying in a nearby hotel when she's discharged. We looked at corporate housing but it's too isolated and farther away from the hospital. She's not allowed to be around people, but I still need to see them, even if it's only in the lobby.

We'll have a suite with a full kitchen and living room, so it's more like an apartment. It's projected we'll be here for more than a 100 days post-transplant and have appointments at the hospital two to three times a week.

It's an exciting time for us. We are getting close to the big discharge milestone. There'll be some separation anxiety as we leave the security of the medical team's eyes on her, but we're ready to move forward.

JANUARY 23, 2008

Jonnae still presses forward, expecting a Saturday discharge. Monday or Tuesday is more realistic, but she's standing firm on her prediction. The counts that went haywire with VOD are either normal or close. She's been off the oxygen all day today. Her weight is down more, which means the fluid is finding its way out. The best news today is the ultrasound showed there is normal blood flow in the vessel that had been reversed. Praise God!

We walked more today and even went downstairs to the physical therapy clinic for a "mini workout." Jonnae's been asking for small hand weights and they took the two of us down to see what they had. The physical therapy room is a good distance away from our unit. We got down there and Jonnae said, "Am I even hooked up to that?"

I was wheeling her empty IV pole all over the hospital. There was nothing she could be hooked to. It's the first time since we've been here that she's been free of tubes and cords. We are so used to it being "an accessory," none of us even noticed. It was hysterical. Sometimes being a "dork" is a blessing.

Whether it's lifting each other up or setting one another straight, Jonnae and I are good at doing both for one another. Today was my turn to do some straightening. She got upset and started crying in the shower because the shower head's not one that can be adjusted.

I said, "Jonnae, you were diagnosed with VOD and puked up feeding tubes and didn't get upset. Don't get hooked by such small bait now. Focus on all the good that's going on. You're getting out of here soon, baby. You've gotten so much good news this week, 'shake this off". It's not worth giving up your joy."

When she got out of the shower, she buried her head in my chest with a big hug and thanked me. We've shared some priceless moments today. Life is good.

JANUARY 25, 2008

We began training for our home health care today and predict Jonnae will be discharged on Monday. I did persuade them to give us a pass for Saturday. Jonnae can still say she "got out" of the hospital on the 26th.

There's not a lot we can do with a four hour pass, but I can take her to see the suite. She can't be around anyone or do anything else, but it will still be a freedom she's not known for the last month and a half. She was a little disheartened with a pass instead of a discharge, but has accepted the scenario as victory.

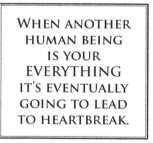

WHEN ANOTHER HUMAN BEING IS YOUR EVERYTHING IT'S EVENTUALLY GOING TO LEAD TO HEARTBREAK.

Today was a day to celebrate with my oldest daughter and cry with my youngest son. He's suffering from a broken heart. He and his girlfriend have shared a lot over the last year. She's been "his everything." When another human being is your EVERYTHING it's eventually going to lead to heartbreak. I dreaded this day coming, and it's here.

He called me after school. When I heard his voice, I knew he needed me home. I asked him, "Would my being home make a difference hon?" He hesitated, but replied, "Probably."

I asked the nurse if she'd mind continuing the home health training tomorrow. I grabbed my purse and hit the road. Jonnae was in complete agreement with my leaving. My mom came on short notice to spend the night with Jonnae and I surprised Layne at his ballgame.

In just a few short hours, I was able to have one-on-one

conversations with my 3 youngest children. They're all so special and so wise for their age. I didn't get the opportunity to have a serious conversation with Nolan, but in the few short minutes I got to see him, he had me smiling with his charm and wit. I miss them all so much and find myself tearing up as I say a prayer of thanks yet again.

JANUARY 27, 2008

We experienced the "air of freedom" from 12 - 5 today. Jonnae approves of our home away from home. I stayed busy unpacking while Johnny watched a ball game and Jonnae slept or played her DS.

She often gets a stomachache after eating and that was the case while we were out today. She was crying from the pain and went into the bedroom to lie down. She asked if I would lay down with her. It's been a really long time since I've been able to. Before the BMT, we used to do it all the time. It means a lot to both of us.

She got teary eyed as we were lying there and told me she loved me. As I watched the tears stream down her face, I told her I love her, too. Through the crying, she continued, "You're the best mom in the world."

I smiled and said, "Oh I'm sure there's a better mom out there somewhere."

She replied, "No there's not. I love you."

She cried harder and said, "I wouldn't be alive if it wasn't for you. Thank you! I love you so much!"

(From Jonnae)

Hello everyone! Today has been a good day. I was able to get out of the hospital for four hours and check out the apartment I'll be living in the next couple of months. It's a suite and is really nice. It's the only room with a full kitchen. It has a nice dining room, a living room with a big TV, two couches, and a really comfortable chair. There are two bedrooms and two full baths and six closets. One is huge, which is perfect as a little exercise room for my

mom.

It felt so good to get out. I am getting discharged Monday. Hooray!!! I can't wait. The apartment is going to feel so much like home. I would like to thank everyone for their generous donations that made it possible for us to have such a nice place. It will be such a great time for mother-daughter bonding. We plan on watching all the movies we have with "The Rock" in them, so we can just sit there and daze and drool, LOL. He is so great to look at. I also plan on getting a lot of my school work done. I will pass some time by making cards. I just need to get some tape for the ribbons.

Lydia, I want you to know how glad I am for you. You have an incredible will power and I am proud of the choices you are making with food. Well that's it for now. Talk to you later.

God Bless,

Jonnae

JANUARY 27, 2008

Jonnae and I had another temporary pass today. We spent more than five hours at our little haven. She did homework all day, even after we got back to the hospital. I finished unloading and unpacking. Johnny just shakes his head at all the stuff we have, but Jonnae and I plan on doing more than just lying around.

However, come Tuesday, if we don't have a hospital appointment I will be doing plenty of that. I'm feeling the brunt of everything. I'm beyond exhausted and look forward to replenishing with adequate rest. How glorious it will be to just "be," with no agenda. I give thanks for the restoration that's near.

Jonnae and I have eaten lunch **together** the last two days. She said grace for us today and spoke sweet words of thanks. We've had a really nice day.

As we were leaving the hotel, she fell again. She kept saying she was sorry. It's seems she's always more concerned for me than she is herself. How is it this child thinks she owes me an apology for falling? I told her to stop but she has seen how I jump to her and knows how much it scares me. I give thanks she didn't get hurt and for the love of her caring heart.

Jonnae believes this leukemia is going to be gone forever. She believes there are still miracles in store for her. We believe this, also, and we thank God for the gift of her.

JANUARY 28, 2008

Aaaah! Home Sweet Home (sort of).

It's as close as we are gonna get for now. We're very happy with our new found freedom and dwelling place. Our suite is plenty large enough for us and the staff here is wonderful. I must give thanks for those who've made this possible for us.

When I play golf, sometimes I start off with 20 or so good shots and then hit a bad one. That one bad shot used to stick in my mind and cause me to lose the joy I knew from the good ones. I haven't gotten to play a lot of golf lately, but I have gotten better about "shaking off" the bad shot and enjoying the round. I still have some work to do, but that one shot that would have scarred the round has lost its power over me. Joy shouldn't be misplaced. It is, when focus is on the wrong thing. I've been tested on this lesson today.

The staff was all smiles this morning as they bid us goodbye. Before Jonnae could leave, she needed platelets and blood. Jonnae and I both agreed I should take advantage of someone else's eyes being on her and run some errands.

I ran into a BMT mother on the elevator. She told me that one of the other moms was back with her son (He was discharged a couple of weeks ago). He's relapsed, his leukemia cells are back, and they're doing a bone marrow aspiration to confirm.

The devil threw his first curve ball. I'm ashamed to admit I swung. My thoughts were hung on this boy's relapse instead of Jonnae's discharge. I looked quickly to the Coach. *This is the day the Lord has made let us rejoice and be glad in it! Psalm 118:24NASB.* He kept me from striking out.

The devil was relentless with downright nasty pitches. "Jonnae's going to be like that boy", he said. *"They won't be afraid of bad news; their hearts are steady because they trust the Lord." Psalm 112:7 NCB.* Thank you for covering me with your Word, Lord.

"Relax and rest. God has showered you with blessings." Psalm 116:7MSG I must listen to the Coach and relax. He has showered us with blessings today and will continue to do so.

"Those who hope in the Lord will renew their strength. They will soar on wings like eagles; they will run and not grow weary, they will walk and not be faint." Isaiah 40:31 NIV The pitches kept coming and this is how I kept swinging.

We are on God's winning team. We may not be undefeated, but we will be the Ultimate Champions, this I KNOW for sure.

JANUARY 29, 2008

Today's been nice. Certainly not free of stress, but I'll take it again and again.

Did your parents ever say to you, "I hope you have a child just like you?" Jonnae's tenacity is certainly one of those traits I see coming full circle to get me. Sometimes it's great, sometimes it's a curse. She's determined to show how hard she's trying. She's convinced she's a Wonder Woman and can defy the odds. As we were leaving the hospital yesterday, she fell again.

We were in the parking garage and she stepped on a small bump in the pavement. That kind of thing is just enough to make her lose balance and fall. She's not strong enough to shift her weight to keep herself from falling. She went down hard and skinned up her knees.

I put her in a wheelchair and wheeled her back up to the floor. With her counts low, I didn't know if I would need to take extra precautions about the abrasions. These minor things aren't minor anymore. I can't just blow on it and cover it with a bandage like I did when she was little. They'd just told us that infection of any kind is a super high risk, but they weren't too concerned. Neosporin, gauze, and a bandage was all they used.

We had a couple of other scares that hopefully won't prove to be major mistakes. When we access Jonnae's line for infusions, we are to clamp the line **before** taking off the last syringe. I clamped it **as** I was taking off the syringe. Probably not a major ordeal, but I don't want to risk ANYTHING.

Then as we were coming back into the hotel after an errand run, Jonnae was in the hotel lobby before remembering her mask. She had left it in the car. That **is** major and a much bigger deal than the clamp. We can't afford to make mistakes like those. It's stressful being on our own.

We've deemed Tuesdays as "spa day." We both drew up baths (Again, not relaxing for me. I'm afraid she'll try to get out of the tub on her own). We did facials and pedicures and were in our pj's by five. The only thing that would have made it a perfect mother/daughter day would be one of "the Rock" movies. But there isn't a DVD player here, so we're waiting for Johnny to bring us one on Thursday.

We have a clinic appointment tomorrow and I'll be hearing about the boy who relapsed. But I will do as James tells us in 1:28 and "consider it pure joy, whenever I'm facing trials of many kinds, because I know that the testing of my faith develops perseverance. Perseverance must finish its work so that I may be mature and complete, not lacking anything."

JANUARY 31, 2008

For some time now, our blessing cup has been full. Last night, Jonnae decided it was time to reciprocate and bless others. This hotel has an extremely long corridor. We walk it as part of Jonnae's physical therapy. She started out with the goal of walking six lengths. After 6 she said, "I'm going to do 6 more as an offering."

As we walked, we discussed and prayed for the individual or family we were offering each lap up for. She kept thinking of more people to add and walked 24 laps. Talk about the power of giving. This was amazing for me to witness.

Every time a home health nurse comes into our suite they comment on how much room we have compared to what they usually see. We know we are blessed to have this set up and continually give thanks for the support that's made it possible. We are blessed every day that we are here.

When we arrived earlier in the week, the room smelled a bit musty. I purchased air fresheners for nearly every room. The next comment, after how much space we have, is always on the yummy aroma. It's a strong vanilla scent. I'm thankful for the sense of smell and the air freshening options we have to make the atmosphere even more inviting. It really is a nice touch.

Jonnae got an email from one of her best friends and she giggled so much while reading it. She has the cutest giggle. It's just as contagious as her smile. I'm thankful for Jonnae's being blessed with laughter, and how it blesses me.

FEBRUARY 1, 2008

The doctors are impressed with Jonnae's "problem solving" skills. She covered the large flesh wound on her knee with a dressing made from a sterile mask. It's a hard cover, similar to a cardboard bowl. So air can get to the wound, she used gauze to prop it up off the skin, and medical tape to fix it to her knee. The bandage with Neosporin was sticking to her wound and keeping it from scabbing over. She is destined to be a "healer." and came up with a really good solution. *Score*

I was thinking ahead this morning and wore workout clothes to Jonnae's appointment. While she slept under the watchful eyes of the medical team, I decided to make good use of the time and go to the gym for a great lower body workout. *Score*

On our way out of the hospital, Jonnae's arm in mine, she jerked and pulled on me. Immediately I thought she was going down again. It scared the you-know-what out of me! I believe I even said, "shit" as I grabbed hard on her to keep her from falling. Only she wasn't falling, she dropped her Chapstick and was bending down to pick it up.

She said, "Gosh, mom!"

Only minutes later, I brushed her injured knee as I was I helping her into the car. I felt just horrible as she screamed out and started to cry. Instantly, she giggled through the crying and said," Can we call it even?"

I kissed the top of her head and shut her door. As I got in my side of the car, I said, "There's no score to even baby. I'd rather not have hurt you."

She said, "We just need to shake it off and laugh about it." *Score*

Jonnae and I have renamed some recent "God hugs" as "God giggles." They don't have any poignant meaning, just grab our attention in a light hearted way. She read to me from a school book about Whitney Houston's, "Greatest Love of All." Later we watched a karaoke game show and a contestant chose to sing that very song.

Our suite is called the Mikhail Baryshnikov Suite. Jonnae didn't know who he was and I had explained to her he was a famous Russian dancer. Later, she was channel surfing and I laughed and said, "Stop! There he is Jonnae, the man this suite's named after."

His costar made mention of his suite and the beautiful hotel he was staying in. Jonnae and I just looked at each other and giggled. Big or small, coincidence is a God incident to remind us that He's with us. We are so small in the creation of His world, but He is forever present.

We have no doubt that He is always by our side. When we cry, He cries with us and sometimes gives us a God hug. Today He asked us to giggle with Him. I pray we never stop picking up on His presence and give thanks for the blessings we know because of it.

FEBRUARY 2, 2008

Jonnae woke up with a headache this morning. She's had one just about every day that we've been out of the hospital. The doctors believe it is from how quickly she was weaned from the pain medication. They also believe she may not be drinking enough to flush the meds out of her system. None of us are too concerned. Her body has so much to adjust to!

No falls today. That certainly calls for a "thank you God!" So does the fact that my parents and kids were here today to see Jonnae and me. Now they're home. I give thanks for the visit as well as their safe travel.

Jonnae and I watched "THE ROCK" (Dwayne Johnson) in the *The Scorpion King* tonight. Jonnae's little comments and giggles were priceless. I love hearing my kids laughter and I give thanks for the music of hers.

I just started reading *The Christ Commission,* another Og Mandino book. It's already hooked me, and I experienced another one of those fun, lighthearted reminders from God that He's with me. Matthias is the main character in this Mandino book and was The Rock's name in *The Scorpion King.* Matthias, I haven't heard or seen that name in any instance I can recall and then twice in one day. I love God's "small play."

FEBRUARY 3, 2008

There's a saying, "If what you did yesterday seems big, you haven't done anything today." Ha! The guys playing in tonight's Super Bowl would have a difficult time with that challenge if presented with it tomorrow.

It may not be big to someone else, but I was able to accomplish quite a bit today considering the circumstances. That's enough to label it a BIG day for me.

FEBRUARY 4, 2008

Clinic went well today. Jonnae is happy to get out of the room, even it's just for a ride to the hospital. Cabin fever has set in.

I keep reminding her that we need to embrace the things we GET TO do here that we will miss once we are home. We may be tired of making bracelets and cards and watching movies, but we will long for one-on-one time after we've left this place.

If life isn't about waiting for the storm to pass, but learning to dance in the rain, Jonnae and I are becoming really nice dancers. We giggled and enjoyed another girl's night in our *cabin*. I give thanks that we get along so well, that we understand one another so deeply, and that we share a bond that is truly "Heaven sent."

> IF LIFE ISN'T ABOUT WAITING FOR THE STORM TO PASS, BUT LEARNING TO DANCE IN THE RAIN, JONNAE AND I ARE BECOMING REALLY NICE DANCERS.

FEBRUARY 5, 2008

Because we didn't have an appointment today, Jonnae slept in until 11:30. She laid down for another good long nap around two o'clock. I had a "just be" day as well. We did watch *Run Down* together (another movie with The Rock), *American Idol,* and *The Biggest Loser.* We both agree there can't be anyone who cries as much as I do watching these two shows.

Every week I find myself experiencing the emotions of these contestants right along with them. Tonight, while on her way to the auditions, a contestant received a call that her father had just been killed in a car accident. It was amazing to hear her dedicate "How Do

I Live Without You," to her father. She did an awesome job, showing poise and strength that only a girl with the help of a higher power could exude. Experiencing that kind of spirit, even if on a TV show, adds to the quality of my day.

Last week I prayed for a {Hug} from God. Nearly every day since, He's playfully responded. We've shared a lot of giggles. He's made His presence known in a fun way, both last night and today. Yesterday, I posted on a message board, "No matter how strong you are, at some point life is going to throw you a test. One that will "rock you to your core." I debated on whether or not "rock you to the core" was the phrase I wanted to use and decided indeed it was.

Jonnae and I had planned on watching *Run Down* last night, but decided to watch *Ratatouille* instead. At the end of the movie, a food critic is giving his poignant take on his last dining experience and says, "the meal and its maker rocked me to my core." I laughed out loud. God is so AWESOME. Oh, how I love Him!

Today, we got the biggest laugh of all when I asked Johnny if he would pick up ginger and garlic at the grocery.

He said, "Are they good looking?"

I said, "Ginger might be, but I highly doubt Garlic would be your type." Kind of a lame attempt at joking around, but that's how it went down.

Johnny called me from the store because he was having a hard time locating them in the produce section. I tried to guide him on the phone. He located the garlic and was still having difficulty with the ginger. I said isn't there someone around there to ask? About that time he located someone and said, "Where's ginger?" The woman explained why she looked startled, "My name is Ginger. REALLY."

Austin and Lydia were there and witnessed it. God sure has a great sense of humor.

February 6, 2008

Jonnae got an email from school this morning and was bummed when she realized she's missing spirit week at school. Today's Wacky Wednesday.

I said, "We don't have to be in Sellersburg to be wacky. Do you want it to be "Wacky Wednesday here, too?"

She said, "Sure, are you going to let me dress you?"

I knew I was in trouble, but said, "Of course."

She really "wacked" me out. The wackiest part was we were the ONLY ones wacky. We weren't surrounded by a school full of participants. Walking out of the hotel and around in the hospital with a butterfly tattoo on my nose like a decorated nasal strip, ponytails sticking straight out, and a bright yellow ball cap on with not one stitch of clothing or jewelry that matched. I truly was a wacky sight.

I painted silly eyebrows on her, different colored eye shadow on each lid, pink circles on her cheeks and "Wacky Wednesday Rocks" on the back of her bald head. Johnny's here today and made sure to walk about 20 steps behind us. When we got off the elevator he stayed on. Little kids waved at me in the cafeteria. I think they thought I was a clown. I felt like one for sure.

I've been using this sabbatical as an opportunity to incorporate better self care habits. They include a scheduled rest day during the week and some nice quiet time in the morning. I'm text book Type A, and typically on the go all the time. It's a true test of patience for me to slow down and these are habits I need for healthy balance. I'm thankful for my new appreciation to occasionally just "be".

"The joy of anything, from a blade of grass upwards, is to fulfill its created purpose." (Oswald Chambers) I pray that I never lose enthusiasm to serve my God, fulfill my purpose, or seize everyday as an opportunity to make my existence more

> I DESIRE TO MOVE FORWARD ALWAYS AND LIVE AS A "HUMAN BECOMING," NOT MERELY A HUMAN BEING.

meaningful. I never want to get lazy and reside in the land of "good enough." I desire to move forward always and live as a "human becoming," not merely a human being.

February 7, 2008

We didn't do our "spa day" on Tuesday, so we opted to make up for it today. We made use of the spa day goodies Johnny brought us for Valentine's Day.

I took advantage of his being here and went to the salon downstairs for a haircut. I was pretty nervous about the risk of using a stylist I knew nothing about. One side of my hair is not even with the other, but I couldn't possibly complain about my hair when my daughter longs to just have some.

As we took a walk tonight, Jonnae sang a goofy Sponge Bob song and cracked jokes about what a "fitness freak" I am. On our last lap, I was doing lunges down the long corridor. We always end our walk in prayer. She prayed that we never stop being silly. I pray for that as well.

February 8, 2008

Jonnae noticed stretch marks on her stomach today. They were caused by the fluid retention during VOD. She was really upset. Her stomach's gone down a great deal though. Her weight's even lower than it was when she was first admitted. She's doing remarkably well.

I used our "I GET TO" practice to help her accept the stretch marks and stay in gratitude.

I said, "You get to put cream on these marks. You get to watch them fade. If they don't and you're not comfortable with them, you get to hide them. There are children walking around with large tumors protruding from their faces. There are kids with scars all over their body, people staring at them all the time. Let's not forget there's a child, several children actually, who would trade their places and scars for yours."

Is that cruel of me? I sometimes question if it's too much, but then realize it's truly how I look at things and what lifts me out of the pit. Why wouldn't I share it, in hopes of it lifting her too?

Today, I laughed at how spoiled I've become in expecting hugs, giggles, and phone calls from God daily. Probably a little selfish of me to expect His attention all the time. I have the mind of a child, occasionally. I know He desires that, but I wonder if He's ever annoyed by it; like when I'm praying the Rosary and get distracted. I'm not only Type A, but A.D.D. as well.

I've found a very useful tool in helping me stay focused throughout the decades of the Rosary. www.catholiccompany.com has lovely pictures that reflect the "fruit of the spirit" for each decade and a little reflection to say before each Hail Mary. It helps to keep me in the meditation frame of mind and the only thing I've found that holds my attention to reflect on the life of Christ throughout the prayer. I'm thankful for this gem of a site and how it's contributed to my Rosary prayer.

FEBRUARY 10, 2008

Overall, Jonnae's still feeling pretty good. She's straightened up her room and made several cards. We watched *The Game Plan* with Johnny tonight. I just can't get enough of that child's giggle. It's SO contagious and such a blessing to hear. I give thanks for the feelings of joy that radiate from her.

As a part of my Lenten plan, I've committed to "offer more up." There is no limit to the amount of offerings that can be made in a day. I'm finding more ways to sprinkle them throughout the day. If I want to put diet hot chocolate in my decaf, I skip the decaf and just have the hot chocolate or even skip the whole thing, and make it an offering. I might take the stairs instead of the elevator and "offer it up."

FEBRUARY 11, 2008

Jonnae's platelets were up to 19,000 today. That's a far cry from 6 or 9 thousand. That's where they've been. She didn't need platelets, so we got out of clinic early. I'm thankful her counts were good on her own and she didn't need anything transfused.

The doctor was able to shine the light on something Jonnae's not been able to see with my help. Her blood pressure was up today. They wanted to know if she'd eaten Chinese yesterday. (Huh?) Jonnae told her she had not eaten Chinese and the next question was, "You've not had anything like say, ramen noodles?"

Jonnae replied, "How did you know I had ramen noodles?"

The doctor explained Jonnae's blood pressure had not been this high, so the first thought is it's from something in her diet, primarily sodium. Combined with the meds she's on, with her kidneys already having to get rid of so much, the increased sodium and retention of water has caused her blood pressure to go up. Jonnae had a nose bleed last night that we had attributed to low platelets, but of course her platelets weren't low. It was the sodium causing her blood pressure to go up that caused the nose bleed.

Lack of proper nutrition has a bigger effect on our "symptoms" than we give it credit for. I really appreciated the lesson Jonnae got on sodium and the importance of water consumption today. She hasn't wanted to listen to me about them. She will now.

FEBRUARY 12, 2008

I've missed being in God's house on Sunday. I have never gone this long without attending Mass on Sunday. Today, I called the nearest Catholic Church to arrange for us to receive the sacrament of reconciliation. We could pray our daily Rosary while in the beautiful church. I don't know why it hadn't occurred to me before, but Jonnae wouldn't be at risk of crowds, or germs, in an empty church on a week day. It was the perfect solution. She was able to get out of the suite and we were able to visit God in a special way.

Reconciliation is a wonderful sacrament. It is not understood by some and awkward for others, but I have a deep appreciation for it. I feel blessed to be able to pour out my sins and be cleansed of past mistakes.

Jonnae and I talked about God's forgiveness. It's great to know He's forgiven us before we go to confession, but hearing it is so freeing. As human parents, we want to help our children get over the pain of mistakes. When they come to us, we can encourage them with our voice. As His human children, we are relieved, encouraged, and feel much better when we come to Him to *hear* we are forgiven. The priest is God's voice giving us peace with the words, "You are absolved from your sins."

After Jonnae and I had received reconciliation, we prayed the Rosary and decided to sing a few songs while we waited for the shuttle to come back for us. We only had time for two. No surprise that the two our eyes fell on contained words that apply perfectly to us. They were exactly what we needed to hear. Jonnae even requested we sing one of them a second time. I'm so grateful for how comforted, protected, and lifted we are by the Love of our Heavenly Father.

FEBRUARY 14, 2008

It's Valentine's Day!!!

I'm thankful we shared this holiday with other *active children* of God. How blessed I feel on this day of LOVE.

"Love each other just as much as I love you. Your strong love for each other will prove to the world that you are my disciples." John 13:34 &35 (TLB)

Love is a priceless, beautiful thing! We've been able to enjoy awesome company with faith, love, and laughter. A powerful combination of gifts! We prayed the Rosary together, shared a special "offering walk," watched movies, played games, and laughed a lot. It was great fun.

FEBRUARY 15, 2008

Jonnae's clinic visit went well. Her platelets were up to 19,000 Monday and had dropped to 12,000 by Wednesday. The doctor explained to us that the marrow can get "lazy" if we keep transfusing. He wants to see what will happen over the next couple of days if we leave them alone. They've come back up to 15,000 today, so her marrow's doing well on its own and we got out of clinic without needing a transfusion today. We expect it will keep growing and everything continue to progress well. During our offering walk tonight she was walking faster and faster. She is definitely getting stronger and healthier every day.

Today, I was posed the question, "What is it that keeps you motivated?"

My reply was: What motivates me (I anticipate it always will) is Jonnae. She's stayed motivated, when many would have quit. When she had the worst case of mucositis the doctors have ever seen, when she had shingles, when her hair fell out for the fourth time, when she thought she was leukemia free and relapsed, when she was on the brink of renal failure, she drew on her faith and tenacious spirit. She kicked butt & took names. We've developed strong "I will not quit" muscles. Not only do I want to continue to build that muscle, I live to inspire others to do the same.

She's fighting for her life. How can I best honor her and her fight? How do I best show God I'm thankful for being exempt from a fight like hers? Wouldn't it be to take care of myself, because I CAN, and live a full life? Is coasting through the day, without seeking to gain more knowledge, without giving to the world around me, without growing and becoming more, honoring the gift of life?

"Strengthen yourselves so that you will live here on earth doing what God wants." 1 Peter 4:2 (NCV)

I'm adding to my answer. Jonnae's example and God's Word keep me motivated.

FEBRUARY 16, 2008

Jonnae and I have new dreams for our boards. We want to make an annual spa trip to keep the tradition we've started here alive. It will be a good way to revisit the memories, growth, and victories we've known through this experience. With schedules that will make it difficult to slow down for a "just be day," we'll build in a retreat of pampering. I'm thankful for the restoration, renewal, and rest, we are experiencing regularly while secluded from the world.

Shortly after his arrival today, Johnny pushed me out the door. Even with rest and "just be days," I find myself exhausted this week. I could have easily spent the afternoon on the sofa with him. However, it was a nice change of pace to get out and be free to roam. The chance to be out and about, by myself, was different and good.

As I was driving in unfamiliar territory, I was giving thanks for "new adventures." Not because of a shopping trip, but because I again found myself feeling as though I were in a dream. It's odd feeling as though I've been plucked out of my life and dropped into someone else's. I don't want it to be because of a chronic illness, but I do plan on throwing myself into unknown territory from time to time. It's an interesting way to experience the world and live life more fully. I'm thankful for new experiences that push me outside my comfort zone and for a little "retail therapy."

Johnny and I took Jonnae and Lydia to the hotel restaurant for dinner when I got back. Jonnae was pretty excited to leave the room for a meal. The restaurant is never crowded and I thought it would be nice way to treat the girls. I'm thankful for the good food and family dinner we were able to share.

Cancer may try to take away, but it has failed! It's given our family more closeness, strength, patience, and forgiveness than we knew before it. We are surrounded by love wherever we turn. Life is good.

FEBRUARY 17, 2008

It's been a day full of blessing in every sense of the word. This morning, Johnny stayed with Jonnae while Lydia and I attended Mass. From the exquisite mosaics and stain glass windows, to the talented musicians and beautiful choir, to the homily of the priest and the Word of God through scripture and song, it was an amazing way to spend a Sunday morning.

I knelt to pray before we left and said several prayers of thanks. I thanked God ahead of time for the blessings I wish to experience. It was a powerful way to pray. I felt the surge of positive energy as I expect God's favor. I left the church feeling incredibly hopeful.

I reflected on my Lenten promise to offer up what I can for the sake of others. We often perceive Lent as a time to "sacrifice". The funny thing is, as I look back on the different ways I've chosen to "sacrifice," it's apparent to me that although I thought I was giving up a great deal, I received more. God gave me more in return. That's just how God is. You can't out give Him. We serve an awesome God!

I make just about everything I do a competition. It's not that I'm out to beat someone, it's about giving all I've got to reach my potential. Well, today a group of young ladies organized and participated in a real competition and they certainly reached a high bar. They created a cheerleading fundraiser to help us with our growing expenses. I heard from a participant and her mother that the energy and love were high and it was an amazing experience. There are no words to describe the feelings in my heart. Humility and gratitude don't seem to suffice, but they are the best I can come up with.

I may not be able to even the score when it comes to giving more than we've received. I certainly won't mind challenging myself as though it were a competition to do so.

FEBRUARY 18, 2008

Jonnae dropped from 15K to 9K and needed to be transfused with platelets again today. The doctors didn't even flinch. They just congratulated her for making it a week on her own.

> LAUGHTER TRULY IS THE BEST MEDICINE AND THE ONLY SIDE EFFECT IS A SMILE.

We will return for another lab draw on Wednesday and have forewarned the staff we'll indeed be "wacky." Being the goofballs we are, we've decided to make every Wednesday "wacky." Laughter truly is the best medicine and the only side effect is a smile.

Jonnae and I are planning each other's ensembles. No doubt they'll be memorable. How many 40-year-old mothers dress up and "wack out" on a regular basis? I'm sure my boys are glad they are 100 miles away.

I got to hear more of Jonnae's wonderful giggles tonight as we watched a movie. Her voice is sweet, her smile bright, and her giggle contagious. I'm blessed to be sharing this time with her. Under different circumstances, it would be fabulous to experience this kind of one-on-one with each of my children. Not likely to happen, but the blessings we know are many.

Life is grand for those who have the eyes to see it. I'm thankful that I do.

FEBRUARY 19, 2008

I've always lived "in the country." I've always loved when the view outside our window was only of nature and God's creation. The view here is quite different; we're looking down into the streets of Cincinnati. I prefer God's handiwork over that of man, but the urban view is nice for a change of scenery. The snow covered rooftops and the way the light hits the city in the background is reminiscent of a postcard.

We could be home, back to our familiar view in 40 days. Winter and the snow will be gone and we'll be enjoying spring and a different kind of "new life." We're preparing, excited, and thankful.

FEBRUARY 20, 2008

Jonnae had a bow on her head, a rhinestone strip from her forehead to her nose, a blackened tooth and a feather boa. I had a

rhinestone snowflake on my chin, ponytails, tiara, the worst makeup job ever and black lip liner. Wacky Wednesday sure makes a spectacle out of us. It takes courage to be in public all wacked out. We are determined to get the hospital staff on board and make this something they do regularly. We need silliness to replace some of the seriousness in the hospitals. We're two that can make it happen.

Jonnae's counts all look good. We got by without a transfusion and return for labs on Friday. We give thanks for another good day. We are one day closer to kissing Leuk goodbye.

FEBRUARY 22, 2008

Johnny and Lydia were supposed to be coming up today but Nolan has come down with the flu. We can't risk the two of them carrying any illness to Jonnae. We've had a string of "just be days" and were looking forward to their company but accept this as necessary for Jonnae's recovery.

I've been a bit moody as I've been dealing with personal

disappointment. I've gotten my body into fine shape, but realize I still have a lot of inner work to do. It reminds me of a saying I heard years ago. "If we didn't have a downpour, we wouldn't know about the leak in the gutter." The current disappointment just allows me to see where some work needs to be done.

FEBRUARY 23, 2008

We awoke to violin music being played across the hall. That was nice. I gave thanks for that immediately. I've never began my day in that way before.

Jonnae and I kind of "clashed" yesterday. I told her we needed to look at the positive. We've made it over 70 days without our raging hormones getting in the way of our joy. Between her steroids and my own 40ish wacko hormones, it's no wonder we haven't hit a rough spot before now. I ran some errands this morning to give us each some space. While I was out, she played around on the computer. It was nice for us each to have some alone time. Our clash wasn't all that bad, but it was good strategy to part for awhile so emotions didn't escalate.

Jonnae and I will welcome the opportunity to get out for a bit on Monday. The days are growing longer as we get more bored with our sedentary lives in a hotel. It's only a clinic visit, but we're getting out.

FEBRUARY 25, 2008

Jonnae's platelets increased by 1000 and we made it through another day without a transfusion. Her potassium is borderline low. They commented on it Friday and again today. I've tried, without success, to get her to eat some bananas or vegetables to crank it up. After the doctors' discussion of maybe keeping her at the hospital for "a boost" of it, she agreed to eat more potassium-rich foods. Don't know why these kids find it so hard to trust that mom knows what she's talking about.

Jonnae and I got our beads out to make prayer bracelets. I know I will be led to give them away while in Columbus this weekend. I'm thankful for the way these bracelets allow me to "give back" a small token of our appreciation for the support we've been given and as a reminder that we can ALWAYS *Fully Rely On God.*

FEBRUARY 26, 2008

What an amazing day of exhilaration. I felt like a "baby bird" on its first flight. All it took was a trip to an enormous mall. I've never seen one so big. I was all over it just because I could be. Jonnae and I called one another often just to check in. We knew the time apart was good but couldn't stop thinking about each other.

My daughter's winning her war, I have a fun event to attend this weekend, I found a great dress for it on sale, and my husband is doing so much to support and encourage me. I am feeling very blessed today and thank God for His favor.

FEBRUARY 27, 2008

Oh, my gosh, it truly does get better and better every day in every way. We've experienced one blessing after another today. My first one occurred on the treadmill this morning. I'm fit, but I really struggle with cardio. A short debate occurred between a "quitter" and "fighter". It went like this:

"You've done enough, quit a few minutes early today. You don't have to push so hard all the time. You're exhausted. What's five more minutes?"

The strong one counteracted:

"You can't push yourself another 5 minutes? Give me a break!!! Jonnae pushed through 2 1/2 years of chemo. She relapsed and pushed through more chemo, full body radiation, all while feeling like shit. She's gone for three years. You're ready to quit over five minutes?"

Short struggle! If that doesn't propel one to finish strong and not quit, nothing will.

I came back upstairs from my workout and woke Jonnae up. I said, "We're going to the mall, baby!" I figured if we got there when they first opened, she had her gloves and mask on, and we stayed away from everyone, she would be safe. She was all excited about sharing a "Build a Bear" experience with me so off we went. Her first outing since transplant was definitely a blessing. We give thanks.

When I shared my awesome "quit or fight" reflection with Jonnae this morning, she said, "Well, if I quit, I lose my life, you know!"

I said, "Yes, baby. But healthy people are choosing to quit by not taking a higher road. It's their life too and they are quitting on it. You're not. I'm so proud of you!"

We got wacky before heading to clinic and were surprised with an awesome gift basket full of goodies for our next spa day. It's incredible and we can't wait to pamper ourselves with it. Surprise gifts are always a blessing.

We could feel the joy and positive energy all about us today. The staff really laughed it up at our get ups and I think this Wacky Wednesday thing just may stick. Two of the staff and one other patient dressed up today. How awesome is that? I think the wacky fever is catching. That's one fever that's welcome.

FEBRUARY 28, 2008

My mom is getting ready for a health expo that is this weekend. She is going to leave early tomorrow morning so I told her that I would take care of the journal entries until she gets back. So for the next few nights, YOU'RE STUCK WITH ME!!!! MUAHAHAHAHAHA!!!!

Today has been another good day. I made bracelets for several hours so my mom could pass them out to people she meets in Columbus. During those hours my mom was able to get out and have a REAL spa day. My dad gave her a free spa treatment for Christmas. She came back feeling refreshed with a manicure and pedicure. We watched a movie when she got back. It wasn't that good, though. The movies we picked this week are all duds. We're running out of good movies to watch.

My dad got here around 8:30. I thought Lydia was coming too, so I was really disappointed to find out she stayed home. I still plan on having a fun time with my dad, though. I just can't paint his nails, give him a makeover, or do anything like that. He would look pretty goofy going back to work with pink fingernails and lipstick. LOL.

I know that my mom posts scriptures. I have a calendar with a scripture for each day and would like to share today's:

"May the God of peace... equip you with everything good for doing His will..."

-Hebrews 13:20, 21

I have certainly known God's peace during this war with Leuk. I pray to continue to experience His peace while I live my life to serve Him and lead others to know Him.

Dad says, "Bearhug."

Blessings,

Jonnae

FEBRUARY 29, 2008

Our visit to clinic today was short. It took us about an hour and fifteen minutes to get there and get back to the apartment. My counts are good. My platelets are... drumroll please... 24! It has almost been two weeks since my last platelet transfusion. I've drank a lot today. I try to drink at least 40 oz. a day. Today, however, I drank at least 60! I'm going to make myself drink that much, if not more, everyday. I can put forth more effort than I have been. If I continue to do the best I can, I may get to go home soon.

I still can't believe I've been here for over 70 days! It seems like it's been that long, but then again it doesn't (I'm weird like that, LOL.)

My dad and I have bonded a lot today. After we got back from clinic, we hung out and I took a nap. When I woke up we went downstairs to eat dinner. I had salmon. It was okay but I don't know if I liked it enough for a repeat. It didn't seem like it had enough flavor for me. No one else was in the restaurant except for the waiters and a few people in the bar area. It was nice having it to ourselves.

I also gave my dad a makeover. I painted his fingernails pink, his toenails black, and gave him purple eye shadow and red lipstick. I still can't believe I touched his feet! LOL. It wasn't that bad. I thought they would stink but they didn't. But I also didn't take deep whiffs or anything. Afterwards we watched *Shanghai Knights*. That's a really funny movie. It's perfect for action and laughs.

The scripture for today is:

"And everyone who calls on the name of the Lord will be saved..."

- Joel 2:32

This scripture touches me in a way I cannot explain. I truly believe that if you believe in God and do not doubt Him or His work, your prayers will be answered and you will be saved. After all, *"With God all things are possible."*

Blessings, Jonnae

MARCH 1, 2008

Today has been a slower day. I spent most of the day doing homework (which is why the day went so slowly.) I also took a nap. When my mom got back we went downstairs and ate at the restaurant. When we got back upstairs my dad left and my mom fell asleep as soon as she hit the cushions on the couch. She's exhausted and is sleeping right now. I told her I wouldn't mind posting for her again tonight.

I've drank more than 60 oz. again today. I can tell I'm getting better and better every day. The doctor even said if all continues to go well, there's a possibility I'll get to go home in a few weeks. I, on the other hand, am determined and have already starting packing (a little ambitious, don't you think?) I know I'll be ready and healthy enough to go home soon.

Today's scripture:

"May she who gave you birth rejoice!"

- Proverbs 23:25

The woman who gave birth to me has rejoiced all weekend and said to let you know she'll tell you all about it tomorrow. For now she's rejoicing in her dreams. LOL.

Blessings,

Jonnae

MARCH 2, 2008

Jonnae's posts, in my absence, were so true to her spirit. Now you must know why I treasure my time with her so. I hope she'll share her gift of writing more often.

It was an emotional weekend of reflection for both Jonnae and myself. She experienced God's presence in a strong way these last three days. Yesterday morning as the first scheduled seminar began I received a text from her that was written exactly like this:

"These last couple of days I have felt a different feeling in me that is so DIVINE! EVERYTIME I THINK OF ANYTHING GOOD, I THINK, 'HOW GREAT IS OUR GOD!' I have felt the feeling of being thankful before, BUT THIS .....THIS IS A GREATER FEELING BY FAR. THESE WORDS DON'T DESCRIBE IT, IT IS MAGICAL!"

Today, as we were saying the Rosary, she got teary-eyed when she again felt God's presence very strongly. She asked, "Why haven't I felt this before? Why can't I feel it more often?" It's a question I've asked myself. I guess we wouldn't experience the gift of being overwhelmed by His presence if we felt it all the time.

MARCH 3, 2008

I'm still processing all that I experienced over the weekend. My spiritualness was overcome by my humanness. God has put the dream on my heart to be an inspirational speaker and author. I had hoped to be given a chance to speak and thank the group in attendance for support they've given us. I felt a brief share would be powerful for all. I know in His time, I will be given the chance, but it wasn't in God's timing for it to be this weekend. I felt like I was *watching the game from the bench*. I should be more gracious for a place on God's team and forgot that for a while. There were some very inspirational thoughts shared and I was blessed with the company of lovely people. This weekend wasn't provided for me to sharpen my speaking skill, it was given so that I realize I have listening skills to improve as well.

"The most effective means the enemy has to keep believers from being full of the spirit is to keep us full of ourselves." (Beth Moore)

It's not about me. It's about us as a team. I'm at peace again. I will wait. I will listen. I will be attentive and give thanks. When the Coach calls me up to play, I'll be ready.

MARCH 4, 2008

Jonnae's clinic appointment went well today. Her platelets are holding at 24,000 where they were Friday. The doctor said she's definitely making her own platelets. All her numbers look good. Jonnae's eyelashes are starting to grow back and there is darkness where her eyebrows will be. Proof positive she's healing. Thank you, God!

The doctor didn't promise she'll release Jonnae next week, but she's definitely considering it. I think her concern at this point is that it's flu season. We'll need to be extremely cautious with visitors and be on the lookout for any symptoms the kids might bring home. A lot can happen in a week. I think that's one reason the doctor wouldn't say for sure. Friday will confirm more, but the Taylors are expecting to finally be returning home next weekend. Praise God!

MARCH 6, 2008

I reached one of my personal milestones today. The 12-week physical challenge I began as Jonnae started conditioning for her transplant, ended today. It feels quite fantastic to have made it to the finish line in victory. I thank God for the amazing weapon it's been for me, as well as the lessons that were contained within it. On the first day, with a "code blue" on our floor, I was ready to run and hide with a piece of chocolate cake, but I didn't. When pizza was brought up and I could have dug in, I didn't. When platters of cookies and Christmas treats were left in the family lounge and I was tired and ready to just eat one, I walked past them. Instead of "drugging" with food, I "drug" my behind out of bed and worked out every morning. I celebrate the strength I've acquired physically, emotionally, mentally, and most importantly, spiritually.

Jonnae spent the day packing. She's understandably excited about our return home. I pray the doctor continues to support our idea of going home next Saturday. We have friends preparing a special homecoming based on our afternoon arrival. It's going to be awesome.

Easter is fast approaching and spring promises to bring new life. We are ready to "resurrect into new life with Christ" as we prepare to come home and LIVE again. I think I feel like skipping.

MARCH 7, 2008

Jonnae's appointment went well today. The doctor gave us the okay for our return home next Saturday. She made it a point to remind us there's always uncertainty. If a fever arises or counts get funky, the plan will change. Jonnae came back to the room and continued to pack up. She's floating on air.

Wish I could report the same. I'm sick of the "spiritual warfare" that's hit this week. The struggle between darkness and light baffles me. How can I be in the light for so long and then, just as this snowstorm that swept in on the back of beautiful warm days, the devil hovers over me trying to steal my long fought for joy.

Pride replaced humility. Again I was full of myself instead of being full of the Holy Spirit. It sickens me, the disguises the enemy will use. He knows my weakness and continues to play on it. I refuse to give in. It's no time to weaken and fall prey to him. "Sorry looks back, worry looks around, faith looks up." I don't know who said it, but darkness will not prevail over the celebration of our finally coming home.

MARCH 8, 2008

Apparently I'm not the only one who's been experiencing turmoil. Mom reported to me that Lydia's had a rough day today, (total melt down actually.) Nolan communicated that Johnny must have had a bad day at work, and Jonnae showed me a picture she drew to capture what I've been like the last two days. It was monstrous.

Our fatigue reminds me of the triathlon I did in Sept. I wanted to rejoice and sprint to the finish line, but was too drained to do anything more than trot wearily and fall across it. I think we're all on our last leg. It's hard to be patient with the finish line so near, but I want to finish with grace.

Jonnae didn't want to ride the elevator up from the restaurant. We decided to try the steps, since she'll be using them when we get home. We thought she would make a couple flights before resorting to the elevator. She walked up the entire 7 flights! She came straight in to call Johnny and tell him. It's going to be a great week!

My parents will get to return to their simpler life and experience rest and renewal. Jonnae will have her Sassy to love on and we'll be a family together again. I'm going to be in the arms of my husband every night as I go to sleep and every morning as I wake up. I'm going to be able to pray my kids off to school and be there when they get home. I'm going to see for myself that they're doing well or having a tough day. I'll be there to be their mom again.

So much to be thankful for! I can hardly wait! But I must, so in the meantime, I'll use this last week to visualize and prepare for a smooth transition. Starting with the zzzzz's I'm getting ready to catch. Can't wait to see what God's gonna serve my soul for breakfast.

MARCH 11, 2008

The latest news is not the usual, but not completely unexpected. These things happen and it won't affect our coming home Saturday. Jonnae's central line started causing problems last Friday. They are going to remove it and she'll just be "stuck" each time they draw blood or she needs an IV.

After waiting five hours for a decision, she was admitted today. It will speed up the scheduling of the line removal. It's been an upsetting day for her, not because she's in-patient for a day, but because the IV they put in her hand has caused her some pain. The incision, where the central line goes in, is very raw also.

Even through tears, she was able to see the glass half full and focus on the fact that we've made it. It's almost time to go home!

MARCH 12, 2008

It's been a long day. Jonnae was an "add on" today. Her procedure was supposed to be between 11 and 12. It wasn't until 3:00. Of course she was starving and anxious about the whole thing by the time the

procedure took place. The line came out fine; she recovered from anesthesia without any problems.

Even though Jonnae was in-patient, we still managed to get "wacked out" for Wacky Wednesday. It was quite fun wheeling down to O.R. and sharing our concept with staff who have not observed our wackiness before.

MARCH 13, 2008

Jonnae's feeling well; no aftermath from yesterday's procedure. She's getting more excited with every passing moment. I think she's a little apprehensive about her appearance, the steroids having caused her cheeks to get so full.

Today she said, "My head is so small and my cheeks are so fat. They're so much bigger than the rest of my head." Then she said, "If this hump on the back of my neck doesn't go down, you can just start calling me Quasimodo."

She's had the swelling at the base of her neck before. Everything will go down with the steroid reduction. Such a cross for a teenager to carry, but she does it with strength, humor, and grace. Oh, how I love her so.

I had a crying spell that came from out of nowhere today. I was discussing it with Jonnae, for I knew she would understand. Our stay in the suite has been like a slow, quiet, peaceful flowing stream. Saturday the pace of the water's flow will change drastically. Very quickly, it's going to go from slow to rapid.

It's a change I'm looking forward to and prepared for. It's going to require patience and understanding from everyone, as we make the transition back to normal. We aren't going back to our "old normal." We've learned many lessons and I don't expect we'll have a "normal" day.

My normal will not ever again be what society sees as normal. I will not forget the gift of life. I want to contribute to others' experience of it--EVERY DAY! It will be my mission and my goal to create sparks of love, peace, joy, happiness and gratitude for everyone I can. This is as important to me as eating, working out, bathing, and breathing.

THE THIRD "TRIMESTER"

MARCH 14, 2008

Jonnae's found a reason to smile with every passing second, giddy and beside herself with joy. During lunch today, she shared with me how everyone in the dining room had something about them that made her smile.

Just as she was going to bed, she let out a squeal. I was in the kitchen cleaning up the last of the dishes and was startled by the noise. She came to me and buried her face in my chest as she cried tears of joy.

"Just 12 more hours!" she said.

I'll workout and shower before getting Jonnae up. We'll enjoy a nice breakfast before I load up the car and will leave by 11. Exciting things await us and our 1 o'clock arrival. The community will not be quiet as we're pulling into town. I expect it's going to be another amazing "gift" offered from this journey.

Who would imagine one could experience such indescribable blessings from an illness that's been relentless? Leuk's been no opponent for my girl. Jonnae's standing, with her foot in its back and her hands victorious over her head, as she claims the title of God's miraculous champion.

> JONNAE'S STANDING, WITH HER FOOT IN ITS BACK AND HER HANDS VICTORIOUS OVER HER HEAD, AS SHE CLAIMS THE TITLE OF GOD'S MIRACULOUS CHAMPION.

MARCH 15, 2008

It was an incredible day. The "extreme homecoming" was phenomenal. I had no idea the turnout was going to be so grand and that the hundreds of people with balloons, posters, and cheering would produce so much energy. Our homecoming ROCKED!

On the way in, we passed a couple of business marquees that read, "Welcome home, Jonnae! F.R.O.G. rules." Two police cars escorted us with lights and sirens, until we reached our home. At the subdivision entrance, we were greeted by a large crowd with balloons and posters. All the way through the subdivision, there were colorful latex balloons and mylar frogs on every mailbox; families everywhere, waving and flashing posters. The closer we got to our house, the bigger the crowd. Huge colorful helium balloons arches at our street and driveway. There was a fire pit, tent, snacks, and hot cider for the two to three hundred people who'd come to celebrate with us.

Jonnae can't be around crowds and it was beginning to mist rain, so she couldn't stay outside. Johnny felt bad about leaving the crowd to come into the house. It was so surreal; I seemed to be in a fog. I still am actually.

I'm processing a lot as I unpack and sort through everything we've brought back. One would think it simple to return to a loving family, beautiful home, and much missed community, but it's complicated.

Cincinnati was very different. I feel like Alice in Wonderland or Dorothy from the Wizard of Oz. Only being back isn't as easy as waking up from a dream. It's hard to explain.

Part of the old normal that I don't want to return to, is pushing myself to go, go, go. I'm not off to a good start. With much to do, I was pouring myself into unpacking and cleaning. A new gym opened while I was away and Johnny knew I wouldn't pull myself away from work long enough to check it out. He got me to go by taking me down there himself. That took some real effort on his part and for his persistent support, I'm grateful.

I'm the only one that seems dazed by our return. I'm overwhelmed by things needing my attention. It's a test in patience. I still have so much to learn in this area.

As "The Passion" (story of Christ's condemnation and crucifixion) was read in church this morning, I drew several comparisons to Christ's cross and Jonnae's. The disciples couldn't stay awake to pray with Him during his last hours. We had our family, close friends, and complete strangers crying out in prayer during what looked to be Jonnae's. Jesus had Simeon help carry his cross when it got heavy. We had numerous "Simeons" helping to ease the burden of our "financial cross," as we faced debt incurred from this illness.

Jonnae was "born" at Christmas time with Nolan's donation of bone marrow and now she's resurrected to new life at Easter. We're experiencing the Miracles of God in a magnificent way. I give thanks that He provided what we needed to carry this cross. The power of His blessing is indescribable.

Jonnae starts her first 12-week challenge tomorrow. I am doing it with her, piggybacking this one on top of another. I have three weeks left to the Transformation challenge I started in January. She's very excited, determined, and committed to having a powerful experience with this program. She realizes there's a difference between surviving and thriving.

She's embracing a chance to reach higher, shine brighter, and LIVE more fully by setting goals and achieving them. We understand better

> WE UNDERSTAND BETTER THAN MOST THAT LIFE IS A PRECIOUS GIFT. WE WON'T LEAVE IT UNWRAPPED AND SITTING IN THE BOX. WE'RE GOING TO MAKE THE MOST OF IT!

than most that life is a precious gift. We won't leave it unwrapped and sitting in the box. We're going to make the most of it!

MARCH 17, 2008

Jonnae and I have made our lists of things we want to accomplish through this 12-week challenge. I want Johnny and I to reintroduce "date night" back into our schedules. I have a Bible study to complete. I have a book to write and speaking engagements to find. I'm going to get this Wacky Wednesday Project going in the hospitals.

Jonnae wants to lose the 20 pounds she's put on from steroids. The weaning of those drugs will help, but she wants to incorporate permanent healthier habits. She's going to read 6 books and complete 3 of her subjects for school by this challenge's end. She's exercising to build her strength and helping Lydia to get healthier too. She's organizing her room and keeping a checklist of things she can do to best utilize her time. It's been a good first day of our challenge. We should be quite content with our accomplishments come early June.

The Bible study I'm doing is about breaking out of mental, emotional, physical, or spiritual imprisonment. I imagine there's always going to be a snare that wants to hold us back from knowing and accepting peace. Transformation is about manifesting the power we each have within us. That's not to be confused with pride. That's a big part of the lesson I'm working on right now. I pray I never forget humility. I've made my biggest mistakes in life when I've been full of myself. Focus was on what I needed or had obtained. I am who I am because of the grace and mercy of our Coach and Heavenly Father. I'm nothing on my own and wasn't created to be.

> I'M NOTHING ON MY OWN AND WASN'T CREATED TO BE.

MARCH 19, 2008

School was cancelled today because of area flooding (so much for easing back into the mom routine). It didn't take the kids long to get bored. Their source of entertainment became picking on one another. The black and white striped shirt came out of the closet and my "referee" job resumed today. They weren't that bad, but it was certainly a different kind of day than the peaceful ones Jonnae and I experienced.

Johnny says I look tired tonight. I am pretty drained, but the LOVE of so many is refreshing me.

I'm blessed in so many special ways. I feel the seeds of my faith sprouting with strong new growth and vision. I will continue to fertilize them with scripture, positive attitude, and perseverance. I'll be certain to nurture the gardens of others too. Blessings come from paying it forward. It's not the reason I do it, it's just the way it is.

MARCH 20, 2008

We went back to Cincinnati for a follow up today. It was agreed by all to share Jonnae's care with Cincinnati and our local hospital. We will go to Cincinnati once a month, and in between visits we will have labs at home.

My Bible study comes at a perfect time to help me deal with sin, forgiveness, and bondage of shame. I've seen several times, "Every saint has a past. Every sinner has a future." It's so awesome when we receive God's forgiveness and then give it to those who've hurt us, allowing it to replace anger and resentment.

Good Friday is tomorrow. As I reflect on the death of the Savior, I will let all negative thoughts and emotions die with Him. Where negativity lives, peace and joy will not. I choose life and all that's good.

MARCH 22, 2008

Jonnae has charted another successful day with her new physical challenges. She's about 20 years ahead of where I was at her age. I'm very proud and excited, for both her and Lydia. They're applying great effort and successfully making difficult, but healthy, choices.

God gave me "hugs" all day today. I'm finding that His plan and my part in it are quite different than I had perceived. Things I used to need, that had power over me, no longer have a place in my life. The best choice I can make is to let go of my plan, to follow His. I pray I stay focused and committed in letting Him do His work on, in, and through me.

MARCH 23, 2008

It wasn't a traditional Easter by any stretch. Normally, we'd be in our hometown having dinner with both my extended family and Johnny's. But it's no ordinary Easter. In regards to feasts and gathering of family members, it fell short. In regards to the parallels we can draw from our journey this year, to the journey of Christ and the Resurrection, no Easter will ever be able to compare.

As we were on our way to church this morning and the song "With All of My Heart" was playing, I belted out the words to the song.

And then the parallels of Jonnae's cross, sacrifice, and victory began filling my head. I continue to grow in my love for my King (my Coach!) Although she's not the Messiah or Son of God, Jonnae is His daughter. Although she wasn't brutally beaten, tortured, or crucified by humans, she was beaten down and tortured by the brutality of leukemia and harsh medications.

Although she didn't wipe away our past sins by the spilling of her blood, we should all sin less, as she's shown us how to F.R.O.G. She didn't miraculously rise from the dead to give us a "new life in Christ" but I believe she's a miracle and we have a "new life in Christ" because of her.

I want to alleviate the suffering; I want to eliminate the sorrow. I want everyone to experience the peace, joy, and happiness I know, that Jonnae knows, that God wants us to know. There is a key hidden deep within us that will unlock the treasure where these gifts exist in abundance. High or low, peaceful waters or rocky waves, we can prevail and know peace, joy, and happiness when we find and use the key.

Today, in the midst of many beautiful thoughts translated in my Beth Moore Bible study, I found this to be most awesome: **"The path to peace is paved with knee prints."** I just love that. Beth Moore is so good!

MARCH 25, 2008

Well, so much for uneventful days. Jonnae called out to me, crying and quite panicked. Rightfully so! Her body was covered with a rash. She was miserable with itchiness and couldn't find relief.

Doctors check for rash at every visit. They are an indicator of GVH (graft vs. host). The donor's graft "realizes" it's in a foreign body and attacks the host (marrow recipient). It's common in transplants and can be acute or chronic; acute being when it occurs within 3 months, and chronic, after. It was a reality check for us--the trees are thinning, but we're nowhere close to being out of the woods.

I called the doctor to give her the details. I was ready to jump in the car with Jonnae and my purse and head to Cincy. She assured me that GVH doesn't normally appear so suddenly. Normally there would be a rash, but Jonnae's entire body had turned pink. There was no swelling of the tongue or difficulty in breathing, something the doctor said would warrant an emergency trip.

She believed Jonnae was having an allergic reaction. We couldn't pinpoint anything she'd been exposed to, by mouth or touch, other than a load of clothes she had folded about 30 minutes before the itching began. We ran to the pharmacy for some Benadryl. We were told it would give her relief and it did. The itching stopped and the pinkness began to disappear.

The river of life continues to flow, sometimes calm, sometimes fierce. I'm not going to get worked into a frenzy over something that may not happen. It doesn't make sense to swim upstream. I'll let go and let God and conserve my energy. While I'm going with the flow, I'll continue to count my blessings. They are still abundant, even when the current is swift.

MARCH 27, 2008

This morning Jonnae awoke itch-and-pink-free. I am happy to report that our regular scheduled appt for a lab check at our local hospital is still all that's in order. No trip to Cincinnati is necessary.

The local medical team was happy to see Jonnae back and looking so good. Her hair's starting to come in, her eyelashes are thick, her skin color good, and eyes bright. All signs of healthy cell growth. They haven't seen her since November and honestly I never got the feeling they were holding out much hope for her. A few of them had tears in their eyes when they first saw her today.

Even with the warm welcome, I found myself challenged to use "get to" today. It takes practice. This is one of those things Jonnae and I've done enough for it to instinctively kick in at the first sign of negativity.

I was filling out forms; they have us fill them out every single visit with info they already have: insurance, address, birthday, yada yada yada. My first thought was "I hate *having* to fill these stupid forms out here. We never had to do this in Cincinnati." I heard a whisper in my head, "Uh hum.....you **GET** to fill out these forms. There are people who can't see to fill forms out. There are people who can't read forms. There are people who can't write." The voice didn't need to go on. Immediately, my want to complain was replaced with my want to give thanks. "Yes! I GET TO fill out forms."

Later I found myself thinking, "I can't believe we've *had* to sit here and wait for 2 hours and we haven't gotten any lab results or seen the doctor yet."

Again, the voice from within reminded me, "You **GET** to sit here and wait. Even if you wouldn't have to wait in Cincy, you would have spent two hours in the car just to get there. You GET to sit here in clinic and wait for labs, not in a hospital for something worse."

It's almost 10:30 p.m. and because Jonnae wasn't home to do her cardio this morning, she is in the living room doing it now. I am so proud of her commitment and determination. She is working hard for her health and fitness.

Earlier, I was showing a friend my before and after pics from the physical challenge I completed in Cincinnati. She pointed at my before picture and made a pouty face and said, "This is what I look like now. It's not fair." I was shocked and felt compelled to point out there was nothing unfair about my weight loss. I worked hard! I fought a lot of "demons" and applied a ton of effort. How is it unfair that the ones who work for it get a healthy body, and the ones who don't, don't?

MARCH 28, 2008

A journalist was here today and asked Jonnae if she ever thought her journey was "unfair" (funny how the subject of fairness came up again today). Jonnae and I can honestly say we've never had that thought.

With Jonnae's initial diagnosis in '05 and this relapse, I immediately ran to God and obediently turned it all over to Him. Jonnae's learned to do the same. This isn't a place I've always been; Jonnae found it much sooner than I. Living through trials that seem "unfair" show us the good to be found in the bad.

I'm thankful I traded in the "shack of feeling sorry for myself" for the "house that Faith built."

> I'M THANKFUL I TRADED IN THE "SHACK OF FEELING SORRY FOR MYSELF" FOR THE "HOUSE THAT FAITH BUILT."

Jonnae has taken the liberty to stick spiritual Post-it notes in different places for me to find sporadically. She's put them in books I'm reading, my Bible, and a small photo album in my purse. She's always been a selfless, giving, thoughtful young girl. On her own accord, even as a preschooler, she would share her school party favors and "goody bags" with her siblings. Any souvenir money she had on a trip, she spent buying gifts for the kids.

This child has been through so much and continually offsets life's disappointments with gratitude and positive thinking. This Sunday marks her day +100. That's the day they estimate a transplant patient will get to go home and a big milestone for a transplant patient. Jonnae chose to aim for a higher bar and she reached it. She's celebrating the victory with friends. I continually learn from her example. Life is meant to be embraced.

MARCH 30, 2008

Now that we're home at the start of a month, I'm eager to use one of the Christmas presents we received. We have *The Ultimate Gift* Family Experience Kit and I've been waiting for our family to be together so we can experience it as ONE, the way it was designed. It's based on the movie and assigns the family a different gift to celebrate and share each month.

This month's focus is the Gift of Laughter. We'll be making an effort to laugh more as well as share that gift with others.

I won't be foolish and squander the days, letting opportunities go by to leave an everlasting legacy. Life is the ultimate gift. As I enjoy it, I'll choose to bless others with it also!

APRIL 1, 2008

Jonnae's clinic appointment went well today. She's cruising right along and we're thrilled with her progress. After next week, she'll be off the Prednisone and down to only one med three days a week. This is yet again a rare scenario after transplant. Jonnae rocks!

Today a woman spoke up in the clinic waiting room. She said, "I feel like I know you because I read your journal." I'm not sure exactly how she worded the next part, but she let me know we impacted her in a positive way because of the journal and our faith. This is what I live for.

Allowing God to speak through me is invigorating. It fills me with energy. Sometimes I wonder, "Did I touch someone today?" "Did they feel what I wanted to give them?" I'm working on that part of myself that doesn't need to know; that doesn't need outside validation. I'm a perfectionist and sometimes need to hear I've hit the mark. I've teetered back and forth on whether my perfectionism is a blessing or a curse. Beth Moore helped me with that this week, when her Bible study said, "Dissatisfaction is a God thing. It's only bad when we don't' let it lead us to Christ." Most of the time, I look to God in my dissatisfaction. I think He placed perfectionism in my heart so I feel the void and seek Him. He is wise and merciful in placing that "God-shaped" void in me. I will seek to fill it with Him and only Him.

APRIL 3, 2008

The enemy often uses the voice of those we love the most to hurt us. Today it was my husband's. In an attempt to help me recover, Jonnae had placed more scripture Post-it's for me to find. One said, "Make every effort to live in peace with all men and to be holy." Hebrews 12:14. We laughed together as I said, "Can I paraphrase this to say, 'You are holy if you can be with men and live in peace?"

This time of year is rainy and cloudy. One thought of where we were not so long ago and the gloomy weather doesn't have much effect on me. All I need to do is recall a 12-by-12 room, accessorized with hospital equipment and my child sick in a bed. I remember escaping that room only to see more sick children and weary parents, exhausted and sometimes shedding tears.

Tomorrow may bring sunshine or it may not, but one thing is for sure. Warm weather and sunny skies are just around the corner. There is a blanket of green sprouting from the ground. There IS color out there--it's just not overhead.

APRIL 4, 2008

We had a glorious day. Jonnae and I went to a salon, one that participates in a program that provides free custom-made wigs to cancer patients. Jonnae had taken several pics of her dream hair. I was a bit concerned with the length of it and was correct with my reservation. After making a phone call, the salon owner came back and said, because of its length, the wig would be $400 and take 10 weeks to make.

As she was talking, she realized how disappointed Jonnae was. She looked up to see a sample wig that was dark brown and long in length. She retrieved it to see if it fit. It did! Jonnae sat there with tears of joy in her eyes. They talked while the hairdresser styled Jonnae's new hair. It will take some getting used to, but it's a beautiful, thick head of hair.

The boys, Johnny included, have mixed feelings. Jonnae's been adamant about not wanting a wig for so long. It's hard for them to understand and accept the change in her desires. But she IS a fifteen-year-old girl. Most young women find something they're insecure with, in their own skin. The wig is something that makes it easier for Jonnae to be more confident.

Hair is a big thing for most women, certainly a teenage girl. I think it's great she's so comfortable with her bald head, but I completely understand her wanting to have the option of hair. Those occasions where she'll be anticipating stares because of her baldness, will be made easier with the wig.

"God does not see the same way people see. People look at the outside of a person, but the LORD looks at the heart" 1 Samuel 16:7 (NCV). As humans we have a tendency to get hung up on the outside. Wouldn't it be great if everyone strived to be more like the Lord, and let the inside override appearances?

APRIL 6, 2008

Jonnae struggled a bit through the weekend with her moods. The weaning off steroids has messed with her appetite. The weaning, combined with lack of nutrients from no appetite, has messed with her moods. It was difficult for her to hang on to her joy today.

The enemy's a hard opponent. She was outside only long enough to shoot one hoop when I reminded her she needed sunscreen (the sun activates GVH, graft vs. host). The tears began to flow and she bee-lined into the house for a breakdown. I found her downstairs, crouched in a corner. She cried as she talked about feeling alone. Her friends haven't been around because they've had cold symptoms or been around illness. She wants to be outside and hates covering up with sunscreen and light clothing.

I mentioned her wig, trying to relight a spark of excitement. She's lost the giddiness since her brothers and dad haven't been enthusiastic with their feedback. She decided to lather up her face and don a light, hooded jacket. We went for a walk and spirits lifted.

As we were walking she named off her "joy moments." She smiled at the kids playing, neighbors mingling, and the sunshine. As we walked past a couple of children she's babysat for, she mentioned how much she missed it. Hopefully once summer's here, flu season's over, and her counts have climbed a little more, the doctor will lift that restriction and she'll be able to resume babysitting again. Instead of the things we miss, we talked about what we have and had a nice walk.

The family has embraced the Joy Calendar from the family experience kit. I expected Nolan and Johnny to need a push, but beyond the first day, they've willingly participated. I'm really happy about that.

TUESDAY, APRIL 8, 2008

Yesterday Jonnae asked if she was letting the devil win by wearing a wig and being bothered by others staring at her bald head. I told her the devil wins when we don't do what makes us joyful because we're worried about what others think. I explained how she had been doing it backwards.

I said, "If it brings you joy to have hair on your head and you're not wearing it because of what someone else thinks, you're giving "the win" to the devil. If you like the wig, WEAR IT! All that matters is how YOU feel in it."

We went out and she wore the wig. I caught her fiddling with it often (twirling it in her fingers, playing with the bangs). She had a comfortable afternoon because of the confidence it provided. She claimed her joy and victory.

APRIL 9, 2008

I've heard Jonnae tell reporters, doctors, and even the hair stylist last week, "I don't regret any of what's happened the last three years. It's taught me a lot and brought me closer to God."

This experience has brought us closer to God and given my young family a giant leap in life as a result. My youngest brought that to light as she stunned me with a comment today.

Report cards came and we've always rewarded the children for A's. Lydia, my 10-year-old, informed me that she didn't want her money.

When I asked why, she said, "$20 for report cards, $20 for the Joy calendar, it could cost you a lot of money, mom."

I said, "Yes, you're right! But you've earned it baby."

She said, "I've earned being a smarter person, that's enough."

Later when we went to her band registration and she saw the

instrument rental fee, she started to second guess whether she should do it or not. On one hand, I think it's good that my children have become conscious of spending. On the other, as children, I think it's sad that they need to be.

For months, Nolan's been saying he's not going to prom. He's said he doesn't really care for dancing, but I can't help but wonder if he's thinking about the expense of it. Yesterday, he asked me if it was okay that he's decided to go. Of course it is. I don't know what transpired to change his mind and I really don't care. I'm happy he's not going to miss it or have regrets about not going.

One of his teachers called me today with very nice things to say about Nolan. Of course, none of them surprised me, but that kind of feedback provides great joy to a mother. The comments, as well as the loving support the school continues to provide us, humble me greatly.

APRIL 12, 2008

I'm not big on typical. I look for ways to create something special out of mediocre. Today I decided to do something out of the ordinary for the kids. I don't slow down to play with them enough. Something I know I'll live to regret, actually already do. It doesn't take anything too outlandish. Most of the time, my attention, time, and some fun are all that's required to create joy. That small effort transformed mediocre into special.

APRIL 13, 2008

Jonnae's not been feeling well. Her appetite has been nil and she's had some headaches the past couple of days. She wasn't able to do schooling today because one got so bad. I still believe it's the detox of the steroids. This is her 3rd day off of them and her symptoms have been present for the same. I'm waiting to hear back from the BMT coordinator to get her opinion. She's feeling a little better tonight. We played Scrabble and now she and Lydia are downstairs working out.

APRIL 15, 2008

Jonnae's appetite is still very poor. She has headaches and nausea, too. She needed to quit schooling today when a headache was too bad for her to continue. I'm wondering if it's possibly a stomach bug of some kind. The BMT coordinator said they aren't overly concerned. She said we'll discuss Jonnae's symptoms during our appointment on Friday.

It's been difficult for me to muster the energy for even small projects. I've drawn the parallel to the likes of plate spinning. In Cincinnati, I only had a couple, here more plates have been added and a few are going to drop before they start spinning smoothly. I imagine I'll find the harmony eventually.

I could complete all the menial tasks there are and it wouldn't compare to receiving one email or letter like the one I got today. I heard from a mother who's lost a baby to heart complications. She said she's using me as an example to help pull her from the hole of despair. A day where I make a difference in the life of another is a day lived well.

> A DAY WHERE
> I MAKE A
> DIFFERENCE
> IN THE LIFE OF
> ANOTHER IS A
> DAY LIVED WELL.

APRIL 17, 2008

I'm anxious for Jonnae's doctor's appointment tomorrow. She has no appetite. It makes sense to me that the headaches, nausea, and fatigue have to do with hunger and lack of nutrition, but I'll feel better getting an opinion from the doctor.

The last few days she's experienced mood swings that were common with the steroid use before the transplant. When those moments come up, I'm tough with her. Not ugly, just real. It's tough to get her to settle down and listen sometimes, but she's always appreciative once we get through the talk. She wants to be "normal" so bad. But the truth of the matter is her normal is never going to be like anyone else's normal.

One of the influences that Jonnae's inherited from me is the need to be perfect - the best. The Joy Calendar was doing the opposite of what it's designed to do. It was stealing her joy. She wanted to win and was struggling with the fact that she might not get the prize.

Whether or not she gets the $20 prize, she's still the winner. She's blowing the others out of the water. But she couldn't see that. Through tears she said, "I'm competitive mom. Just like you!"

I replied with a smile, "Yes, babe. But I've never been about the prize. I've always been about being the best. It's not even about what the others can do. I know if I do MY best, it's probably enough to win, because most people don't drive themselves to their highest potential."

That's a lesson that's been really tough for me to wrap my head (and heart) around. What it's boiled down to is outside validation and recognition. It's robbed me of joy. I'm better about it now and want to make sure she doesn't take as long as I did to get it. Joy can't reside with focus on the wrong thing.

Later I found a small piece of dark chocolate with a handwritten note from Jonnae inside my Bible: "You are one of my GREATEST joys and the devil could never take that away."

DEVASTATING DEVELOPMENT

APRIL 18, 2008

Today's visit went as expected. The doctor explained that the symptoms Jonnae was feeling were indeed typical with the steroid schedule Jonnae's been on. She gave us an exuberant, "Be off and we'll see ya next month."

We had an enjoyable lunch with my sister and two nieces and came home to go to Layne's ballgame. While there, I got a phone call from the doctor. She said Jonnae's platelet count dropped to 22,000 and she was worried. She said a slide of Jonnae's cells didn't look good. We're returning to Cincinnati for a bone marrow aspiration on Monday.

Jonnae could have some funky virus, but by the sound of the doctor's voice and the choice of her words, I think she fears leukemia's back. She apologized repetitively and asked me if I was okay. I assured her, I AM. I don't know how to explain it other than God's prepared me to play this *game* His way. I trust Him as my Coach completely.

As I watched the rest of Layne's game, I observed how both the batters and pitchers look to their coach for a sign. Even the pros look to the Coach before EVERY pitch. God's calling the shots and I'll continue to step out of the box and look to Him before every single pitch. It doesn't matter how much time we have left in the game. My eyes are on the eternal prize. Our Coach has prepared a victory crown for each of us. That's all that matters.

I haven't told her yet. The right time did not present itself tonight. Is there a right time? No, not really. But it certainly wasn't tonight. She was giggly and feeling better than she has for days. I couldn't bear to deflate her spirit. I won't be surprised by her reaction tomorrow. It could go either way. I expect her to cry at first and then throw on her shield of strength. But then again, I'm not so inhuman I don't realize she may be too tired to fight anymore.

This morning I read "God in Heaven appoints each person's work." John 3:27(NLT) Adversities happen in our lives as a push towards that work. Sometimes pain is divinely woven into our lives. If we let it do what God intended, it aids us to complete our work.

This war with leukemia has always been a part of God's plan. It's necessary for my family to go through it in order to do our appointed work. We can reject it or accept it. We can fight against Him, or devote our lives to please Him. I will do the latter and try my hardest to lead the rest of my family to do the same.

APRIL 19, 2008

This morning I said to Jonnae, "The doctor called. Your platelets have dropped. She wants us to check into the hospital tomorrow for a bone marrow aspiration on Monday."

My eyes looking directly into hers, I watched her closely. She never faltered, flinched, nothing.

She said, "I'm bruised and my platelets are getting chewed up. I'm not worried."

And she isn't. She's ready to pack up for a several day stay and wants to go paint pottery today. She continues to blow me away. We should all follow her example. Let go and let God! Find joy, stay positive, and have no fear!

We experienced a wonderful day because Jonnae chose to create one. She shows no signs of worry, fear, frustration, disappointment, or anything other than complete confidence. She's proven she's strong enough to get through whatever happens. The thought of low platelets and tests for leukemia have not shaken her.

She, Lydia and I had a great time painting pottery. We went to Olive Garden and shopped around at Hobby Lobby and the Dollar Tree. She was rather ornery and giddy today, a lot more than usual. She was in a fabulous mood. As her mother, I could tell it was no act. It was genuine joy. Once again, I'm reminded to mimic the heart and mind of a child, particularly mine.

Nolan even surprised me today. I told him Jonnae had gotten a bad report and they were running tests. Without skipping a beat, he said, "Do I need to give her more marrow?" That was it! And that's not typical of how Nolan responds to such news. When her diagnosis and first relapse occurred, he was angry, retreated, and didn't want to talk about anything.

In church tonight I told God I wanted to follow Him and know the signs, but that Jonnae's and Nolan's lead were so much easier. They aren't overanalyzing. They've made it clear what they intend to do and where they're going. But then my mind flashed back to the first bone marrow aspiration she had after relapse, when she told me God wanted her in Heaven.

Don't put a question mark where God put a period. I'll continue to submit to whatever plan He has orchestrated, not questioning why. I'll try to figure out how I best execute my part in it and contribute to the lives of not just my children, but everyone I can.

APRIL 20, 2008

Jonnae's slept a lot today, on the trip up and since we've been here. In the car she was napping and I was listening to the music I love so much--those words of faith, scripture, and conviction that really speak to me.

I was listening to "The Voice of Truth" by Casting Crowns. When the words about David and Goliath fell on my ears, I came to attention. Jonnae is our "David." As armies of prayer warriors surround her, worried, fearful, and in doubt, she says, "Enough already! The giant is no match for me!"

She's our Lil' Davie. (When I called her David earlier and explained my reference, she told me to call her Davie.) I pray that Davie will be victorious once more and the giant's going to be buried forever.

APRIL 21, 2008

The *giant* lives. Jonnae has one last stone to take him out.

The bone marrow aspiration has confirmed leukemia's back. Actually, this means it was never completely gone. Apparently one cell can be hiding out. It splits, multiplies, and eventually explodes into blasts of cells. That's what's happened. So here we go again.

We were given the news and immediately Jonnae's response was, "Well, I've gone through this twice. I can do it again." How does this child take such news and not let it faze her?

Each time she relapses, the odds are more against her. The doctors aren't hopeful and have painted a grim picture. It hasn't shaken her. She's a ROCK. The words amazing, strong, unbelievable aren't enough to adequately describe this child. I'm blessed to call her daughter.

I don't want to think about losing her, but I must not turn a blind eye to that possibility. I feel I'm as prepared as a mother can be, but don't really know if I am. How could I be? All I can do is F.R.O.G. Live by His word, knowing and trusting that we are exactly where we're supposed to be.

Chemo will begin next week. We're going home tomorrow and will recheck labs on Thursday. She's planning a sleep over for Friday and looking forward to watching Nolan get ready for his prom on Saturday. Sunday, we'll have a family reunion for all relatives to see her, possibly for the last time. In typical Jonnae fashion, it will be a full weekend.

APRIL 22, 2008

How many cleansing breaths can a person take in a day? I think I've broken a record I don't care to have. Many wars, all at once: war with Leuk, war of the heart, war for strength, and a war of the voices. A constant tug of war ensues between hope and fear, fitness and fatigue, gratitude and pain, joy and sadness, and strength and weakness.

I watched yesterday as they punctured Jonnae's back four times, trying to get enough marrow for a sample. Even then it was miniscule. These procedures normally take one try and cause her a couple days of pain. I can imagine what pain will result from four tries. The pain she feels from the punctures is overshadowed by the pain of the evidence that's come from them.

Today they had trouble finding a vein for her chemo. As I watched her get stuck another three times, tears rolling down her face, I couldn't help but ask why is this lovely child being asked to go through so much? Why can't something go smoothly, without complications? Who is she paying a price for? I'm lost, Lord!

In response, my mind was filled with Mary. She was asked to watch her child suffer, too--a horrendous, violent death caused by sin and hatred. No one is doing this to Jonnae out of hate. Our suffering is nowhere near the magnitude of that of Mary or Jesus. They carried their crosses. They trusted. They felt the love of their Father. So must we.

I've been here before. We've been here before. I've had this same tug of war before. The voice of despair is relentless as it tries to take over the voice of hope. It's been a long time since despair has won. It's not going to claim another victory. I will win this one, too. Not without tears and more heartache, but I will prevail.

I was running on the treadmill early this morning at the RMH. There is a mirrored wall directly in front of it. Normally, the image of a strong woman is looking back at me and gives me a turbo kick of energy. The strength of that physical body spills over to my emotional and spiritual ones. Today I saw that image, and although it looked strong, I didn't feel any power coming from it. My grip is slipping, I need to hang on!

Jonnae's quieter today. I sense her wall crumbling too. I need to let her know, whatever she's feeling, it's okay. I need her to know I'm here for her whenever she's ready to share her innermost thoughts. Even though I don't have the answers, I pray God gives her some. Whether it's peace knowing she's going to be victorious, or peace knowing she will join Him in Heaven, I pray for my baby's peace.

APRIL 23, 2008

Last night, I said to Jonnae, "Keep your eyes on the Coach. As long as Peter was looking at Jesus and trusting, he was walking on water. Don't doubt or you will start to sink, baby."

Her reply was, "I haven't doubted, mom, and I've started to sink twice. It's hard."

We had a short spell of tears. Not much was said, just a quiet understanding between the two of us that this is sad and difficult.

We've announced to the friends and family coming to the reunion that they're to put on their "happy faces" and carry on like this is any other family get together. We've been cracking jokes about me being a bouncer and forcing people to leave the party if their energy is negative or heavy.

We've come up with a onetime warning and then "you're out" rule. Normally we don't mind lifting others out of their sorrow or distress, but this is a difficult time for us. It would hurt Jonnae more than help her. My girl is the best there is at focusing on the good and celebration. We will have nothing but fun for her this weekend.

APRIL 24, 2008

Jonnae's appointment went pretty much as expected, but did come with a few surprises. The doctor found a new protocol for Jonnae. It includes a different drug than the one we were initially looking at and has a higher success rate. It's still going to be a concern with her liver. The success rate of these studies is based on subjects who are second relapse patients who haven't made it one month drug free before relapse. We didn't know there had been enough patients like her to have a study to guide us. Also, there were no leukemia cells in her lab work today.

Mornings are always the roughest for me. Waking up to the harsh reality of where we are yet again takes some real, "I will not quit" perseverance. I refuel and pump up that spiritual muscle with prayer, reflection, and my morning workouts.

On my way home, I prayed fervently for a God hug today. I've been so longing of one. I ended up getting several. God is so good.

APRIL 25, 2008

It's been a good day; different but good.

Jonnae wanted a new top for this weekend. We were at the mall when she said, "I would do this every day of my life, if I could."

I said, "What's that, baby?"

She said, "Just spend the day with you."

I told her how much I love her and we continued to enjoy our time together.

I received a strong message before bed last night and it's been heavy on my mind today. I was watching a recorded sermon and it began with David and Goliath. This after I've just deemed my girl our modern day Davie. The message it delivered was very powerful and has me wondering if the chemo isn't like Saul's armor.

Even though it's the weapon typically used, it doesn't appear to be what's going to work with this giant called, Leuk. In true "let go, let God" fashion, what if she did like David? Set down the expected artillery, and relied on God? Either let Him heal with His miraculous hand, or call her home?

Jonnae's so mature, so willing to be obedient to the Coach, and so strong. She can talk candidly and openly about anything. We watched the recorded sermon together and discussed her options. We're in agreement that she's the one who needs direction from God, not me. We'll be patient as we continue to pray for a clear sign for her.

I was deep in thought while working out tonight. I don't see why God wouldn't choose to heal this child. I can envision the nonbelievers becoming believers by the droves if He performed a miracle in her. What could possibly be gained by His not saving her? The only thing I came up with is as a nation, as a world, we've fallen away from Him. Maybe there's a shortage of souls making it through the pearly gates to join Him? Maybe it's just time for her to know something better than what we know here on earth. She mentions tooth pain and headaches bothering her constantly. Are we are supposed to keep subjecting her to more suffering when the stronger chemo hasn't been able to take the giant called Leuk down?

Despite her discomfort, she's having a good time with her friends tonight. We're embracing the weekend and having fun while we wait. In the next couple of days, if STRONG discernment doesn't come to her, that we should step out of the boat and F.R.O.G. for healing, we'll proceed with chemo on Monday.

APRIL 26, 2008

Last night, Jonnae lost her grip and the real struggle began. I laid down behind Jonnae to watch a movie with her and her friends, and could see she was crying. We acted like we were taking Sassy out and, once outside, she broke down.

She said she was stuck and didn't know what to do. She's tired of feeling so bad from leukemia and the chemo, but she doesn't want to die. Her sobbing continued and I found myself repeating the same words she's heard from me over and over again.

"Keep your eyes on the Coach. This is exactly what the enemy wants. For you to fear! God doesn't want you to be afraid, baby. I know it's hard, but shake off the enemy and grasp the hand of God. He loves you, HE REALLY DOES LOVE YOU! I know it seems like He's abandoned you, but I promise He hasn't."

She was tired, her head and mouth had been bothering her all day from Vincristine. I encouraged her to go to bed and offered to explain to her company that she was not feeling well. I told her she would feel better in the morning.

Only she didn't. She was too tired to get out of bed. I took the girls home and when I got back she had decided to take a long bath. She said it wasn't as relaxing as she thought it would be, but she was feeling better.

I asked her if she was praying, reading her devotions for encouragement, or journaling to clear her head. She admitted she hadn't been. I told her I felt like she was on the phone with the enemy and God was on call waiting. I told her to hang up with fear and switch over to the other line and hear what God had to say. He can't reach you if you don't answer His call. In times like this He doesn't want us to run *away* from Him, He wants us to run TO Him. She shared with me that she felt like she would be a quitter if she DIDN'T do the chemo.

Then I said, "It's your choice, baby. If your gut is saying go for it with chemo, then GO FOR IT. I just want you to fight, honey. It's your call what weapon you use. But fear won't work."

She found her grip again.

While she was in the tub, I waited on her, the way she often does me. She'll bring me a glass of water or maybe a glass of wine if I'm up for one. She might turn on the music or hand me my razor. Anything I've forgotten to do before getting into the water, she takes care of for me.

I was taking her a bottle of water and a piece of chocolate and decided to stick a scripture Post-it on her bottle. It said, "This is the day the Lord has made. Rejoice and be glad in it." It put a smile on her face. The first one I had seen for a while. I was relieved as she said, "Thank you."

I also put a note in her medicine cabinet for her to find later: "Do not fear the future, God is already there." I could see her getting traction and coming out of the rut. Once again we're ready to fight.

We watched Nolan get ready for prom

and followed him to the meeting place for pictures with friends. Jonnae's spirits continued to soar. As a result, she's made more entries in her "happy book." She's a warrior and the fight is on!

We've made the decision to do the chemo here versus returning to Cincinnati. She wouldn't be likely to get out of the hospital if we went back to Cincy. Here they'll allow us to come back and forth since we aren't but a 15-minute commute away.

We're to check in at 8 in the morning. They'll give her platelets to prep her for surgery and place another central line. Chemo will start either tomorrow afternoon or Tuesday.

APRIL 28, 2008

Yesterday, the family reunion was absolutely wonderful. Jonnae's smile was bright, her spirits up, and a good time had by all. We had good weather, a good turnout, and got back home late last night.

She's been the warrior we're used to seeing. Today was another test Jonnae's aced with flying colors. Nothing went as planned.

This morning her platelets were lower than they've been since transplant and her WBC is just over 1. She needed two units of platelets before today's procedure could take place. Poor thing NPOed all day for a scheduled central line placement that was supposed to happen at 1:30. She wasn't taken back to OR until 3:30, where they gave her anesthesia and sent us to the waiting room.

They got to see Jonnae's true colors today. Before they took her back she impressed them with her knowledge of all the meds they use in her anesthesia cocktail. She could teach a class on all of them. Then she had me taking pictures of her as she started feeling silly. They wheeled her back to OR as she smiled, held her Rosary, and proclaimed her love for us.

They came back out only 15 minutes later to tell us the two units only took her platelets to 44,000.(they needed them to be at least 60K) The procedure is cancelled until tomorrow morning. We went into

Jonnae's room to comfort her. But instead of showing disappointment with the postponement, she said, "Wasn't that fast?" and smiled that amazing smile of hers. She continued to focus on the positive, saying now she could eat.

She's still talking about yesterday and how much fun she had. We've had several relatives with hurt feelings, anger, resentment, and bitterness towards one another. It's gone on for far too long. Yesterday was a day they left the past behind. Hopefully they'll never pick it back up.

I truly believe part of the reason for Jonnae's suffering is to show us the way to live. In spite of everything, we are to love. Her cross is meant to show us how to free ourselves from the snares of the devil and chains of negativity. Christ said, "Love one another as I have loved you!" Everyone did yesterday. What a blessing.

APRIL 29, 2008

Things went smoothly today with Jonnae's line placement and chemo was administered this afternoon. Her steroids are already kicking in. What a beast they are. Her cravings are uncontrollable and food's all she thinks of. She had a milkshake and banana bread immediately after her procedure today, followed with brownies and cheese ravioli.

The sweet treats are always a test for me as a sugar addict and past binger. Being surrounded by the junk food Jonnae eats presents a never ending challenge for me. Often she sends me on a run for something sweet and before I'm even back her appetite has disappeared. So then, the food is left to tempt me with not much to divert my attention in this small room. I'm holding steady. I have come too far and feel too good, to hand my joy to an apple turnover.

Jonnae's spirits are great. She's still ever the trooper, fighting this war one day at a time. The grimness of everyone here, with their low expectations of her outcome, is not affecting her or me. I'm keeping my eyes on the Coach (and on her--she's a rock) and am doing well also.

MAY 1, 2008

When I wake up to devotions like this:

"I am the resurrection and the life. He who believes in me will live, even though he dies." John 11:25 (NIV)

Surprisingly, I find the strength to say, "I hear you Lord! I get it and I'm okay! I'm not afraid of letting Jonnae go. Just lead me."

It can only be that our Heavenly Father's preparing me, gently letting me know the time is coming. But then I look to my daughter, I hear her words, and see her eyes, and she truly believes she's going to slay this giant. I'm confused. I want to believe, too. Why is my spiritual intuitiveness telling me something different than hers is? Our Coach is the same.

Johnny says it's because I have more information. But does that matter? Isn't it only what SHE believes that matters? I believe she can slay this giant if God performs a miracle. I'm just not sure He wants to. I want to believe He does, but I keep getting "calls" that tell me different. Is that lacking faith? One hand says it's not, the other says it is.

The only thing certain is that I trust Him. I trust Him and I want to do what pleases Him. Is it pleasing to Him that I continually ask for her to be one of His miracles? For freedom from Leuk, when I feel He has a different plan? The voice of God tells me one thing, the voice of the world sometimes tells me another, and the voice of the enemy still something different. At times, it's difficult to decipher whose voice I'm hearing.

I pray Jonnae is left here to deliver her testimony personally, not that I'm the one who is to share it as her legacy. Am I being a spoiled child? Am I annoying my Father? He knows I'm not wanting to. I realize I'm being selfish and as any child who's respectful and loving of their Father would, I will accept His answer. In the meantime, I will enjoy the gift she is to me.

MAY 2, 2008

Yesterday the doctors were certain we'd be here for a while. Today, a different plan's been revealed. After "tanking her up" with platelets and blood, they are sending us home tomorrow. We'll come in every other day for counts and check her bone marrow in a couple of weeks.

Jonnae was beaming with the news. Of course, I'm anxious to return home as well. I have a little anxiety about leaving, but that's something I've experienced and gotten over several times already. A lot can happen in a day, or even a couple of hours, that could change the doctors' minds. But as of now, the plan is for us to go home tomorrow. One day at a time, we'll march forward.

MAY 4, 2008

Sometimes God supernaturally opens doors, sometimes He closes them. It's always to propel us to a higher place. He doesn't always create the problem, but He will allow it to happen. It can be turned around to work for His Divine purpose. We can choose to be defeated by it, or to use it to rise to higher ground. A big mountain means big victory, as long as we continue to climb. We are doing things we didn't even know we were capable of because we are being "pushed out of the nest" and "forced to fly."

Jonnae had fun driving me in the golf cart tonight, while Johnny and I enjoyed a round of nine holes. Her energy seems to be fairly normal. Overall, we're feeling really good and just waiting for Leuk to give up the fight. He should be getting tired of his butt getting kicked right about now. Hopefully he'll throw up the white flag within a couple of weeks.

MAY 5, 2008

Jonnae's white cell count and her platelets are way down. That's not good for her immunity, but it means the chemo's doing what we expected it would do. There's no way to wipe Leuk out without driving the counts down.

Jonnae thinks she's in remission. She said, "I FEEL it" and followed with, "I think I'm going to cry."

I don't know if it's remission she's feeling, but she was overcome by something divine. It was a beautiful moment. Several times today she smiled and said, "It's a really good day." And it was!

The Ultimate Gift Family Experience for April was focus on joy. May is the month for giving in all ways. Jonnae and I will still continue with our participation. We have the opportunity to give several times a day. Whatever it is we don't want to do, we'll do it anyway, and offer it up as a prayer, a gift, for someone. It's a gift that will keep on giving.

MAY 6, 2008

Not without trials, not without having jumped hurdles, but Jonnae goes to bed tonight with another victorious day behind her. She continues to amaze and inspire the medical professionals who care for her. She walked out of the hospital today, (no wheelchair, thank you) after three "peg" shots, a spinal tap, and a bone marrow aspiration. After resting a couple of hours at home, she fixed a dessert as a gift for a friend. She's embracing May's "giving project."

The left hand didn't know what the right hand was doing at the hospital today. I was quite proud of how both Jonnae and I handled it. We could have easily gotten worked up. We held our composure, all of course by the grace of God, and kept a constant eye on Him.

Without faith no one can please God. Anyone who comes to God must believe that he is real and that he rewards those who truly want to find him. Hebrews 11:6 (NCV)

I don't think there is any greater feeling than reading scripture and knowing you are living it. It's the most exhilarating powerful truth there is to know. It's what makes life beautiful, regardless of the trials and tribulations that come. God is awesome, His Word life giving, and all is right with my soul.

MAY 7, 2008

"Live your life in such a way that when your feet hit the floor in the morning, Satan shudders & says, 'Oh no....she's awake!!' "

I can't wait to share that quote with Jonnae in the morning. She's fast asleep, after a full day.

We got a call reporting Jonnae's latest aspiration results. Jonnae's marrow is 90% leukemia blast cells. Not good. Not a lot of marrow there, either. Again, not good! But we're told by an encouraging doctor not to be disheartened. It's way too early to expect response from the chemo. We may not see much change next week either, when they do another bone marrow aspiration to check again. We'll continue on with the action plan as laid out. God knows the plays. We continue to trust Him and give thanks for our place on His team.

We had an amazing night, as we've been made a part of another awesome team. Team Transformation. Bill Phillips himself, the author of *Body For Life* and *Transformation*, surprised us with a visit tonight. HE WAS HERE... in our home... He gave Jonnae an early birthday present, a Nissan Sentra (her dream car) and announced me as one of his Transformation Champions. Jonnae was beside herself with joy. We all were.

If only I could give you the feelings in my heart. If only I could plug into you so that you may know what we know and feel, and experience what we're experiencing. I heard Jonnae say, as Bill's crew interviewed her. "We've had the most amazing day. We will never forget it." I'm certain we won't!

MAY 8, 2008

Jonnae's had a rough day. I believe we've both caught a stomach bug from one of the boys, only her body doesn't have the ability to fight it like mine does.

She's wanted to get sick all day in hopes it would allow her to feel better. She did only moments ago and is sleeping now. I pray she rests comfortably tonight and wakes in the morning with no queasiness. I called the doctors about it, they weren't concerned. We have an appointment in the morning, anyway. Had it been an ordinary day, the discomfort would have been harder to deal with, but this was no ordinary day. We're still on cloud nine from the most amazing experience we were blessed with last night.

Bill posed a question as I began one of his challenges in '04. "On a scale of 1-10 where are you? What is holding you back from being your best self, a *ten*?" Even leukemia is not holding Jonnae or me as her mother, back from being our best. Not on our own, but with the strength God provides, we will continue to push for our *ten*.

MAY 9, 2008

At 2a.m., I got a text from Jonnae, asking me to come to her room (The cell phones are our grown up version of baby monitors). She was running a fever, so we headed straight for the hospital.

Bacteria are growing in her blood. Cultures grew quickly, proving the bacteria are strong. This isn't uncommon. The "healthy" bacteria we have on our skin and in our mouths create havoc when counts are low. The doctors reminded us last week that a fever was pretty much inevitable with the low counts, so we're not alarmed. She'll remain on an IV antibiotic for 2 to 3 weeks but will be released from the hospital as soon as the labs come back negative and she's been without fever for 48 hours.

Our hearts are full of God and our love for Him. Neither leukemia nor the enemy will be allowed to set up pity or sorrow to weigh us down.

MAY 10, 2008

Today has not been a great day for our warrior, but today's been better than yesterday. Her stomach's still queasy and she's just not up to speed. Her temperature is holding and her blood pressure not as low. Last night they were monitoring it pretty closely. After MRIs and CTs they've ruled out typhlitis and are keeping her NPO until tomorrow, so they can monitor her colon.

It's been a long day. Sedentary living works for the patient who's not feeling well, but not so much for the healthier, active parent. It's difficult not having something to occupy my mind and keep it from one way dialogue. I found myself asking questions again today; questions that I can't answer and may not want answers to. They come more frequently with the restriction of her hospital room.

I had an epiphany tonight as Jonnae and I were watching a movie. There are a lot of movies about cancer and dying. Somehow they manage to find us with timing that seems orchestrated by a higher power. I don't believe in coincidences and often when these movies show up in these ways, I feel as if God's trying to tell me something.

Jonnae doesn't seem to read as much into the movie's events, or words, as I do. It's difficult to allow myself to feel the emotion these films conjure up in front of her. Mostly because I don't want to trigger a thought she's not having, but also because Jonnae hates to see me cry. Sometimes I manage to let the tears flow without her noticing. Times that I haven't been able to, I've been able to give a partial explanation that's honest, without revealing the main reason I'm crying.

Tonight the room was dark. I wasn't lying in bed right next to her as I often am, (she's too uncomfortable) so I let the tears flow. I told myself, "You know this isn't like you, but it's been a different kind of day. Just let it out. Go ahead. Feel the sorrow. Allow yourself to be something other than strong! Make this your 'free' day."

I couldn't do it for more than a few minutes. In reasoning with myself as to why I couldn't, this is what came to me. In the BFL challenges, a free day is suggested. This is a day to forget about exercising, planning, or restrictive eating. Basically, let go for a day.

Eat what you want or need. Only what I've found is, it's never what I think it'll be. It's never really satisfying. It certainly doesn't get me any closer to my goal. In the same way, the crying wasn't making me feel any better. It was making me feel worse. I would rather think about our Father's grace and mercy, and His rewards for serving Him, than my sorrow as a mother. Feeling sadness just wasn't the choice I needed to make tonight.

There's nothing wrong with "free days" or crying, but just as my habits of clean eating kick in to keep me from falling off the "healthy wagon," my habits of remaining in gratitude, and in the embrace of my Heavenly Father, keep me from falling into a deep pit of sorrow. I'll pass on the "free day" for now.

MAY 11, 2008

Jonnae has been NPO again all day today. Poor thing, it seems so cruel to put a child on steroids that make them obsessed with food, and tell them they can't eat. Yesterday she was feeling nauseous and didn't want anything. Today she's been more like herself on steroids, and is sensitive and irritable because she's hungry.

Apparently, she has an infection in her gut and food will feed the bacteria. They want her gut to have a break and therefore are starving it. I'm having a hard time agreeing with their philosophy. She has hunger headaches, she's nauseous from having an empty stomach, and has no energy from lack of nutrition. The body is made to have food to function. It is so frustrating.

It's encouraging that she wants food today. She hasn't for the past three or four. I'm going to stay focused on that and expect a better day tomorrow.

I awoke this morning to find a Mother's Day E-card from her. She had ordered it days ago.

She also made a CD for me of our favorite Christian music. While listening to it, I could feel my heart breaking as I thought about her and how I want better for her. I want so desperately to be able to heal her, for us to be able to move forward, happy and healthy, forever.

As soon as my heart begins to sink, there is a warmth, strength, and LOVE, that I know is HIM. He picks it up, holds it, and calms it. The heart break is replaced with peace. It's as though God is crying with me, wraps me in His embrace, and then, all is right again. He is my strong tower, shelter, and refuge. He is my strength. His love is like the sun, breaking up the clouds of sorrow.

I pray for the *SON* to shine tomorrow, as we all seek to LIVE a brighter, fuller day. I pray for my baby girl to take giant steps forward in her healing. I pray that I focus on my every word, action, and deed, so that my Heavenly Father shines through me and gives those around us the strength and comfort they need. I want them to experience what I have found. His love is AMAZING!

MAY 12, 2008

Last night the doctors were very concerned about Jonnae's low heart rate. They put her on oxygen before doing an EKG. This would be unsettling any time of day, but occurred after we had been in deep sleep. Awaking with this news was startling.

Sleeping was pointless, so I logged on to the computer. Just as I did, the first devotion for the day popped up on my screen. "I tell you the truth, this day you will be with me in paradise!" Luke 23:43 (NIV)

How else would I interpret that? My morning was heavy as I wondered if there was more in store for the day than what was apparent by watching her. Although she's uncomfortable and tired, she doesn't look like she's on the brink of death. The sign seemed so strong though. My mind stayed consumed with "get ready." As the day went on and the doctors came in for rounds, it became clear that today is NOT the day.

Her infection and temperature are gone and her labs came back negative. The fluids they had her on caused the issues with her blood pressure, so no concern there anymore either.

She was allowed clear liquids today and has tolerated them fine. Tomorrow they will advance her diet and allow her to have food. The big concern now is her liver. Her bilirubin is high and they are afraid to administer her scheduled chemo tomorrow. They'll wait to see what the lab report indicates, but apparently her liver is not functioning at a level to tolerate chemo.

The question is will leukemia have too big an advantage if we don't proceed with the drugs? A bone marrow aspiration is going to be done. If the leukemia hasn't weakened, we may need to take the risk and go on.

As her mother, the one who's connected to her in the most unimaginable, beautiful way, I don't stay in a place of darkness, sorrow, and pain. In looking to the life of Christ and his mother, Mary, I realize our cross is not near the weight theirs was. I look to them as the example of how to be. I know our rewards for following them will be great. Even with a cross such as ours, LIFE IS MAGNIFICENT. It is beyond human understanding, but that's what happens when one chooses to follow the way of Christ, instead of the way of the world. It's a shame more people won't try it.

Before she napped today, Jonnae told me with confidence she'll be out of here by Sunday. Joel Osteen will be in town and we've been looking forward to attending his service for a very long time. She has told me, and several of her friends, she'll bust out of here to go see him and they can't stop her.

Her fighting spirit is so cool to witness. She is a young, sweet, small girl, but her conviction is always bold, confident, and strong. I asked if she had considered the risk of going with no counts. Her white count and ANC are both 0. We'll use a special entrance where there are no crowds. She'll wear a mask and sit in a wheel chair away from everyone. This IS doable and it's going to happen. Anything is possible with God.

MAY 13, 2008

Jonnae's had a better day, but her stomach's causing her discomfort and seems to be swelling. This is concerning. They've done a liver ultrasound to see if she's again a victim of V.O.D. (Veno Occlusive Disease). She amazed the doctors and defied all odds in January and says she will again if V.O.D. has returned. If V.O.D. is ruled out, she'll get chemo tomorrow. It was scheduled for today, but postponed because of her high bilirubin.

We informed the doctors that we're making arrangements to go see Joel Osteen on Sunday, with precautions in place. They were hesitant, but understand we're serious. I'm certain the service will be a spiritual feast and we're not about to miss the opportunity to be nourished by it. At this point, I can't imagine anything better than soul food.

She's not eating much, even though the restrictions have been lifted. She informed me this morning, "I feel it, and I'm getting better!"

Earlier I believed her; tonight she's less convincing.

I pray she's well enough to see Joel this weekend. I pray we all continue to move through this storm, with strength and refuge our Heavenly Father provides.

MAY 14, 2008

The ultrasound concluded there wasn't any V.O.D. Thank God! So she got the scheduled chemo for today. She's on high blood pressure medication and antibiotics. She's not been able to eat anything. Not because of restrictions, but because her stomach is distended and she's too uncomfortable to put anything in it. She's been given a laxative and hopefully will experience some relief by morning.

Focusing on something that's more positive, Jonnae's counts are slowly coming up. I laughed when the doctor said, "so, they may be up by Sunday," like that's going to make a difference in our plans. I can't believe that they don't know by now you can't keep a Taylor down.

Today, as I vowed to stay on the piece of cardio equipment I was on for 20 minutes, I heard myself saying, "You are not getting off of this machine! I don't care how tired you are. Do it for Jonnae and all of the sick kids pushing themselves through Hell today. In comparison, this is nothing!"

I thought about the difference between where I am today versus yesterday. I was flying so high yesterday and today, I'm struggling to keep my feet under me. I'm reminded once again of golf. I can shoot a really sweet round, where every shot seems effortless. The swing is smooth and the click of the club as it hits the ball is proof positive I've just hit a sweet shot. The gorgeous flight of the ball, and the scorecard, reflect a beautiful round of pars and birdies.

Then out of nowhere a double, or worse, triple bogey happens. It doesn't make sense. Where the heck did the swing change? It's imperative to maintain focus, stay loose, and not get uptight. That's how I'm keeping my spirit up today. Can't say I've mastered the practice on the golf course, but I did well in real life today.

I acknowledged I was having a rough morning and even though I couldn't pinpoint where the "swing changed," I decided to focus, relax, and loosen up. Let go and let God! I'm keeping my eyes on the pin, not worrying about the rough, the water, or out of bounds. A wonderful golf instructor, Caroline Gowan, once told me, "If you focus on where you don't want to hit the ball, that's where you'll hit it. You go where your focus is."

I'm keeping my eyes on victory. I can't control Leuk. I can't do the job of the doctors. I don't know what the future holds for Jonnae. Ultimately the calls are God's to make. His plan is perfect. On His team there is no losing.

MAY 15, 2008

Jonnae's had a better day. Even though she's gotten platelets every day since we've been back, her platelets were very low this morning. Her stomach discomfort isn't as bad as yesterday, but she still isn't eating much.

These long hospital stays, with me here and Johnny at work, take their toll on the other children, also. Happenings at school are affecting them more than they normally would. Johnny is spending tomorrow and Saturday night here with Jonnae. Maybe I can work on healing the kids' emotional states at home. They have a low tolerance of one another and school work is slipping. It's understandable.

MAY 16, 2008

Jonnae's gotten so much better, they're talking about discharging us on Sunday. She's eaten a bit more, up and walking more, and not nearly as uncomfortable. Her temperature is down and even though her blood pressure likes to jump around, the doctors are not concerned.

She's gearing up for Sunday's big event and has prepared a list of things for me to get ready. (Clothes, bandana, jewelry, etc.) Joel Osteen has been a big source of "fuel" for our *fires* the last 3 years. It's going to be an unforgettable experience, no doubt.

My excessive talking can be annoying to people at times, myself included. I've been annoyed with the endless self-chatter going on in my head this week. It reminds me of ballgames where parents are adamant about shouting unnecessary things to their kids.

The coaches are there to instruct the children, but parents want to chime in and overrule. It's not enjoyable. That's what's going on in this little head of mine. I can't turn it off. I told someone this morning it's like those remotes that don't always work. You think you've turned off the television, but the screen just 'clicks' to black and comes back up. If anyone has ever thought, "just get to the point, wrap it up," they'd have a hard time being me. I can't get away from myself. I refer to my analytical mind as a "hamster on a wheel." Lately, it's even wearing me out.

One of the things that keeps coming to mind is this weekend's event with Joel Osteen. Is God preparing us for a grand finale? Are these "heavy hitters," like Bill Phillips and Joel Osteen, coming into our lives for a reason we've not realized? What is it? I'm distracted by so much, the doctors, statistics, symptoms, and signs. It's unsettling to say the least. I've got to stop jumping ahead and trying to figure out the score. The only place I find peace is with my eyes on the Coach.

MAY 17, 2008

We're still on the mark for going home tomorrow. The highs and lows have been more extreme this week. I'm a bit worn. I've noticed it in the gym and in the way I've responded to the kids. I've also found it in my will for her to keep fighting.

Yesterday, one of the doctors reminded me that each time she relapses she goes through even more "crap" (his word) than she's had to before. To expect her to go through 2 - 3 more years of this, as they are suggesting will be necessary, seems selfish. Do we really want to drag her through this?

I don't want to give up on her, or on God, but as I think of what lies ahead for her, my family at home, and me, too, I feel my fatigue. I find myself asking God for the verdict NOW. And then I get sick to my stomach thinking about what it might be.

At home, my kids are all running on low levels, too. I know we're in need of some high octane fuel, but I'm not certain how to get it to last longer. We're not getting the same mileage we were.

My husband, our other children, and I, may find ourselves dragging, but Little Miss Jonnae doesn't appear to be. This week is toughest on her and she hasn't cried, complained, or shown any signs of weariness in spirit. As a matter of fact, it's been quite the opposite. When they ran tests for V.O.D., she simply stated to me, "Mom, I don't have V.O.D. And if I do, I beat it before, I'll beat it again."

Her hair's come out again, AGAIN. It had just barely begun to "sprout" and came out in a rather odd way. It all fell out, except this one little strip right at her hairline with a point in the middle from her Widow's Peak. She asked if someone would bring a hair trimmer up here because she's "tired of having a mustache on her forehead." She is so darn cute and funny.

The *student* has surpassed the *teacher*. I learn something from her every day.

SURPRISING COMPLICATIONS

MAY 19, 2008

Jonnae is in ICU. We didn't make it to Joel Osteen's service. We got home from the hospital yesterday around 2:30. Jonnae wanted to take a nap before getting ready for the big event. When I awoke her an hour later, she could not see. She was scared and delusional. I rushed her to the hospital ER, where she became more delirious. They did a CAT scan and, after 3 hours of waiting, sent us to ICU. We were not there for very long before she had a horrifying seizure. I have never witnessed anything so horrible in my life. She was in a weird coma-like state for hours. This morning she's not herself at all (very defiant and still not recognizing who we are).

As I was driving Jonnae to ER, many of our friends were driving to a restaurant where we originally planned to meet. My youngest daughter, Lydia, was with them and was still able to go back stage and meet Joel

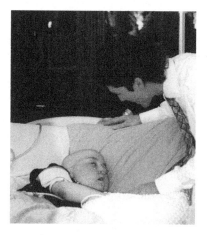

after the service. She gave him a gift we had prepared for him and a letter Jonnae had written. He came to the hospital and prayed with us. What a generous man. It was late and he could have easily gone on, but he chose to bless us instead.

Apparently, Jonnae's suffering from PRES (*Posterior Reversible Encephalopathy Syndrome)*, a fairly common state that can accompany high doses of steroids. It's characterized by headache, confusion, visual disturbances, and seizures. I'm keeping close to God, begging Him to not let me lose my grip. I heard Satan's voice tell me over and over again this is my fault. I refuse to believe him.

Jonnae wanted to go to Joel's service and was adamant about it. Even after losing her sight, she was begging me not to come back to the hospital, to go eat, and to go see Joel. Up until that point, I was only supporting her wishes. Why shouldn't I?

As we were driving to the ER, I imagined the enemy laughing at our defeat. I swear I got in his face and told him he had picked the wrong person to fight. I will not lose sight of my Father, nor will I ever bow down to the sadness, frustration, and hopelessness. All things Satan would have me do.

Like Job, I will stay constant in my love and praise of our Creator. I will use this to weaken the enemy's army and increase the power of God's people. What he has meant for evil, God will use for good. I will let my Lord use me (us) whichever way His plan calls for. It's not easy, but it's the way I choose.

Several tests were run today to confirm there are no tumors, clots, or anything like that. There's swelling in the back lobe of her brain. She's having a hard time processing the data that comes in and cannot communicate. She can't do simple things like say her name, follow a finger, or finish a sentence. What she says makes no sense at all.

We can tell she's frustrated, but her determination is nothing short of AWESOME. At one point, she made the sign of the cross repetitively. Another time she looked directly at me, made eye contact, and winked at me.

The good news is this Pres is reversible. She's already improved over the coma state she was in last night. The bad news is, in order to stave off the seizures and allow her to recover; her chemo will be reduced or cut off. The last bone marrow aspiration showed the chemo hasn't yet made a dent in Leuk's strength. Her marrow was still packed 90% with leukemia cells. No chemo means the door's wide open for Leuk to take over.

Watching that seizure last night and not having any proof that my baby was still with us, I asked the doctors which was going to be hardest on her, the Pres or leukemia. I asked if Leuk was a less violent killer. They told me both are bad.

I don't want to see that beast called Pres ever again. It was horrible. This morning, I pretty much asked God to take her now. It doesn't appear we're ever going to beat this monster. I'm tired of watching her fight like hell. I understand it's all in God's timing. I will never venture away from trusting His plan and doing my part, but I'm begging him to end her suffering.

I can't explain the fatigue I've felt today. Emotionally and spiritually I understand, but physically I've not been able to. I explained the feelings to my husband and asked him if he felt the same way, and he said no. I wondered if it's like "sympathy pains" a husband feels when his wife is pregnant. Am I feeling the effects of her seizure? I likened it to having been drug for miles over horrible terrain. I'm completely exhausted, experiencing an odd soreness all over, and my limbs very heavy. Regardless of how I feel physically and emotionally, spiritually I am certain of one thing. Even when I feel "lost," I'll hang on.

This was God's plan which he had made long ago; he knew all this would happen. Acts 2:23 (NCV)

We have a purpose set before us. It doesn't matter if it's difficult or if we're tired. When asked if we will do our part in God's plan, we say, "Yes!"

MAY 20, 2008

Jonnae's made progress today. She's responded better to questions and has been able to make sense in some conversation. Yesterday, her talk was all gibberish. She focuses on one thing and repeats it over and over, much like Dustin Hoffman's character in *Rain Man*. It's like she's trying to get a running start to get over the hump and get the whole thought out. What she's saying doesn't usually make any sense.

Positive phrases and exercises have kept us steady and strong through this journey. "I'm getting better and better, every day in every way," is a mantra that's kept Jonnae pushing forward with positive attitude in past. Last night as she drifted off to sleep, she began, and continued to softly speak for what must have been at least 10 minutes, "Better and better....better and better....better and better." It was so beautiful. My baby was working hard to "come back" even in her sleep. What an amazing inspiration she continues to be.

I asked her repetitively today if she was going to smile for me. I couldn't see that she would, but I didn't stop trying. We had some friends stop in for a visit and one of them asked if she could have a picture taken with her. When the camera came out, so did Jonnae's smile. So incredible!

"The real voyage of discovery consists not in seeking new landscapes, but in having new eyes." -Marcel Proust

I continue to see life through new eyes, as we realize powerful blessings in carrying this cross. The landscape of Leuk, and of God's grace, hasn't changed, but my eyes are renewed daily to see new blessings and new ways, in every day. She's getting better and better, every day, in every way!

MAY 21, 2008

A meeting was called today and Jonnae's condition was discussed in great length. A bone marrow aspiration will be done tomorrow to see if any progress in reducing the strength of leukemia has been made. If not, the toxicity of drugs is more than Jonnae can tolerate. Administering chemo won't do any good and will only aggravate the Pres Syndrome. If that be the case, the fight will be surrendered and our mission will be to keep her comfortable until God calls her to be with Him.

As an artist, when I create a piece of work I like to use a lot of color and ornate detail. The same holds true with words, as I "paint a picture" of our day. Today I'm struggling to find the words to accurately portray where I am.

On one hand, Jonnae is improving. She remembered her name today and that of her dog. She knew the doctor and one of the nurses when they came in. She's been able to string sentences and thoughts together that make sense. She's walked 2 laps around the floor and picked up the pace when I suggested we make it an offering walk. On the other hand, there are more times she's a lost little girl.

One example is how she struggled with the ABC's today. When she gets stuck, her focus is relentless. It is nothing for her to try for 20 minutes to get one sentence out. She will say five or so words and then go back and repeat. She's hallucinating and gets frustrated with simple tasks. So much so, it brings her to tears. Or she gets really defiant with her words and actions, not like her at all.

I have moments where I hate her experiencing this. Then I realize she's not in pain or aware of any of it. Somehow, that makes it better. It helps that she's quite comical. That's something that's intriguing about this wall we're up against--the humor in the midst of heartbreak.

We've learned another lesson, just how much we take our brains for granted. A healthy body is abundant with blessings. My heart of gratitude has been most focused on that today.

It's time once again for me to walk the talk. In the beginning of this fight with Leuk, I remember saying, "If there are 100 bad things and only one good, we'll focus on the good. That's the only way we'll beat this thing."

> I REMEMBER SAYING, "IF THERE ARE 100 BAD THINGS AND ONLY ONE GOOD, WE'LL FOCUS ON THE GOOD. THAT'S THE ONLY WAY WE'LL BEAT THIS THING."

As every day seems closer to her last, I find myself working hard to stay focused on the good. There are two ways of doing it:

1.) Focus on the good that I have;

2) Giving thanks for the worse that I don't.

I'm certain with the anticipation of the news of her results, I will wrestle back and forth with the hope of a miracle and the acceptance of a loss to Leuk. The episodes of sadness will be replaced with a heart full of gratitude and obedience. I know my Father's wants are not for us to stop living, but to be filled with LIFE. Jonnae has taught us, and will continue to do so. There is an amazing legacy being built here; its contractor is God and its builder, Jonnae. I will reside in it and experience it with gratitude, honoring all that she exemplified and suffered for.

> THERE IS AN AMAZING LEGACY BEING BUILT HERE, ITS CONTRACTOR IS GOD AND ITS BUILDER, JONNAE.

I continue to strengthen my faith. There will be no white flag. I will never give up.

PART IV: LABOR PAINS BEGIN

MAY 22, 2008

We have the results from the aspiration. Whether we proceed with chemo or not, the end is near. The toxicity in Jonnae's body has taken its toll. We could risk her organs and try to get her into remission with more chemo, but we could only administer half the dose called for. We have done far more aggressive chemo, twice already, and it's not been successful in taking Leuk out. The doctors don't believe we should go that route, but rather, try and provide her with some quality days, possibly a few at home.

The first decision we made was whether or not, and when, to tell the kids. The news will get around and would be horrible for them to hear from someone else. Johnny stayed with Jonnae at the hospital, while I came home to tell them. I was so absorbed with figuring out my choice of words to tell them, I didn't think to prepare myself for their responses.

It was the most horrible heartbreaking experience ever. Four children wailing and only one set of arms to embrace them. My parents were present, too. Thank God, each of them could grab a child. Nolan bolted outside and begged to be left alone.

We've not told Jonnae yet. Second to a fearless, peaceful death for her, my biggest prayer is we tell her the right way, at the appropriate time. I pray she doesn't fall into despair at the news.

As far as she's concerned, she's had a really good day. She woke from sedation quickly, walked a couple of laps around the floor, remembered everyone's names, and was quite proud of all of her accomplishments and triumphs. This will be much harder than what I have to draw on from telling her about her diagnosis or relapses. I don't know how to best do it. I'm praying hard for clear direction before tomorrow.

I'm spending the night at home and will return to the hospital in the morning. I'm thinking she'll ask about the results tomorrow, which would end all of the debating in my head. I've always been completely honest with her and would give her the news if she inquires. But then again she isn't thinking as clearly as she was pre-seizure, so it's anyone's guess. She thinks she's coming home tomorrow, even though she was initially scheduled for chemo. That's proof she's not herself. She doesn't normally have an oversight like that.

Eventually we'll all be okay. I pray I give the support and direction the children need to grieve and mourn in a healthy manner, without letting them be consumed by it. I pray that Johnny and I are patient with one another when our personality differences make it challenging to be supportive.

I pray that we never cease in honoring and following the example our lovely Jonnae has set for us. I pray that once she's been received into paradise, I feel her heavenly hugs as strongly as I feel the ones from my Heavenly Father.

MAY 23, 2008

My morning started out with an early trip to the gym. Many have encouraged me to rest and forego that part of my day, but for me, going without my workout is like going without food. Only, it doesn't just fuel my physical body; it fuels my spirit, also. It keeps me strong in more ways than one.

The kids opted to go to school this morning. Their hearts are breaking, but they seemed to be handling the news well. I got back to the hospital to find Jonnae had snuck to the bathroom by herself. I opened the door to see her bed empty, I.V. line trailing into the bathroom, and my husband asleep. I was nervous, yet smiling.

She's not strong enough to get up off the commode on her own. I was half-afraid she might be laying on the floor in there. I smiled because she's so much like her mama, it's not funny. She's inherited that "I'll show you how strong I am" stubborn, independent streak from me. We've seen it kick in several times today.

Confused, upset, and delusional, she was in a fog this morning. On my way to the hospital, I was feeling confident and at peace about telling her today. But when I witnessed the state she was in this morning, I quickly lost my footing.

She hadn't slept well through the night. There's a nocturnal thing that happens with Pres Syndrome and it robs her of her clarity. She slept for the first three hours I was here. Just as she was waking up, the nurse from the adolescent hospice arrived to talk with me. I was hardly prepared for the information she shared with me.

What it boils down to is complete surrender. Not only will Jonnae not be getting chemo, she'll not have any labs drawn, or use any antibiotics to cover her. She'll not return to the hospital or clinic for any care, regardless of what transpires. Basically, we'll treat any symptoms and keep her comfortable, but there will be no treatment with the intent of curing anything, regardless of what it is.

There's nothing to gain by prolonging anything. It's so difficult to think about. I'm a bit overwhelmed by the thought of being the one taking care of her. The anticipation of my child dying, while under my watch, is not something I can describe or anyone would want to know.

I came back to the room and Johnny and I sat down on the bed to break the news to her. He left everything to me and was supportive. Given the fact we weren't going to fight leukemia anymore, I needed to have her input. Did she want to be home or here?

This child's strength and selflessness is mind blowing. She shed only a few silent tears and then immediately asked about the kids. Did they know? Were they okay? She's made several comments throughout the day in regards to others' acceptance and well-being. She doesn't "know" everything, but she knows. She said she would ask the questions when she wanted the answers.

Jonnae's determined to fight to the end. She set goals and reached them all day. We suggested she share the master bedroom with me on the main floor and Johnny would sleep in her room on the second. She says she'll be able to crawl up and down the stairs. "How else am I going to get my strength back?"

She walked a total of eight laps around the floor today, this to her daily average of two. She doesn't want to have another sleepless night, so she pushed herself to stay awake until ten o'clock.

We watched as she struggled to keep her eyes open. Now it's 40 minutes past her goal time and she's gotten a second wind. She doesn't appear to be ready to sleep. However, I'm about to drop from extreme exhaustion.

MAY 24, 2008

After an eventful, restless night, she's sleeping comfortably here at home. Although she was full of spunk and vigor yesterday, ready to crawl up to her room on the second floor, she quickly relinquished the idea today. Her energy and what's left of her health are declining rapidly.

Her liver's getting worse each day. The whites of her eyes are a brighter yellow today, than yesterday. That's where I'm looking for a miracle to present itself first. I keep thinking she's going to open her eyes and they'll be that bright white again.

It was stressful leaving the hospital with a fever, no ANC, liver getting worse, and knowing that this is it. We wanted her be in on the final decision, understanding we're not going back. Johnny and I asked the doctor to give us a few minutes with her. I don't remember how I started, only that I said as much as I could before leading up to the fact the doctors don't believe she has much time--days to be exact. When I told her I didn't want her to be scared, she simply nodded her head and softly said, "God's plan."

It's a nightmare to sign a DNR (do not resuscitate) contract. That was the last thing they had us do before leaving. Of course, it's our choice to make, but we opt to not put her, or our family, through anymore of this pain, should heart failure occur. She told us she didn't want to be put in the ground to rot, that she wanted to be cremated. She has two locations that she's mentioned as her "resting place." She said, "Ashes to ashes, dust to dust."

We discussed her memorial service. She said she'd keep a notebook close to add things as she thought of them. This child endlessly amazes us with her grace, dignity, and strength in the face of death.

The medical team could hardly make eye contact with us. I know their hearts were breaking with ours. I think I'm holding up well, but my body, at times, says something different.

When we first got home, Jonnae slept for a long time. Then, she wanted to change clothes and head to the golf course. She loves driving me around in the golf cart, as Johnny and I play golf. At times, I've felt paralyzed today. I can't feel my arms and legs working, but somehow they are. I felt like I was full of iron, not like I could swing one. We played six holes before she was ready to call it a day, at least on the golf course.

After taking another long nap, she awoke and wanted to watch some home movies. As her mother, I want to know what's going on in that head of hers. She's pretty quiet. I can't stop wondering if there's anything I can say to comfort her.

A lot of family members and friends have expressed the want to come see her. I think it's asking a lot of her. How can she go to the park, or do the things she wants to do, if she's hanging out here to play hostess? I've asked everyone to respect the time she has left and give her freedom. She would forego her desires to provide for others. She's put others first her whole life. It's time to ensure these last days are completely hers, without concern for us.

MAY 25, 2008

Not much has changed with Jonnae's physical status or my emotional one. At times I think Jonnae looks and acts as if she's improving. Then, I see she's not. She's slept a lot more today and her eyes are still very yellow. I'm still seeing signs of dementia, although nothing like what we witnessed in the hospital and she's very quiet, very sad.

This morning I planned on taking the children to church, while Johnny stayed home with her. She felt like taking a long bath and the timing didn't work out, since I was keeping an eye on helping her. Johnny took the children instead.

When I got Jonnae back to bed, I knelt beside her and said, "I'm so ready for your pain to be over, baby."

She said softly, "Me too!"

I said to her, "It's almost over, baby, whether a miracle's performed or you join our Savior in Heaven, your suffering is about to end."

I held her and tried to fight back the tears. I'M GOING TO MISS HER SOOO MUCH!

The one difference between Jonnae and me is that I'm a sap and cry at the drop of a hat and she rarely ever does. She's such a rock. The one thing that will make her cry is seeing me shed a tear for her. As one of my tears dropped, she wiped it as she fought back her own and said, "I'm not going anywhere."

There is a persistent question that keeps resounding in my head: "Am I the one standing in the way of her healing?" I believe in miracles, no doubt about it. Is my questioning whether He's going to create one in her, the very thing that's preventing it from happening?

These signs that I truly believe have been from the Coach to prepare me for her death; were they a sneaky ploy from the enemy that steered me away from what was needed to heal her?

Someone came by today to pray over her and said it's in the Bible that Jonnae is to be healed. This woman said she's not wavering and is standing on the Word. I've had others share the same. Yet, I've had the Word come to me and show me something different. Is my being obedient, my making preparations, my accepting the end is near, are these things preventing her from joining the ones who have been cured?

I know that it's not me. I know that my faith, or difference of, has not been what's harmed her. The voice of the enemy is trying to be louder than the voice of truth. Jonnae has been chosen. Look at the people whose lives have been impacted by her. A crown awaits her that any of us would choose to be graced with.

We came home to be with her siblings and father, but it's still been a lot of just her and me. I can't say I blame the kids for wanting to stay busy and away. It's not a joyful place here. She feels bad, she's sleeping most of the time, and it's difficult to watch.

We used to come home from church and have biscuits, gravy, and eggs. She wanted us to do that today. Nolan was really struggling. He tried to use a baseball cookout as an excuse to not join us, but it wasn't scheduled until several hours later. I encouraged him to just sit at the table with us.

I watched as he fought the tears the entire time. Earlier, I told him it was okay to be angry. When I mentioned God, he retaliated that God was doing a bang up job right now and he doesn't want to hear anymore about Him. My husband feels much the same way. Yesterday Johnny said, "If you want to buy into God's love and glory and it makes you feel better, that's fine. But, I'm not".

I know they're just questioning, "Why her?" and "How could this be happening to someone so sweet and selfless?" I refuse to believe it's for any other reason than to teach us. I read once that God won't do what makes us happy, He'll do what makes us His. Sometimes that means not getting what we want, but what we need instead.

> GOD WON'T DO WHAT MAKES US HAPPY, HE'LL DO WHAT MAKES US HIS.

We've needed the lessons that have come from this journey. I'm not thankful for Jonnae's suffering, but I am thankful for my new perspective of life and how intimate I've become with my Heavenly Father because of it. We should learn much from her and follow her example. We should accept and obey what His purpose and plan is for us. It breaks my heart that I can't help my daughter's physical suffering or the spiritual and emotional suffering of the rest of my family.

I believe God's heart is breaking with ours. I believe we should all do as she has, turn our face to the Father, be thankful, obedient, loving, forgiving, and serve Him. We want to keep her with us, but are acceptant of His will. Now our prayer is for her suffering to cease.

MAY 26, 2008

The day hardly went as planned. The weather wasn't cooperative and Jonnae's energy level is less every day. She's too tired to do anything and sleeps the biggest part of the day. I don't think she's sad so much as she's completely drained.

I drove her up to Mount Saint Francis. The Falls of the Ohio and the Mount are two places she mentioned as her final resting place. She liked the Mount, said she had a good feeling about it, and wanted to come back on a drier day. I took that time to tell her I had observed how quiet she's been. She cried and simply said, "I'm tired. I hate being this tired all the time. I hate this."

I asked her if she was holding on for our sake or for her own. She didn't respond, not because it was too difficult for her to face, but more because she can't hold her eyes open long enough to complete, or hear, an entire sentence. I told her she could "let go." It's hard to make the most of a day if you can't stay awake through it.

Once home, we attempted to play one of her favorite games, Scrabble. She wanted to play, but again, couldn't complete one word without falling asleep. Poor thing. I'm out of patience and ready to give in. I'm done with the selfishness of wanting to hang on to her for my sake.

My prayer was different today than it's been the last two days. I begged God for His mercy. We know the Lord is kind and merciful. I'm begging Him to be most merciful now. Either create PERFECT health in her, where she'll never need medicine again, or take her home. It literally makes me sick to my stomach and weak in my whole body to think of living without her, but I feel so selfish begging for her healing, knowing that she has something so perfect awaiting her in Heaven.

This morning I was overcome, as I often am, with the reality of where we are in Jonnae's fight. Every single morning I awaken to realize it's not a dream. I recall all the giggles and wonderful times we've shared and realize I've experienced the last of them.

After my workout, I retrieved my things from the locker room. I was leaving when the still quiet voice insisted, *Be bold! Go back and tell her*. The louder voice, and the one that used to hold the winning record, said, *Oh come on, just go home. You can't seriously be thinking about going back in there*.

I decided to do the better thing and trust the first voice. I went back into the locker room and approached the woman I had passed on my way out. I said, "I'm going to take my chances here, and believe you have a still quiet voice you listen to also. I was 'told' to come back and share with you that today's a gift. Don't take it for granted. I probably won't see anyone else to share this message with today, so I'm telling you. Hug your loved ones like you've never hugged them. We often take for granted the blessing of a day. I'm reminding you not to."

She asked me if something happened to me. I told her about Jonnae. As both of our eyes welled up with tears, she thanked me.

Tonight we gathered more pictures to use in a video tribute that's being made. Emotional isn't an accurate enough word to describe the experience, but it will do. She's always been a radiant star to us and I'm going to create a memorial service that reflects that.

It's late for me. The last few nights I've literally fallen asleep at the computer. Now, I'm ready to fall into bed beside her.

CELEBRATION OF LIFE

MAY 27, 2008

Jonnae slept the entire day. I gave her a bath and body massage early this evening. She followed them with a short nap and came into the kitchen when she awoke. My husband threw out ideas of things we could do. When he suggested a ride on his four-wheeler, she was all in. I was a bit concerned. She can't hold her eyes open long enough to read a card, how was she going to hang on to him for a ride? The solution was to sandwich her between Johnny and I. It was a nice ride and the longest she's been awake for several days.

Hospice visited today. One of the many unpleasant things we discussed today was what the other children want me to do, should she pass when they're not at home. As I was getting ready for the hospice visit, I was thinking about Jonnae's memorial service. Something came to me. I've been seriously thinking about abandoning the use of a funeral home for a place that's different. When we've attended funerals in the past, we've discussed how we don't want people mourning and wearing black to our services, but rather celebrating our lives and wearing vivid color.

Jonnae had a dream a few nights ago that she was a star. There's a beautiful old theatre downtown that would be the perfect setting to celebrate the life of our "star." I thought we could celebrate her by premiering her tribute video on the big screen. I heard divine guidance telling me not to wait for her to pass, but instead have a memorial service now. Let her see and feel the energy and love we have for her. Celebrate with her in our midst. I am so going to run with it.

I called the theater today and it's available on Sunday. I will determine a time tomorrow. The video's being created, a music group being contacted, and a celebration of Jonnae's life is going to happen, with her there to experience it. I don't know if this'll be the perfect way for her to find peace and let go, or if it's the setting God wants for His next miracle, but I'm certainly going to make it a great experience for everyone, especially her.

Obviously, time is of the essence. Each day the life within her is dwindling. I want to make this a very special event for her, but my time needs to be with her, not occupied by the planning and preparations. I'm going to need help. This is not easy for me to ask for and shows just how much God has changed me through this experience.

God was generous in allowing me to mother this child for 15 years. The last three have been full of heartache, but they've also been full of priceless memories and a one of a kind bond. I'm still counting my blessings today, for I have much to be grateful for.

MAY 28, 2008

The love we feel right now is unimaginable. It's beyond amazing. The celebration is going to be full of LOVE, life, blessings, and the

Holy Spirit. I can feel the glory of it already. What a difference it's made today to look forward to celebrating her, rather than waiting to lose her. I've been full of adrenaline and feel ALIVE. It's a feeling I've missed.

For Jonnae, today was another day consumed with sleep. She woke up around 2 and was determined to get to Buckhead's for a late lunch since it was such a pretty day. She tries so hard, but her body just won't work with her. It's pitiful. We wheeled her into the restaurant and she couldn't even hold her head up long enough to look at a menu or enjoy the view.

She slept with her head on the table, while we waited on our food. Once it came, she could only eat a couple bites. The staff was aware of her imminent death and were honored she'd chosen their restaurant as her last to visit. They covered our tab and wished us well. I know it broke their hearts to watch her.

After napping a while more, Jonnae wanted to watch *Sydney White*. She didn't laugh as much as she did the first time we saw it, but she did seem more like herself than we've seen in a long while. She's a night owl, so we joked about how the Celebration should be from 7 - 11, instead of 3 - 7.

On Sunday, June 1 from 3-7, we're going to roll out the red carpet for a premier of Heaven's newest star. In addition to a live band and the airing of Jonnae's tribute video, there will be a table for making scrapbook pages where guests can share their favorite memories of her. With a small donation to the Leukemia/Lymphoma Society, guests can purchase a star for writing Jonnae a message.

We're encouraging everyone to dress wacky as Jonnae and I are. She's never been a girly girl or enjoyed dressing up. Wacky Wednesday is what she most wants to do and of course, I'm game for whatever brings one of her smiles. Balloons, bookmarks, and a special gift for the guests are all being provided. We are so grateful for the generosity of those who are making those things possible.

MAY 29, 2008

Jonnae woke up at 6:30 a.m. to use the restroom. That's not anything unusual, but the fact that she didn't want to go to bed and stayed awake for 4 hours is. After a nap, she awoke and stayed up for another 6 hours. She painted her nails, searched through quarters for collectors, watched *America's Funniest Home Videos*, and wrote a short letter to be included in the program for Sunday's Celebration.

She's had some bleeding from the nose. I would venture to guess we're getting to the hospital for platelets and blood, just in the nick of time. Not something that's typical of hospice's "comfort care" but everyone agrees it's worth a try to have her feeling good on Sunday. She's still lethargic and easily frustrated. Who could blame her? She can't hold a thought for very long. She has no mental clarity, or memory, and it's most difficult for her to understand. I hope and pray her energy is as good for her celebration as it's been today.

She has slow growing bacteria that just began showing in labs they drew last Saturday. We were presented with the decision of whether or not to treat it. I knew Johnny and I would each want to handle it differently. We met in the middle and are treating her with an antibiotic until Monday. It's so difficult to break away from treating her. I can't stand seeing her cry so much, not having much to smile or laugh about, and feeling so awful.

I'm ready to hop off this ride and let God do His thing. However, Johnny's struggling with that and would prefer to continue to treat problems as they arise. We both understand where the other's coming from. We want mostly to support one another and work as a team. All we can do is bear down, grit our teeth, hold on to one another, and let her go.

On a brighter side, the planning and preparations for the Celebration of Jonnae's Life are exciting. Many who can't make it have ordered balloon bouquets to launch into the sky at 3 o'clock Eastern, when the celebrating begins. What a lovely idea. Others are taking pictures of their loved ones holding signs that wish Jonnae well. Nearly two hundred people on one of our message boards changed their avatars to frogs yesterday. That was such a powerful display of love and support. I'm just so blown away and in awe of the incredible movement of LOVE. It's AWEsome!

MAY 30, 2008

Consistent with the ups and downs of this Leuk war, today provided us with another "low." Yesterday was a "high" with 10 hours of alertness; today was full of tears and sleeping. Jonnae got platelets and a blood transfusion today, but it's had no apparent positive affect. She's slept all day; no awake time or sitting up in a chair. When she's awake for a bathroom visit or mouth care, she's crying. The doctor doesn't anticipate her making it more than a few days past the weekend.

Her fatigue is harder to combat with each passing day, with tears flowing more easily and more often. She cries as she repeatedly says, "I just don't feel good."

I hope the day's one of pleasant rest, with no tears, and Sunday's more like the day we had yesterday, with more smiles. I've slowly watched my smiling angel disappear and I miss her. As much as it pains me to think of not seeing her or holding her, as much as it hurts to know our giddiness, ditziness, and earthly experience of fun and love is over, I'm as ready as I can be to let her go. It's time for her to go where the pain is replaced with the sheer delight of HEAVEN. It is time.

Early in her illness, Jonnae wrote in an online journal. Someone recently went back to read it and shared this excerpt with me today:

"I know it's pointless to worry. Worry doesn't help solve anything. Worry takes away a lot of your energy (Which I have learned from experience). You could waste a lot of your time on worrying, when something might not even happen. So I'm cool with it. And if I can't be strong all the time, I have a wonderful mother

> YOU COULD WASTE A LOT OF YOUR TIME ON WORRYING, WHEN SOMETHING MIGHT NOT EVEN HAPPEN. SO I'M COOL WITH IT.

who can be strong for the both of us."

MAY 31, 2008

Jonnae was awake most of the afternoon. At one point, she decided she was hungry and wanted to go raid the gas station for snacks. I didn't question her, just went along with it.

I wheeled her in and we cruised the short, narrow aisles to find Reese cups, Funyuns and a Yoohoo. At the register she picked up an ice cream drumstick and we were on our way. She ate most of the ice cream, but didn't touch anything else we'd bought. While we were out, we went to a novelty shop to find some accessories for tomorrow's celebration and came home.

She drove her car from the house to the subdivision entrance before we exchanged seats to run our errands. I certainly relied heavily on guardian angels, but she drove just as well as she has any other time and seemed quite content with herself.

I want so much for tomorrow to be perfect. I'm an extreme perfectionist, most of the time depending on myself to get the results I've envisioned. That would definitely not be the scenario here. I only secured the location. I've not seen, prepared, or done anything hands on, for this most important day. I've not heard the band. I've not seen how the chairs are set. I've not tested the media system. I've not been involved in the decorating. I'm so not used to turning everything over. I've definitely "let go and let God" on this test.

JUNE 1, 2008

Jonnae is back home, snug as a bug, in the comfort of our bed. Today was not what I had hoped for in the way of comfort and energy for her. She's one tired little girl. But the experience of today, and the outpouring of love for her, was everything I dreamed it would be.

I have never felt so much adrenaline and energy in my life. When we entered the theatre with her, there were nearly a thousand people standing there, cheering as we exited the limo and wheeled her into the building. The band was playing and everyone was clapping. It sounded and felt like one giant heartbeat. It was an experience I'll never forget.

Jonnae just wanted to sit and take it all in for a few moments. She was fighting the tears, as well as her exhaustion. It was all she could do to stay awake but she wanted to view her tribute video with the crowd. Afterwards, we moved her to a recliner back stage where she could rest. It was my hope that she would rest and come back out, but she fell asleep and stayed there for the rest of the afternoon.

My mom stayed with her while I hugged and thanked nearly everyone, one by one. That's the least I could do after such a turn out. The video tribute was amazing and is an invaluable treasure we will hold close to our hearts forever. I will be forever indebted to Terry Coyle (producer extraordinare) for her talent. She's provided my family with lifelong memories. The entire event definitely passed the perfection meter with flying colors. What an amazing day.

It was declared Jonnae Taylor Day, by the city and state. The children of our neighborhood raised funds for us yesterday and gave us a loving gift. We raised close to $2500 for the Leukemia/Lymphoma Society. I think a hundred families participated in the balloon launch in honor of Jonnae and we received loving videos and pictures of families holding posters of encouragement and love via internet.

What a blessed life we share. Some may not feel He's blessing us with Jonnae's earthly life coming to an end, but she's about to receive the ultimate blessing--a place with our God, in Heaven.

TRANSITION

JUNE 2, 2008

Jonnae was up for a good bit today. We went to Wal-Mart and printed some pictures from yesterday's celebration. As with any exciting event, there's a bit of the "post event blues." With the focus no longer being on the anticipation of a fun-filled day, I've found myself questioning when the sad one will be. I don't like living her last moments with my mind in the future and not on the present, but it's hard not to when she's moaning and crying, both in her sleep and waking hours.

Tonight she started running a fever, which means there's an infection somewhere. We've been told that's one of the ways the end could come. Earlier, she told me she felt weird, like I wasn't her mom and Johnny wasn't her dad. Tears streamed down her face as she told me she felt like she was waiting for her real parents to come and get her. It was heartbreaking for me, but I wondered if this is how God is preparing her to leave us. Was this how He was helping to loosen her grip on earthly life?

My decisions no longer consist of who's going to play the music at a celebration or how can we play a tribute video. Knowing that we are getting closer to the time we let her go, now they consist of what we'll do for her body and burial. Should I awake in the middle of the night to find she's no longer with us, I need to know who to call and what to have them do. She wants to be cremated, and honestly, that's what I thought I wanted for myself. But as I study what the Church teaches, there's a peace I cannot find in that decision.

Normally, I accept the direction of the Church, but I'm struggling with it's stance on cremation. I understand the body is a fine vessel and the temple of the Holy Spirit. I live each day treating it as such. It's a shame, that after such a day full of joy, love and light, yesterday, my thoughts today seem dark and heavy.

As I listen to Jonnae breathe in her deep sleep from the corner of my bedroom, I ask God to grant us the most perfect and peace-filled experience with her death. I thank Him for surrounding us with so many people who want to give us comfort and strength. I ask Him to keep a firm grip on me and my family as we prepare for the most difficult experience we've ever known.

I'm certain that we'll be okay. I'm certain I'll not take my eyes off God. I'm not certain what I'll do if the hour comes tonight or what to do in the way of her burial. I'm praying for speedy discernment and peace in this most difficult, yet important, decision.

JUNE 3, 2008

Today's been much like the last several. Jonnae was awake for a short period, but slept through most of the day. She thought a chocolate lava cake sounded worthy of a trip out. She slept in the car on the way to the restaurant, laid her head on the table waiting for the order to come, and then was only able to eat one bite of cake and a few bites of ice cream before determining it hurt her mouth too much. She returned to bed once we got home and never got back up.

In my search for answers on what to do about the cremation, I was hung up on whether it was wrong to treat the dead body differently than Christ's was treated. I believe the body is the temple of the Holy Spirit and was wondering if destroying it by fire reflected that.

I've guided Jonnae to follow the example of Christ in all things. His body was entombed. Should I be doing the same, even though it's not her desire? I had resolved to speak with her today and confirm her final decision. God was quick to "call me" this morning and put my mind to ease.

Two phone calls came, back-to-back, from a family member and priest friend. They were calling to give me loving direction and peace in the decision to go through with Jonnae's wish to be cremated. A Denise vs. Denise battle is grueling. I realized this morning, that's all this was--my own battle of faith and fear. But faith had the upper hand, for it reminded me Jonnae was the one who has "a connection." Her spirit would not steer her in the wrong direction. When we told her nearly two weeks ago that she was about to die, her first response was, "I want to be cremated." She later told me she didn't want the ashes scattered, she wanted them buried.

I found a peace this morning with that thought, but it was when I came upstairs and pulled out the Catechism of the Catholic Church and it literally fell open to the page with "Respect for the Dead" that I had complete peace. It stated "the church permits cremation, provided it does not demonstrate a denial of faith in the resurrection of the body." These words made a point I'd already read in articles. These words had already been shared with me in conversation. But when the book just opened to the page, (I didn't flip a single one, it just fell open to it) I knew it was discernment. I call that a "phone call from God."

Oddly enough, a different priest called me once I had found peace with Jonnae's desire and our decision to have her cremated. He was calling to encourage me yet again, for we had already spoken about the matter, to respect the body and abandon the idea of cremation. I was made aware of the strength of God's grace when I spoke to thank him for his call and support and to tell him the decision for cremation had been made. It would not be changed. Any other time, I would have begun to second guess myself, but this peace and strength I was feeling was the same I had seen in my daughter. It was not strength of my own, but by God.

I've stepped out of the house when having these conversations. It's not something I normally do, but seemed at the time like a safe place to talk without being overheard. Afterwards, I went into the bedroom where Jonnae was with my mother. She started to cry and said, "Why are you going out on the porch to talk? It's scaring me."

My mom replied, "She's got a loud voice and didn't want to wake you."

I spoke up to say, "I've always had a loud voice and never stepped outside, have I, baby? I've been struggling with the cremation, wondering if the Church approves of it or not."

She interrupted me and said, "It's what I want!"

"And it's what you'll have, babe. I got my 'call' from God and I'm at peace with your decision."

We also agreed that St. Joe Hill, where we go to church, will be nice as her final resting place.

I guess since we were already discussing her mortality, she thought it would be a good time to talk about other things. She wanted to know if she could change her *Make a Wish* dream. She wanted to know how much time she had before she died and said she was afraid and not ready.

I told her I couldn't imagine anyone being more ready and that she had earned a fabulous spot in Heaven because of her faith and her example. I told her to try and play the "get to" game. Instead of saying, "why do I have to die," say, "I get to go to heaven."

I told her most of us have a lot more work to do before we "get to" join her. She cried and said, "I wanted a husband." I tried once again to console her and said "What you don't get in earthly wants you'll be rewarded in Heavenly Gifts." I told her many a woman had a husband, but wouldn't see or experience what she had waiting for her in Heaven.

She said, "I wanted to rescue dogs." I told her I would rescue them for her. She asked how. I told her I'd find a way. She cried some more. "Who will take care of Sassy?" I told her I would. I said, "Baby, just make me a check list. Whatever is important to you, whatever you wanted to do, tell me and I promise I will do it for you."

The only way I could have said those things with such conviction, without shedding a tear, was by the grace of God and the guidance of the Holy Spirit. She quieted down, I rubbed her head, and we laid in silence for a while.

The hospice nurse was here today and said Jonnae's vitals are the same. It's not apparent by physical symptoms that we're within days of her leaving us. However, we know her platelets are bound to be dropping and that she has an infection that's causing a fever. We want it to be the infection rather than a bleed out that takes her. We don't know how long any of it will take, be it the platelets, the infection, or the leukemia. The only thing visible is she's more tired with each passing day.

"A good name is more desirable than great riches...." Proverbs 22:1(WEB)

Her name is GOOD and I'm certain the riches that await her in Heaven far exceed any she would have known here on earth.

JUNE 4, 2008

Jonnae's moaning woke me up around 4 a.m. This happens frequently through the night. Moans, whimpers, talking in her sleep, I normally respond with, "What can I do for you, baby?" She usually keeps on sleeping. This time there was something bothering her that was visible, a nose bleed. Something we've almost been waiting for, knowing her platelets are low. It started out as a slow drip and she was able to sleep with a tissue next to her nose.

I cuddled up next to her, wrapped my arm around her, and rubbed her soft, slick head. Off and on for the next four hours I'd drift off to sleep and then awake startled, afraid she wasn't breathing any more. I was really frustrated with myself for not being able to stay awake. I could hear Jesus' voice as He said to the disciples, "Can you not watch and pray one hour with me?"

I don't want to miss her final moment. Mothers who've lost children have shared their beautiful last moment experiences with me. I'm praying for that beautiful moment.

The nose bleed worsened. I called the hospice nurse and she came and packed her nostril with lubed up gauze. She stayed for a while to make sure it slowed down. Jonnae's gums started bleeding slightly as well. She rolled up a piece of a lunch bag and packed it up under her lip, applying just enough pressure to get the bleeding to stop. She suggested we keep Jonnae drugged with Atavan, in hopes to keep her calm and asleep. It's working. There haven't been any moans or cries today, only snoring.

It's a very surreal time. I know I'm not ready for the void her death will leave in my life, but it almost seems like I'm anxious for the time to come. I'm extremely exhausted. Not like I need sleep, but like my body is made of something other than flesh and blood, more like a suit of armor. I feel numb, yet heavy. The days are very long and I'm just watching her slip away. Her moaning, crying, and the absence of her spirit are hard to endure.

JUNE 5, 2008

The nurse thinks we are looking at days, not weeks. That's all she could tell us today, after evaluating Jonnae. My girl is no longer able to stand on her own, or even with help for that matter. It hurts her when we try to help her up, down, or just to roll her over. She's very weak, frustrated, confused, and sad. Her words are soft and mottled, so even if she's awake enough to try and communicate something, it's very difficult to understand.

We were able to understand her when she asked what day it was. She cried because she thought she'd missed her brother's birthday (it's next Tuesday). Just like her to be thinking of someone else in her weakest, darkest moments. She's the epitome of selflessness.

Her nose is packed with blood from yesterday's bleeds. We need to leave her nose alone because her platelets are low; anything could trigger bleeding difficult to stop. She wants to blow it or pick the stuff out of it and gets very upset with us for not allowing her to clean it out.

Even in her sleep, she's trying to put her finger in her nose. It's bound to feel awful. I'm constantly pulling her hand away from her face and asking her to stop. She's upset with me. How I hate that. All I want is to pick her up, hold her, and tell her how much I love her. The closest I'll probably come happened today as she lay on her side and reached up to put her arm around my neck. She held me for several minutes like that. I completely took it in and cherished every second. Her hands are so soft; her touch is still ever so sweet, and her presence angelic. There's so much I'm going to miss about her. Sweet love is at the top.

Earlier today, she awoke for a moment and mumbled she wanted to donate it. When I asked what, she said, "Money." I said to whom, and she said the animals. I've even thought about contacting the Make a Wish Foundation to see if something along these lines could be done as her "wish," since traveling and a family vacation is out of the question.

I had a friend call me yesterday to see if she could pick anything up for me while she was at the store. My request was tennis balls. Granted, that's an odd request, but I explained to her that I had a really annoying catch in my back. I figured rolling around on them would loosen it up and relieve me of the discomfort. A couple hours later, she showed up at my house with another friend and a masseuse. I enjoyed the best massage I've ever had, right here in my own home. LOVE knows no boundaries. I am blessed.

Before crawling into bed with her earlier, I took Jonnae's hand away from her nose, and she said, "I don't know what to do."

I said, "About your nose?"

She said, "About all of it."

I said, "Look for Jesus, baby. Look for Him! I know He's there with His arms open. Find Him and RUN to Him!"

She whimpered a little and said, "I can't run."

I said, "You can't here, baby, but when you see Him you'll be able to. You'll be able to run and jump and feel no pain. It'll all be replaced with JOY. Leave us behind. We'll be okay. RUN to your place in Heaven."

I've heard our loved ones share glimpses of what they're seeing with us as they're about to "crossover" into eternal life. She said, "There are *so many people*."

I know we're in her final days. I know she's sharing glimpses of what to look forward to with me. I think I'm ready to say goodbye, but when she leaves this house for the last time, the void is going to be debilitating. I'm as ready as I'm going to be. I know she has a fabulous crown awaiting her.

I'm blessed by the company of others. I'm blessed by how many have shared the way this child and our story has touched their lives. More and more are sharing with me how they've found their way back to the Church. They'd turned their backs, now they're crawling up into the lap of our Father.

Yes! I am blessed! The way I see it, my daughter's been sacrificed to show not only me, but all of us, how blessed we are. I refuse to let a day go by, where I don't acknowledge the multitude of blessings given to me, regardless of the trials and tribulations presented in that day.

> I REFUSE TO LET A DAY GO BY, WHERE I DON'T ACKNOWLEDGE THE MULTITUDE OF BLESSINGS GIVEN TO ME, REGARDLESS OF THE TRIALS AND TRIBULATIONS PRESENTED IN THAT DAY.

There's nothing more rewarding, nothing that makes it more apparent that we're serving our purpose, than to know people are finding peace through our Father's Loving Care. He is an awesome GOD. It may not appear to be so, but we're on the WINNING team and will be celebrating the ultimate victory with *"so many people"* when the time comes for this earthly game to be over.

JUNE 6, 2008

Jonnae's still with us. I recall the saying that goes, "God is never early, never late, but always on time." and I find myself thinking,

"He's late!" I try not to question why, although I find myself doing just that.

Jonnae's nose would still be bleeding if there wasn't so much old blood blocking its way. Her mouth's bled all day. I can't even clean it out anymore. I can't tell where the blood is even coming from. It's clotted and stuck to the insides of her cheeks, under her tongue, in the roof of her mouth and her teeth. There's not room in there for much more, the clumps just keep growing. It's an awful mess and there isn't anything to do about it.

I can't determine if it's going down her throat. I'm concerned it could cause her to choke or drown. I try to keep her on her side, as it occasionally drains out onto her shirt or the bed sheets. It's hard to witness. There's no way for me to explain where I'm at right now. It's not going to reverse and it's not going to go away, so I just want it to be over. All that's left is to let her go. And I'm ready to do so.

If a friend had offered me a fine piece of exquisite jewelry and came to retrieve it, I would understand and happily give it back with gratitude for her having shared it with me. How could I not do the same with the most precious

> IF A FRIEND HAD OFFERED ME A FINE PIECE OF EXQUISITE JEWELRY AND CAME TO RETRIEVE IT, I WOULD UNDERSTAND AND HAPPILY GIVE IT BACK WITH GRATITUDE FOR HER HAVING SHARED IT WITH ME.

jewel we'll ever know? What favor I've been shown to be this child's mother.

Johnny wrote this last night:

I walked into the bedroom to see how my baby was doing and Denise was lying beside her and had been crying. I held them both to provide what little comfort my arms could give. While I was holding them, I whispered to Jonnae to keep fighting back and not to give up. Denise looked up at me and said she was telling her to let go and run to Jesus. That hit me hard because, all this time, I've been waiting for her to wake up as from a bad dream, and everything be all right. But I too must let her go and be

with Jesus. She's suffering a very cruel death and I have been selfish in wanting her to stay. It's ripping my heart out to see her disappearing from me.

To touch her causes great pain and all I want to do is pick her up and squeeze her to me and protect her from the poison inside her body. She came to focus today and asked what day it was, scared that she had missed Layne's birthday while she was out of it - perfect example of Jonnae. No matter that she's suffering a cruel death; she'll never put herself above her brother. It seems she is still living her life in her subconscious and she is still living it the right way! When I lay with her in bed, I place her hand on my face or neck, hoping that my love for her can find its way from my heart to hers.

So she knows I am here for her, by her side, holding her hand and proudly giving her over to Jesus. I am so very glad that after all of those late nights at work I took a few moments to walk upstairs, ensure they were tucked in, and give them a hug and kiss goodnight. I would ask them if they remembered it and they always said no. Now I realize it was more for me than for them.

My other children's days continue to be as normal as possible. Ballgames, birthday parties, playing with friends, and errands, have gone on all week. I haven't left the house since Sunday. I'm afraid I'll miss something or she'll ask for me in my absence.

My love for our Heavenly Father, even in the midst of this confusion and suffering, is all the more obvious to me. Nothing can separate me from His love, not even death. His Love is unconditional for us; my love is unconditional for Him. By His grace, I have peace and understanding. That's the only way to explain it. I'm not responsible for it; I'm just willing to receive it.

We're told to live in the present, but I find myself looking to the future; one full of hope, dreams, and purpose. I know God has a plan, an incredible plan for me to share my life and Jonnae's legacy. I know when I can leap again, instead of crawl, the beauty of her life and it's affect on us, will be all the more evident. Until then, I pray. I pray for wisdom in how I lead my family to know the peace and acceptance I do. We all appear to be ready, but I know it's going to be more difficult than we're predicting. Jonnae was always ready to embrace what guidance I offered her. It's my prayer God will continue to guide me in how to lead the rest of the family as well, and that they'll follow.

Life is a gift. Today, Tomorrow and Always! I pray none of us let a day go by that we don't accept it graciously, use it most effectively, and give of ourselves more fully, so that each one is more beautiful than the one we experienced before it.

JUNE 7, 2008

Jonnae's weaker. She can only open her eyes halfway, for only a second or two. When she does, I don't think she's seeing anything. There's no contact with them. She's sleeping most of the time; only awake to say a few muffled words that most of the time we can't interpret.

One thing did happen about 4 a.m. this morning. She woke up, and even though it wasn't clear, I understood her ask me to get Nolan. I went downstairs, woke him up, and got him to come upstairs. When we were by the bed and I told her he was here, she said, "Tell him to get in bed," and then she giggled. Nolan didn't look too enthused. His look was more like, "Are you kidding me?" But it was funny.

Today I've found myself *tripping* continuously. I've not been moving forward with my eyes on the Coach. It's reminiscent of my triathlon experience last September where I wanted to finish the race sprinting, upright, and strong, but mustered up everything I had just to fall sloppily across the finish line. I'm tired! I'm tired of her suffering. I'm tired of looking at her frail tiny bruised body. I'm tired of pulling her bloody finger out of her bloody nose.

I'm tired of seeing her mouth full of dried, clotted blood. I'm tired of not being able to understand what she's trying so hard to say. I'm tired of her crying and moaning in pain. I'm tired of sitting here in this dark room staring at a computer screen trying to pass the time.

I'm tired of feeling ashamed because I feel like a prisoner and because I feel like my life has been on hold for so long. How awful is that?

I'm tired of not executing what I know works for me and now, I'm tired of complaining. Basically, I've allowed myself to be a victim today and I know better. I'm a victor! I'm tired of not acting like one. Oh, I know I'm entitled to days like this, but that doesn't mean I like them.

Whatever tomorrow brings, I have what I need to champion over it. It's all about choices. I need to see the opportunities as they're presented and decide to overcome the hurdles.

THE "CROWNING"

JUNE 8, 2008

This morning I headed out for a run. I used to love running, now I don't care for it so much. When I set out to do any kind of cardio, I do what I do throughout the day. I listen for God's voice to guide me.

This morning I set out to run a couple to 3 miles, but that voice, my Divine Coach, suggested I run more. So I set out to finish the task, figuring I would further develop my "I will not quit muscle." The Coach threw out more instruction. *No stopping, no walking.*

I don't like cardio because I get bored and I get tired. This morning it was hot, so that factored into my displeasure all the more. I made sure to run through a couple of sprinklers.

I varied the run by running backwards up the hills and did some side shuffles around the cul-de-sacs. So I didn't stop and I didn't walk. Mission accomplished. When I shared this with my husband, he said I'm a nut case. I smiled and told him I even moved my arms to and fro at certain points, just like a child might, thinking about how Jonnae would "get me." She wouldn't think I'm nuts, she's just like me.

Throughout the run, I prayed and offered up sprint intervals for those "who have rope burn from trying to hang on," or think the end of the rope has no knot. For those who are struggling to get a grip, regardless of their challenges, I prayed for victory and for peace.

As I entered our own street and approached our driveway at the end of my run, I looked up to the sky and raised my hands. God's response was an eagle soaring with its wing expansion wide and beautiful as it glided about the sky. It looked just like the eagle at the end of Jonnae's Tribute video. I came in and wanted to share my awesome "God hug," so I went upstairs to tell my husband, assuming he would be moved as much as I was.

He said, "A bald eagle?" I said, "No just an eagle."

He said, "It was probably just a hawk."

To which I replied, "Hawk, eagle, I don't care, it was the most beautiful flight of a bird I've ever seen and it was meant to symbolize the eagle in Jonnae's video."

I have strength in God right now that won't allow me to be suckered by the devil's tactics. The best weapons in his artillery are the ones you love and respect the most. So now, he was trying to use Johnny's voice to rob me of my joy. I didn't engage in the devil's pathetic little game. My joy is mine as long as I choose to possess it.

The hospice nurse come out today to implant a catheter. Turns out it's probably too late to benefit her. Her kidneys are shutting down. Tonight her hands and feet have gotten cold and her breathing is rapid with some short gasps and pauses. All signs indicate the end is near. She isn't responding to anything and probably won't make it through the night. Lord knows she's surprised us before.

Without any knowledge of the latest update, our community blessed us tonight. Around dusk, Johnny looked out the window and called me to come see. About 200 lit candles were moving down the street and stopped in our yard, just outside her window. They stood and sung the chorus to *He is Here*.

They said the Our Father and repeated the chorus several more times. My dad and I went out to join them and he led us through the

Rosary. I felt a breeze blow up through the grass that I know was no ordinary breeze. I'll never forget how it literally came from the grass up through my body, pulling me to sit straight up, as though it were lifting me. I hugged as many as I could before rejoining my family back in the house to be at her side.

In addition to our community's expression of support, there continues to be an outpouring of love across the country as a result of the impact Jonnae's had on many. I received an announcement that purple wristbands are being created to say, "I GET TO." They will remind us of Jonnae's strength and enable us to enlist our own. They can be ordered at www.wegetto.com. SO AWESOME!

THE HEAVENLY BIRTH

JUNE 9, 2008

It is finished. Jonnae's battle is over. Her Heavenly Birth happened around 4 a.m. this morning.

Where to begin…. I lay down at Jonnae's side last night, completely exhausted, and nuzzled up close to her with no anxiety about falling to sleep. I experienced an awakening this morning like I've never felt. I can't even explain it. It was like that breeze I described as the Holy Spirit last night; this unexplainable, peaceful, stirring occurred. As it pulled me up out of my sleep, I looked at my baby and knew she was gone.

A wave of emotion has hovered over me. Just as I feel like I'm about to be engulfed by it, there's a shift in the air and the pending storm of sadness subsides. Of course, the shift is Jonnae. She will probably always have that affect on me. At least, I pray she does.

When she was here with me, if I felt compelled to shed a tear over, or for her, she would look at me as though she were seeing into my soul and beg me, "Don't, mom." Just like that, I could shut off the leaky faucet to protect her from any water damage. Knowing she would not want me to cry, I've been pretty solid today.

It's a balance of sorts. She wouldn't want me crying, and although I hated seeing her uncomfortable and in pain these last few weeks, it's by staying focused on those dreadful memories, rather than the good ones, that I'm finding relief today. All I need do is think of how pitiful she looked, and how awful she felt, and the letting go becomes easier. I rejoice that it's all over for her. If I go back to memories that are pleasant, the ones where we were laughing, living, and loving, then the wave is dangerously close to crashing down around me. Sadness has a chance of consuming me. I've fought hard to not let that happen today.

As the evening came on, I got weaker, wanting to release the tears. Still, she won't have it. As always, I am doing whatever I can to please her. Even though I'm certain there's nothing I could or couldn't do to affect her pleasure now.

She was a beautiful, peaceful sight this morning. She looked as though an angel had come in and cleaned her up. All the blood that had been so messy, protruding from her nose, was out of sight. Her lips had a little smirk of a smile to them, and her perfect little nose with the evidence of so many "angel kisses" (what we called her freckles) was beautiful.

Johnny took her passing the hardest this morning. He wailed when I woke him to let him know she was no longer with us. The kids, with the exception of Nolan, all came into the room briefly to see her one last time. They didn't shed any tears and eventually went back to bed. Nolan cried when I first told him. He had spent the night at a friends' house, so I gave him the news over the phone.

I myself stayed on the bed, lay up close to her, and kept my hand under her back where the last bit of warmth could be felt, as the rest of her body turned hard and cold. At some point there'll be a breaking point and it'll probably be a welcome release, but for now, I can't seem to let it happen.

JUNE 10, 2008

I find it difficult to write now. I'm used to starting with an update on Jonnae. Things kind of just flowed from there. I guess I just start with the events of the day.

I woke up and headed to the gym. I worked out in the basement all last week because I couldn't stand the thought of being more than a shout away from Jonnae. I really wanted to hit my "10's" today, but I couldn't seem to. To lift properly, you need to be able to breathe. My lungs weren't cooperating. I needed to take a lot of deep cleansing breaths.

Layne's having his birthday party at a friend's house tonight. Her parents were gracious enough to offer their backyard. With his evening occupied, we decided to have a breakfast birthday celebration for the family. We enjoyed our meal and the company. Johnny, Nolan, and even Layne, have been quick with their wit today. We've had a fair amount of laughter which feels really good.

I've always had a high tolerance for physical pain. I think that level of tolerance has crossed over into my emotional and spiritual capacities. I understand the need and importance of letting tears flow. I know I need them to. But they haven't come at the right place and time.

I explained it to a friend like this: I've felt the presence of God so strongly before that I've wanted to throw myself down face first in awesome praise of Him. But those feelings don't come at an appropriate time, I'm in the car or at a ballgame. I need them to come when I'm at church in adoration. It's the same with the overwhelming emotions of not having Jonnae with me anymore. When they come to the surface, it doesn't seem to be the time to let them flow, so I stuff them back down for a while.

I spent several hours planning the funeral mass; selecting music, readings, and participants for different parts of it. I want everything to be a perfect reflection of her, but struggle with contentment that it will.

I find myself praying and looking for a "Jonnae Hug." It will be a huge chunk of healing, of peace, when I strongly feel her presence. So long as it's a strong sign, I don't care if it's only for a second.

I know she's in Heaven! I have no doubt that she's with God, amazed at the glory of the place He's prepared for her. Yet in my selfishness, I just want to FEEL her. Johnny's gotten hugs from her all day today. I am not jealous, I am happy for him. But I do feel a bit like a child in wanting it to be my turn.

I've read *90 Minutes in Heaven* and the author says there's no awareness of time there. Maybe she hasn't realized how long she's been gone from us. Is my patience ever going to stop being tested? Johnny referred to the JOY principle (Jesus, Others, Yourself) about a week or so ago in describing Jonnae. Today he came back from running errands and said a cashier named JOY waited on him today. That was enough for him to feel like Jonnae was with him.

Later he was reading the paper and said you're never going to guess what school's in the paper today. I made a few attempts and then he said, "JOY Elementary! Who's ever heard of JOY Elementary?" Then he was reading a post to one of our guestbooks and a visitor had used the word JOY three times in her post. He's deserving of such a hug.

Here's an excerpt from Johnny:

Sunday night we were in bed with Jonnae whispering I love yous in her ear and holding her hands while the TV was playing old home videos. I happened to look out our window and see a sea of candles walking up the sidewalk toward our house. Our incredible community had come to pray for Jonnae and sing songs of prayer. I turned off the TV and raised the window hoping that Jonnae would somehow be able to hear the love for her. I thank you for that with all my heart! Denise and Jan thought that it would be that night that we would lose her, but I kept hearing Jonnae say, "Fully Rely On God." I just knew that Jesus would take her by the hand and breathe the healing air back into my baby and she would wake up and tell me she was hungry and ready to get out of bed.

Later that night I snuck back into the room to watch over her while Denise slept with her. They were keeping a perfect snoring rhythm, so I went on to bed thinking she would be here in the morning. But God answered my prayer for mercy and took her while she was sleeping.

When Denise came to tell me at 4 a.m., I ran to her with complete despair as I had failed to stay by her side until the end. I ran outside to see if I could see her ascend into heaven. I begged her to come to me with some kind of sign to let me know she was okay. I sat down and cried and Lydia came out and sat with me trying to console me. My kids are so strong and so loving, it amazes me. I kept waiting for Jonnae to come whooshing by me with her new wings and say look at what I can do daddy! Life is already less without Jonnae.

I'm certain, like Johnny has today, I will feel her when God's decided it's time.

On a more joyful note, Nolan won the Golden Glove award at his sports banquet tonight. That would've been enough to put a smile in my heart, but it was the words the coach chose to lead up to the announcement that were the real prize.

The trophy was a reward for how he plays on the field; the words were a reward for the way Nolan's chooses to live life. The coach said the highest compliment he could pay a player would be to say if he had a son, he would want him to be just like the player. Tonight, the coach said that's how he felt about the Golden Glove recipient, Nolan Taylor. He was fighting emotion as he spoke the words and then embraced Nolan. As I experienced this moment any mother would cherish, I heard myself say the words we speak in Mass, "Lord, I am not worthy."

I may not be worthy, but I'm fortunate enough to have been chosen. Each of my children is as remarkable as the others. I am so blessed, and yes, proud. I give God the glory, if not by his grace and mercy, I wouldn't have what I've been given.

It's time for bed. It's there that I find myself letting down, shedding tears, and sobbing. I'm not sure it won't happen again, as I crawl into that place I shared with my baby as she left, but it is time. And with time, it'll get easier. Of this, I'm certain.

JUNE 11, 2008

The clarity, focus, and direction that I obtain, while spending my first moments of the morning in silence, is amazing. This morning I was driving to the gym when the still quiet voice said, *Why are you so desperate for a sign from her? You had this child for nearly 16 years. You witnessed her amazing spirit nearly 24/7 for the last three of them. You've been blessed beyond measure. Why are you asking for more? Be still and know that she is with ME.*

Wow! Forever, I will have a void that no one else can fill, but this thought is so powerful. I am not "having to" bury my child tomorrow, not knowing if she lived her life well enough to spend eternity with Christ. "I GET TO" release her into the arms of our loving Father, knowing not only did she live a good life, she's left a legacy that's going to grow, as people by the masses are inspired to live more like her. There's no arguing that! I GOT TO be her mother and I don't need to be given anything more.

It's been a different kind of "long day." Not exhausting in the same way as with Jonnae's illness; an entirely different kind. I shopped all day for an aqua-colored top to go with a skirt in my closet, for Jonnae's funeral. I forgot how draining shopping is. One of the many things that's transformed my life is I don't spend my time, I invest it. And not on purchasing things I don't need.

The top that came with the skirt is dark brown. Jonnae and I have discussed on many occasions how bright colors should be worn to a funeral to celebrate the person's life on earth and Heavenly Birth. As it is, I'm tired and still don't know what I'm going to wear to my daughter's funeral. I've told myself she would not be upset if I wear the dark brown shirt. The skirt and shoes are colorful and I certainly made the effort. She would tell me it's okay and to not be burdened by it anymore. I hope I'm at peace with it soon. I've over-invested both time and energy on this desire.

I stepped into the first store and the void and loneliness from her absence tried to get a hold of me. I have heard the first birthday, the first Christmas, the first of all the holidays is very difficult. There are going to be many "first" hurdles ahead to clear. Monday it was eating out without our little "steroid princess." That was hard.

Today, shopping without her, for the first time, was hard. Getting my first text from Austin this afternoon was hard. (I'll explain) Jonnae left her cell phone to Austin and she had set my phone to open her picture on the screen each time she called or texted me. When my phone beeped that I had a message, I looked down to see Jonnae's picture. My heart was in my throat. Was I really getting a text from her?

I don't think I was breathing when I opened it. Then I realized what was going on. Austin was doing as they each have upon receipt of a new phone. He's turned into a texting fool. After several messages from him, I couldn't take it anymore. I decided to delete her picture and name from my phone's contact list so that Austin's name would come through. "Deleting" my angel as a contact, THAT WAS HARD!

One of the last text's I got from Jonnae was a mantra we used to help heal her with the power of positive words, only this time it applied to something different. Jonnae repeatedly said, "I'm getting better and better, every day in every way." It was borrowed from a quote of a turn of the century French healer, Emil Coue.

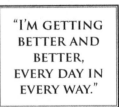

"I'M GETTING BETTER AND BETTER, EVERY DAY IN EVERY WAY."

No one has ever celebrated a bowel movement as much as we have. With the drugs these kids are on, the body can't do what it was created to do. I got a text from Jonnae saying, "I just pooped again. It was probably twice as much as yesterday. I'm getting better and better every day in every way." She was such a cute jokester.

GOING HOME

JUNE 12, 2008

It was a gorgeous day. I couldn't have asked for anything more in the way of Jonnae's funeral mass. We arrived at 10:20 for the 11 o'clock service and the church was already full. I don't know how many people ended up staying outside, but

> HE USED A CANDLE TO SYMBOLIZE THE LIFE OF MY BABY. THE CANDLE USES ITSELF UP, IN ORDER TO PROVIDE LIGHT. JONNAE GAVE OF HERSELF, TO BE A LIGHT FOR US.

it was an incredible display of love for a child that used her life to lead us. Father's homily was absolutely perfect. I sat there smiling in agreement with everything he said. He used a candle to symbolize the life of my baby. The candle uses itself up, in order to provide light. Jonnae gave of herself, to be a light for us.

I won't get this exactly right, but I'm going to do my best to relay a point Fr. made. He said he hated to burst any bubbles, but those who think she's earned her wings, and is now an angel, are mistaken. Not to belittle the angels, but humans were made in the likeness of God. We weren't created as angels or to become angels. However, we can become saints. He reiterated that today was not a canonization, but he did believe Jonnae lived in such a way to become a saint.

> "SUFFERING CREATES ONE OF TWO THINGS. IT EITHER CREATES BITTERNESS OR IT CREATES A PATHWAY TO SAINTHOOD."

He said, "Suffering creates one of two things. It either creates bitterness or it creates a pathway to sainthood." Jonnae accepted her suffering, she was never bitter. She only used her life in a way that was pleasing to God, leading us to a life of strength through faith.

I was strong today. I wasn't sure what to expect, although I envisioned myself being strong and unshaken. My source is faith.

I trust my Heavenly Father's taking care of Jonnae in a way we can't even comprehend. I'll never stop missing her, but my happiness for her far exceeds the sadness I feel for myself. I'm blessed to have been the one she called, "mom."

Johnny and I have four other amazing children to parent. They were strong today too. Their peers who showed up to support them were nothing short of amazing, also. Anyone who thinks there isn't enough respect or good in our youth, obviously haven't been exposed to these kids. They're incredible.

At the mass' conclusion, I carried Jonnae's ashes down to the gravesite. A massive crowd gathered around us. We waited for Father to close the service and then my dad read a poem. At the completion of it I released a white dove, symbolic of Jonnae's spirit. Then my husband opened a basket to release six more representing how the rest of us will follow her.

My family has gotten a kick out of mocking my release. The woman that raised these beautiful birds told me to keep a tight grip on the single bird, that it was anxious to take flight. It was fighting pretty good in my loosely clasped hands. The fight was being felt under my fingers, it wasn't evident in my posture or position of hands, but the bird was rapid flutter of the birds wings made it obvious to me, it was ready to be free. I anticipated the bird would take off as soon as I opened my hands. However, when I pushed my hands up to release and give the bird its start, it didn't move. I feared it was going to fall to the ground, so I quickly pumped my hands down and back up. It took off. It looked like I "stuttered" with my hands. I didn't think it was that bad, and not even remotely funny, but my family sure has enjoyed teasing me about it. I guess we can find laughter in anything.

PART IX: POSTPARTUM: WHERE I AM A YEAR LATER....

Reconstruction continues from the devastating storm known as "Leuk." It's been an exhausting year, but with the craftsmanship and majesty of God's amazing Hand, some incredible rooms have been built.

Since Jonnae's Heavenly Birth, I've experienced great sadness, as well as incredible joy. God continues to mold me into something more. With His stern, yet loving guidance, I continue to build a stronger body, a heart more loving, and a lighter spirit.

Through many years of confusion and discontentment, my focus was on the structure and not the foundation. It was more important for me to win praise and adoration with my body, than to praise and adore my Creator with all my soul. I still workout, but what I love most about being in the gym is how it's developing my spirit into something more. My body is just along for the ride.

The journey we know as life is fascinating. I'm so far from where I started. Before "Leuk" and Jonnae's Heavenly Birth, I was lost. I was consumed with who I was on my own, instead of who God is in me. Like the finest GPS, Jonnae's courage, selflessness, and love steered me in the direction I'm meant to go. Through acceptance and forgiveness of all my mistakes and those of others, the ride's become more enjoyable and I have found peace.

I've pulled off the road a time or two, as if I were at one of those breathtaking "lookout points" (we have those here in the mountains). It's not a place to invest a lot of time or take up residence. It's merely a place to take a moment and appreciate the magnificent creation of God's hand. As I observe the point where I am, and the road it took to get me here, I'm in awe.

As the construction and journey continue, I encourage and inspire others through writing, speaking to organizations of all kinds, and building the dream of Wacky Wednesday. Casual Friday began in one office somewhere and spread across the country. It is my hope that before my own Heavenly Birth, every children's hospital in the country will be wacky on Wednesdays.

Whether He's my Coach, Potter, Contractor, or compass, I look forward to what God still has in store for me. As we prepared for Jonnae's Heavenly Birth, I said, "These are the worst of times but the best of times." As I feel the void of her not being with me physically, yet continue to experience the beautiful gift of life, I'm saying it still.

"Day by day, I'm getting better and better, every day in every way." Emil Coue

READERS GUIDE

GENERAL QUESTIONS

1) How do you think you would respond to news of a chronic illness or relapse? If you have, share your initial reaction.

2) Would you be public or private about your thoughts and feelings? What is the benefit of your answer?

3) Jonnae and Denise both felt God's presence in profound ways. Recall when you felt a surge of something powerful stir within. Explain the event and how it made you feel. Was it during a time of adversity or peace? How can you open yourself up to experience that more often?

4) How often does God speak to you? Do you call on Him, or wait for Him to call on you? What's the most unusual way He's spoken to you?

5) Have you tried replacing "I have to" or "I've got to" with "I GET TO?" Was there something that caused you to feel burdened today? How could the situation have been worse? Who would trade places with you and embrace it as a blessing? Initially you felt you "had to" deal with it. With your new perspective state how you "got to." Explain the shift you experience.

6) What did you think about Denise's focus on fitness during Jonnae's illness? Did it, or didn't it, serve her well? What could you take from her experience to enhance your path to health; mind, body, and spirit?

7) In what way has this book affected the way you experience your day? How is that change affecting your life and the lives of those around you? Are you a *"deposit"* or *"withdrawl"* in the *"life account"* of others?

FIRST TRIMESTER

1) This mother/daughter duo continually took the lemons in their life and made lemonade. Think of an occasion where you took what appeared to be a negative situation and turned it into a positive one. Is there currently something making you sour, that with a different perspective, could turn into something "sweet?" Elaborate.

2) How often do you write in a gratitude journal? Name one "uncommon" thing you could give thanks for today. If you had acknowledged that blessing, as it occurred, how would it have affected your day?

3) Jonnae stayed strong and positive through her relapse and treatment when most would have felt defeated. Denise completed a triathlon when she wanted more than anything to quit. When is the last time you gave your "I WILL NOT QUIT" muscle a good workout? How did you feel afterwards?

4) Denise introduces the reader to many analogies. (baseball, boxing, cars, balloons) Which one can you see yourself using to shift from victim to victor? Share a different analogy that you personally draw strength from often?

5) The Taylor family found the support they needed through their church, community, and each other. Denise also found inspiration and strength through books. Where do you turn for support? Do you spend more time seeking it or offering it? Does one come more naturally than the other? Does one empower you more than the other? How can you incorporate more support into your life?

SECOND TRIMESTER

1) Denise and Jonnae were constantly challenged with fear and worry but did not allow it to consume them. Denise prayed, exercised,

and wrote her way through it. Jonnae used scripture, prayer, and positive affirmations. They found ways to reclaim their power, instead of give it away. What things do you worry about that you cannot change? How is that "what if" way of thinking serving you? Are you exhausted or empowered? Could you "lean on" someone who's been there? Consider reading, watching documentaries, or going to a support group. What would be the best fit for you?

2)   Jonnae created a dream board to keep her focused on "fighting for her future." What strategies do you use to keep you moving forward? What visuals would motivate you to stay positive, take care of your health, perform better at work, and keep your dreams alive?

3)   Denise and Jonnae's spirits were lifted when they received "snail mail." Who last sent you a card for no reason other than to express love or gratitude? How did you feel? When is the last time you mailed someone a card, or letter? Who could you bless with a mailed sentiment now?

4)   On several occasions, childhood and Christmas memories filled this mother with joy. How often do you reflect on 'the right' memories? Take a moment to reflect on your happiest ones. What are they and who were you with?

5)   Denise reminded Jonnae that she had made it through a painful bone marrow transplant, VOD, and higher obstacles than a nonadjustable shower head. It shifted Jonnae's focus and she reclaimed her joy. What is the biggest obstacle you've overcome to date? How does that compare to what you're challenged with now? What can you use now, from the experiences you championed over in the past, to help you turn your stumbling block into a stepping stone?

6)   Denise and Jonnae received special "God Hugs" (divinely planned instances that are often dismissed as coincidence). Name an experience that you first chalked up as coincidence, but in hindsight felt was something more. What effect would it have on you, if you started recognizing coincidence as God's presence in your life?

7)   Jonnae and Denise both experienced "spiritual warfare."

Recall a time when the enemy tricked you into the wrong way of thinking. Why do you think darkness sometimes comes so swiftly, just as the dawn is about to be experienced?

8) If laughter is the best medicine, Wacky Wednesdays provided Jonnae and Denise with a healthy dose of it. How have you used humor to get you through a tough time? How can you invite more laughter in your life?

THIRD TRIMESTER

1) If today is a gift from God, what are we telling Him when we say, "It's been a bad day"? Are we saying God gives bad gifts? What would be a better word choice?

2) When is the last time you set a goal and accomplished it? Make a list of five things you want to accomplish this month, and another list of things you want to accomplish this year. What would happen, if you took a step towards your intentions every day?

3) Denise and Jonnae influenced one another's spiritual growth. Who do you credit as the most influential person in your life? Do you contribute to those around you in the same kind of way? In what way can you enhance your contribution?

4) Are you living in the "shack of feeling sorry for yourself" or the "house that faith built?" When it's time to relocate to "the Mansion–," will you be ready? What would you need time to do? What's keeping you from doing it?

5) Jonnae's giddiness over her wig was effected by others reaction to it. How has the judgment of others muted your joy? Do you judge? Do you judge yourself as harshly as you judge others?

6) Denise and Jonnae sometimes struggled with perfectionism. Do you typically set low, or high, bars? Do you think striving for perfection is a positive or negative trait? Is it attainable?

DEVASTATING DEVELOPMENT

1) Denise drew great strength from the Biblical examples of David, Mary, and Jesus. Who in the Bible can you relate most to? How would regular reflection enhance your spirit?

2) Do you think God creates adversity in our life, or simply allows it? Explain your chosen perspective and how one view or the other makes a difference.

3) Denise and Jonnae used small sacrifices as offerings for others. What sacrifices could you offer up as a prayer? How have you experienced joy from an anonymous act of kindness? Which gives you more joy, being the giver, or the receiver?

4) What is keeping you from living your best life? What choices can you make to experience something better than you are now? What's keeping you from making them?

5) Denise and Jonnae used scripture, prayer, exercising, and creating memorable moments to release them from the grip of despair. When you are disappointed or discouraged, who, or what, do you turn to? What practices relieve you from negative emotion and get you going in a more positive direction? How would it benefit you and those around you, if you tapped into your spirit at the first sign of an "energy leak?"

SURPRISING COMPLICATIONS

1) When Jonnae suffered her seizure, Denise struggled as she heard, "This is your fault." Who did that voice belong to? What makes it difficult to decipher whose voice is being *heard*? How is the voice of goodness different than the voice of darkness?

2) Jonnae's seizure shed light on the miracle that is our brain. Have you ever been around someone who suffered head trauma? What

awareness did it give you about the ingeniousness of the brain? When is the last time you gave thanks for your brain? What ways do you protect and strengthen it?

LABOR PAINS BEGIN

1) Denise was always forthcoming with information about Jonnae's illness to all of her chidren. How do you think she handled delivering the devastating news of Jonnae's prognosis to both her family and Jonnae? Would you have handled it differently? If yes, in what way?

2) Sadness was definitely a natural emotion to feel during this part of the Taylor story. What other emotions did you experience?

3) Denise questioned the way she prayed. Explain what you believe makes a prayer right or wrong. How are your prayers consistently the same? Are prayers during hardship more important than prayers in the midst of joy?

4) How have you stepped outside your comfort zone to compliment a stranger? Do you find it easy to tell a stranger about the obstacles you're being faced with? Why do you think it is easier to share a compliment than it is to share a valuable lesson we've learned? Why do you think we voice our hardships more often than we do our blessings?

CELEBRATION OF LIFE

1) Denise decided to replace a funeral visitation with a Celebration of Life. Do you choose to celebrate or mourn when someone departs from the world? Why is your choice the best one for healing?

2) Do you think the Celebration was a bigger gift for Jonnae or those in attendance? How so?

Transition

1) Jonnae wanted to be cremated. What are your thoughts about cremation? How would you handle such a request from a loved one? In what way would your religion influence your decision?

2) What do you think happens as the soul is about to leave the body? What experiences have given you a glimpse into Heaven? What thoughts were provoked by the statements Jonnae made just before she experienced her Heavenly Birth?

3) Johnny was asking Jonnae to hang on, as Denise was encouraging her to let go. How did Denise and Johnny's candid sharing, in the days leading up to Jonnae's Heavenly Birth, affect you? What different perspective of life and death do you have as a result?

4) Even with rapidly failing health, Jonnae was more concerned about others than she was for herself. She wanted to make a difference with her life. How has this child's life had an impact on yours? What gift did she give you? How could you further her ripple and pass on the gift she's given you?

THE CROWNING

1) Denise felt a strong breeze come up through the grass during the candle vigil. What do you think that breeze was? Have you ever felt the breath of the Holy Spirit? Revisit that experience.

THE HEAVENLY BIRTH

1) In regard to her being chosen to mother incredible children, Denise stated, "I am not worthy." Explain how we are worthy, or not, of the blessings we receive?

2) How much time do you spend in silence with God? Have you already gotten the answers you need, or could you use some Divine

Guidance? Do you think it might change your day to be still, quiet, and listen for God's voice, first thing in the morning? If you already do, share its benefit.

GOING HOME

1) The priest who spoke at Jonnae's funeral suggested humans aren't created to become angels. Why do you agree or disagree with his philosophy? Explain the difference either view makes.

2) Denise explains a shift on the day of Jonnae's funeral. What and who does she credit for the strength she was given? Is this strength available for everyone to tap into?

3) How do you want to be remembered after your Heavenly Birth? How are you using your life to create a legacy? When you last thought about it, how did it change your course of action for the day? Was your heightened consciousness more beneficial to you or more beneficial to those around you?

POSTPARTUM

1) Denise and Jonnae obviously shared a very unique bond. Denise handled Jonnae's passing and first year without her daughter's earthly presence differently than most. Tell of a time you felt like it was both the best and worst time of your life? Explain how one can experience joy in the midst of pain.

2) Denise admits to having put too much focus on her body and the approval of others. Where can love that is enduring be found? If you've discovered where real love abides, share the moment you realized it.

3) What experiences have increased your belief of eternal life? Do you believe those who've been born into Heaven "visit" us? Share an experience you believe was the presence of one who's crossed over.

4) Denise intimately shared her flaws, her strengths, and her journey, as she prepared for Jonnae's *Heavenly Birth*. Through the adversity and pain, she grew into something more and was enlightened with a new passion and purpose. Having read "Heavenly Birth" how will you face adversity differently? In what way has your thinking about life changed? How will you actively use your new perspective so that when it's time for your *Heavenly Birth*, you will be at peace?

Resource Page

Share I GET TO stories and order I GET TO wristbands at www.wegetto.com   (Proceeds help support Wacky Wednesday)

Online Daily Devotions

Girlfriends in God – www.girlfriendsingod.com

Encouragement for Today – www.crosswalk.com

Today's Word with Joel and Victoria- www.joelosteen.com

Daily Devotional with Max Lucado- www.maxlucado.com

Daily Devotion Books

Hugs, Daily Inspiration Words of Promise

Praying God's Word Day by Day – Beth Moore

BOOKS OF INSPIRATION

Joel Osteen - Your Best Life Now

Become a Better You

Beth Moore - Breaking Free (Bible Study)

Jim Stovall - The Ultimate Gift

Og Mandino - The Greatest Miracle in the World

The Greatest Mystery in the World

The Twelfth Angel

The Christ Commission

The Choice

The Spellbinders Gift

FINANCIAL ASSISTANCE FOR TRANSPLANTS

National Transplant Assistance Fund

National Children's Cancer Society

CHANGING YOUR VIEW
OF WHAT
HOSPICE CARE CAN DO.

The time to begin hospice care is just after you've learned you, or someone you love, has a life-limiting illness. By contacting Hosparus early, patients immediately benefit from our expert counseling, exceptional pain management, and compassionate care. This allows them to live each of their remaining days to the fullest. To learn more about Hosparus, the region's premier hospice provider, call or visit us on the Web.

HOSPARUS

Because the end of life is part of living

1-800-264-0521 • www.hosparus.org • A non-profit organization

Made in the USA
Monee, IL
18 June 2023

35893456R00174